Revenge

Margaret S. Mahler Series

This series of yearly volumes began appearing in 1991 and is based upon the panel discussions presented at the prestigious annual Margaret S. Mahler Symposium held in Philadelphia. Each volume consists of three papers and their discussions presented at the most recent Symposium. A thorough introduction and a comprehensive conclusion that pulls all the material together are specially written for the book. Occasionally, one or two papers that were not presented at the meeting but represent the cutting-edge thinking on the topic are also included. While this format and organization gives these books a friendly familiarity, the books' contents vary greatly and are invariably a source of excitement and clinical enthusiasm. Volumes published so far have addressed topics as diverse as hatred and cultural differences in childhood development, extramarital affairs and sibling relationship, mourning and self psychology, and resilience and boundary violations. Among the distinguished psychoanalysts whose work has appeared in this series are Salman Akhtar, Anni Bergman, Harold Blum, Ruth Fischer, Alvin Frank, Dorothy Holmes, Otto Kernberg, Selma Kramer, Peter Neubauer, Henri Parens, Fred Pine, John Munder Ross, and Ernest Wolf, to name a few. The vantage point is always broad-based and includes developmental, clinical, and cultural variables but the end point is consistently an enhancement of the technical armamentarium of the therapist.

Books Based Upon The Margaret S. Mahler Symposia

- *The Trauma of Transgression* (1991)
- *When the Body Speaks* (1992)
- *Prevention in Mental Health* (1993)
- *Mahler and Kohut* (1994)
- *The Birth of Hatred* (1995)
- *The Internal Mother* (1995)
- *Intimacy and Infidelity* (1996)
- *The Seasons of Life* (1997)
- *The Colors of Childhood* (1998)
- *Thicker Than Blood* (1999)
- *Does God Help?* (2000)
- *Three Faces of Mourning* (2001)
- *Real and Imaginary Fathers* (2004)
- *The Language of Emotions* (2005)
- *Interpersonal Boundaries* (2006)
- *Listening to Others* (2007)
- *The Unbroken Soul* (2008)
- *Lying, Cheating, and Carrying On* (2009)
- *The Wound of Mortality* (2010)
- *The Electrified Mind* (2011)
- *The Mother and Her Child* (2012)
- *Guilt* (2013)
- *Revenge* (2014)

Revenge

Narcissistic Injury, Rage, and Retaliation

Edited by
Salman Akhtar and Henri Parens

JASON ARONSON
Lanham • Boulder • New York • Toronto • Plymouth, UK

Published by Jason Aronson
A wholly owned subsidiary of Rowman & Littlefield
4501 Forbes Boulevard, Suite 200, Lanham, Maryland 20706
www.rowman.com

10 Thornbury Road, Plymouth PL6 7PP, United Kingdom

Chapter 1 is reprinted here, with permission, from Salman Akhtar's book, *Sources of Suffering: Fear, Greed, Guilt, Deception, Betrayal, and Revenge* (London: Karnac Books, 2014), 147–168.

British Library Cataloguing in Publication Information Available

Library of Congress Cataloging-in-Publication Data

Revenge : narcissistic injury, rage, and retaliation / edited by Salman Akhtar and Henri Parens.
pages cm. -- (Margaret S. Mahler series)
Includes bibliographical references and index.
ISBN 978-0-7657-1013-0 (cloth : alk. paper) -- ISBN 978-0-7657-1014-7 (electronic)
1. Revenge. 2. Anger. I. Akhtar, Salman, 1946 July 31- II. Parens, Henri, 1928-
BF637.R48R49 2014
155.9'2--dc23

2013037806

∞™ The paper used in this publication meets the minimum requirements of American National Standard for Information Sciences Permanence of Paper for Printed Library Materials, ANSI/NISO Z39.48-1992.

Printed in the United States of America

To

the Memory of

MARGARET S. MAHLER and SELMA KRAMER

Contents

Acknowledgments

All the chapters in this book, except chapters 1, 8, 9, and 10, were originally presented as papers at the 44th Annual Margaret S. Mahler Symposium on Child Development, held on April 20, 2013. We wish to express gratitude to the Department of Psychiatry of Jefferson Medical College, the main sponsor of this event. We are especially indebted to Dr. Michael Vergare, Chairman of the Department of Psychiatry and Human Behavior of the Jefferson Medical College; Bernard Friedberg, President of the Psychoanalytic Foundation of the Psychoanalytic Center of Philadelphia; and William Singletary, President of the Margaret S. Mahler Foundation for their continued kind support. There are many others who helped in subtle and not-so-subtle ways. To them, our most sincere thanks indeed. Finally, we wish to acknowledge deep appreciation of Ms. Jan Wright, for her superb organization of the Symposium and for her skillful preparation of this book's manuscript.

Chapter One

Revenge

An Overview

Salman Akhtar

The history of human civilization is replete with examples of man's destructiveness towards man. Some of these outbursts are impulsive, passionate, and transient. Others are calculated, deliberate, and longstanding. Some involve individuals. Others involve masses. Some occur only in fantasy and, under fortunate circumstances, are turned into defiant poetry, biting fiction, and provocative theater. Others slit throats, ruin families, and cause bloodshed. Regardless of their extent, all destructive actions somehow or other get justified in the mind of the perpetrator. One's violence is given a patina of reasonableness through all sorts of rationales and rationalizations regardless of whether it involves the plebeian tit-for-tat of children or the awesome 'messianic sadism' (Akhtar, 2007) of paranoid fundamentalists. Matters of the former variety fall under the purview of parents, elementary school teachers, and benevolent clergy. Matters of the latter variety belong to interdisciplinary think tanks that can inform sociopolitical praxis.

These two extremes are not encountered in clinical situations. What one does witness are 'mid-level' destructive aims and fantasies directed at old and new objects as well as their re-creations in the transference. Any therapist who has worked with narcissistic, paranoid, and sociopathic individuals would vouch for the veracity of this observation. Given this, it is surprising that the theme of revenge has attracted very little attention from psychoanalysts. The PEP web, which contains over 88,000 entries, comes up with only thirty papers with 'revenge' in their titles over the one-hundred-and-thirteen-year history of psychoanalysis. Clearly, something is remiss here.

This overview is intended to summarize the scattered writings—psychoanalytic or otherwise—on the topic of revenge and to create some phenomenological and psychodynamic order out of this chaos. In addition, the contribution will make a brief foray in the literary realm and close with elucidating the clinical implications of the observations made during the effort to unfold the nuances of the issues involved here.

PHENOMENOLOGICAL ASPECTS

The English word 'revenge' is derived from the Old French *vengier*, meaning 'to avenge.' Its dictionary definition includes phrases such as (i) to avenge by retaliating in kind or degree; (ii) to inflict injury in return for an insult; and (iii) an opportunity for getting satisfaction (*Merriam-Webster*, 1998, p. 1009). An unmistakable implication is that revenge has ideational, emotional, and behavioral aspects. In the ideational sphere, revenge is accompanied by a fantasy (conscious or unconscious) of having been grievously harmed by someone and of finding relief from inflicting damage upon the perpetrator. In the emotional sphere, revenge is accompanied by feelings of 'mental pain' (Freud, 1926; Weiss, 1934; Ramzy and Wallerstein, 1958; Akhtar, 2000), bitterness, rage, and defensive exaltation; the vengeful person is often euphoric. In the behavioral sphere, common manifestations of revenge include verbal and physical assaults of varying degrees, ranging from sarcasm, denigration, and hurling obscenities to slapping, hitting, punching, throwing things at someone, knifing, maiming, shooting, and killing. However, gross actions of such sort do not exhaust the behavioral manifestations of revenge. The phenomena associated with it are complex in many ways.

First, acts of revenge are not always directed at the individual or organization that is viewed as having caused harm. Often the rage emanating from feeling hurt is aimed at objects that symbolically stand for the injuring party or are weak and vulnerable, hence suitable for being attacked. Nearly a hundred years ago, Rank (1913) pointed out that neurotic acts of revenge are often directed against the 'wrong' people. Revenge fantasies in terrorist acts especially depict how victims of the destructive impulse are not truly the targets of it (Akhtar, 2003); innocent civilians are killed and maimed not for rage directed at them but because they are dispensable pawns in a violent game of chess with their governments.

Second, redirection of vengeful affects and behaviors can involve the self. Thus, the chronic self-effacement, self-deprivation, self-denigration, self-mutilation, and self-destructiveness of severely masochistic patients contain a powerful, though unconscious, element of revenge. Freud (1917, 1921) had long ago discerned this element in the symptomatology of depression. He stated that

> a leading characteristic of these cases is a cruel self-depreciation of the ego combined with relentless self-criticism and bitter self-reproaches. Analyses

> have shown that this disparagement and these reproaches apply at bottom to the object and represent the ego's revenge upon it. (1921, p. 109)

It is as if the patient, in his misery, has become a walking billboard of the parental misconduct during his childhood. His ongoing pain and suffering shouts at the parents with the whole world as their mutual audience: "Look how much you have damaged me! I am a total failure compared to everyone else. I am retarded. I cannot grow and it is all your fault!" (Kramer, 1987, p. 217). Procci's (1987) concept of 'mockery through compliance,' whereby the individual acts out his or her parents' destructive intent towards himself or herself in an exaggerated way, also applies here. And, so does Ferenczi's (1929) somber delineation of how the unwanted child turns pessimistic and devoid of life energy. Even more dark is the description of 'spite suicides' (Zilboorg, 1936) referring to taking one's life due more to sadism and sarcasm than depressive hopelessness. Maltsberger and Buie (1980) offer a more recent and lucid description of this phenomenon:

> Would-be suicides often daydream of the guilt and sorrow of others gathered about the coffin, an imaginary spectacle which provides much satisfaction. While the contemplation of such a scene is a pleasure in itself, the patient may also consciously entertain the illusion that after the act of suicide he will be present as an unseen observer to enjoy the anguish of those who view his dead body. Such an illusion may be held with such intensity that it supersedes reality in emotional value and forms the basis for action. (p. 61)

Third, even direct acts of revenge take many forms. Some of them are active (e.g., sarcasm, physical violence), while others are passive (e.g., gaze aversion, refusal to eat). Some involve aggression while others deploy sexuality as a medium. Behaviors that have been linked with an underlying theme of revenge are as varied as frigidity, euphemistically referred to as "revenge on the man" (Fenichel, 1945, p. 174); incestuous acting out (Gordon, 1955); pathological stealing (Castelnuovo-Tedesco, 1974); primal scene reversals (Arlow, 1980); shoplifting (Ornstein et al, 1983); serial killing (Stone, 1989); and sexual betrayal (Akhtar, 2013a). At times, an individual's sexual object choice can also express his or her rebellion and revenge against the cultural strictures of the family (Freud, 1920b). Neurotic fears of being bitten by animals too can contain elements of revenge being taken against oneself for one's original hostility towards parents (Freud, 1926).

Finally, there exists a relationship between the level of character organization and the nature of revenge fantasy. At the 'higher level of character organization' (Kernberg, 1970), where identity is well-consolidated and defenses center around repression, revenge fantasies—if they even exist—involve oedipal issues. Childhood exposure to parental sexuality fuels such fantasies and their subtle and disguised seepage into actual behavior. At the 'intermediate' and 'lower' levels of character organization (Kernberg, 1970), characterized by identity diffusion and preponderance of splitting mechanisms, matters appear more stark. Revenge, in this context, is usually overt, cold-blooded, and accompanied by conscious sadistic pleasure. Rosenfeld's (1971) description of narcissistic personalities who idealize their destructive capacity and Kernberg's (1984) delineation of the syndrome of malignant narcissism which combines grandiosity, paranoid traits, and antisocial tendencies are highly pertinent here. Fantasies and actions of violent revenge are common among such individuals and are founded upon severe childhood frustrations and actual trauma; their vindictiveness constitutes the reversal of betrayal and abuse by their parents.

PSYCHODYNAMICS

Freud's first comment upon revenge was in the context of trauma, which, he believed, became more pathogenic when suffered in silence. Taking revenge holds the possibility of getting over the injury, though speaking about what has happened also helps. Here are Freud's own words on this matter:

> An injury that has been repaid, even if only in words, is recollected quite differently from one that has to be accepted. Language recognizes this distinction, too, in its mental and physical consequences; it very characteristically describes an injury that has been suffered in silence as "a mortification" (*Krankung*, literally "making ill"). The injured person's reaction to the trauma only exercises a completely "cathartic" effect if it is an *adequate* reaction—as, for instance, revenge. But language serves as a substitute for action; by its help, an affect can be "abreacted" almost as effectively. (1895, p. 8, italics in the original)

Freud later evoked the idea of revenge in his elucidation of the dynamics of Little Hans (1909a) and the Wolf Man (1918). He regarded their fears of being bitten and devoured by animals (in reality and in dreams, respectively) as a boomerang effect of their own hostile fantasies towards their parents, especially in the context of the latter's sexual lives. In *Inhibitions, Symptoms, and Anxiety*, written nearly two decades later, Freud reiterated this idea:

> The case of the "Wolf Man" and the somewhat less complicated one of "Little Hans" raise a number of further considerations. . . . There can be no doubt that the instinctual impulse which was repressed in both phobias was a hostile one against the father. One might say that that impulse had been repressed by the process of being transformed into its opposite. Instead of aggressiveness on the part of the subject towards his father, there appeared aggressiveness (in the shape of revenge) on the part of his father towards the subject. Since this aggressiveness is in any case rooted in to sadistic phase of the libido, only a certain amount of degradation is needed to reduce it to the oral stage. This

> stage, while only hinted at in "Little Hans's" fear being bitten, was blatantly exhibited in the "Wolf Man's" terror of being devoured. (1926, p. 106)

The linkage between a child's sense of betrayal at the discovery of parental sexuality and the resulting devise to take revenge is nowhere more clear in Freud's writings than in his 1910 paper titled "A Special Type of Object Choice Made by Men." Explicating the oedipal situation of the boy, Freud stated:

> He does not forgive his mother for having granted the favour of sexual intercourse not to himself but to his father, and he regards it as an act of unfaithfulness. If these impulses do not quickly pass, there is no outlet for them other than to run their course in phantasies which have as their subject his mother's sexual activities under the most diverse circumstances; and the consequent tension leads particularly readily to his finding relief in masturbation. As a result of the constant combined operation of the two driving forces, [sexual] drive and thirst for revenge, phantasies of his mother's unfaithfulness are by far the most preferred. (1910, p. 171)

Freud's 1909b paper on family romances and 1920 paper on a case of female homosexuality repeated that revenge originated in the child's feeling humiliation and injury vis-à-vis parental sexuality. A new perspective on revenge was, however, evident in "Mourning and Melancholia" (1917), where the self-reproaches of both the obsessional and the melancholic were seen as acts of revenge upon the subject's own ego:

> The self-tormenting in melancholia, which is without doubt enjoyable, signifies, just like the corresponding phenomenon in obsessional neurosis, a satisfaction of trends of sadism and hate which relate to an object, and which have been turned around upon the subject's own self. In both disorders, the patients usually still succeed, by the circuitous path of self-punishment, in taking revenge on the original object and in tormenting their loved ones by their illness, having resorted to it in order to express their hostility to him openly. (1917, p. 251)

Freud repeated these ideas in "Group Psychology and the Analysis of the Ego" (1921, p. 109), though conceding, in "Civilization and Its Discontents" (1930, p. 130), that the severity of self-reproaches and the underlying revenge motif is only partly due to experiential factors (either via narcissistic injury in the oedipal phase or via loss of an ambivalently held but needed object); inborn constitutional factors also contribute to the ferocity of superego and to the overall propensity for rage and revenge in one's character.

Following Freud, many psychoanalysts enriched the understanding of revenge-related phenomena. Abraham (1920) described a 'revenge-type of female castration complex' which, reflecting the phallocentric theorization of the era, was alleged to cause attacks on the 'luckier' male by castrating him. To deprive him of the satisfaction that he has given her sexual pleasure, the woman might become incapable of orgasm. Or, a certain kind of aggressive hypersexuality might develop in her; this is often accompanied by the exploitative fantasies of being a prostitute. Fenichel (1945) later added that since the infantile oral pregnancy themes often include the idea that the woman eats the man's penis, revenge-type of female castration complex might also result in eating inhibitions. Similarly loyal to the drive theory of psychoanalysis, Klein (1933, 1940) spoke of externalization of death instinct and the subsequent creation of 'bad objects'; these can then be feared and therefore justifiably attacked. Though the word 'revenge' does not constitute an element of her vocabulary (see Hinshelwood, 1991), Klein's description of 'paranoid position' centers upon infantile persecutory anxieties and fantasies of retaliation against 'bad objects.'

Moving away from this drive-based model, Winnicott (1956) traced stealing and outrageousness toward others to actual deprivation in childhood. He did not use the word 'revenge' (Abram, 2007), but his ideas on what he called 'antisocial tendency' are certainly applicable to revenge as well. In his inimitable fashion, Winnicott suggested that insofar as it compels the environment to respond, 'antisocial tendency' is an expression of hope. The delinquent's outrageousness is a cry for help. Winnicott (1956) noted that there are always two trends in antisocial tendency:

> One trend is represented typically in stealing and the other in destructiveness. By one trend, the child is looking for something, somewhere, and failing to find it seeks elsewhere, when hopeful. By the other the child is seeking the amount of environmental stability which will stand the strain resulting from impulsive behavior. This is a search for environmental provision that has been lost, a human attitude, which, because it can be relied on, gives freedom to the individual to move, to act, and to get excited. (p. 310)

The tension between a drive-based and a deprivation-based etiological model of revenge tilted over time (just as psychoanalytic theory at large did) towards the latter view. Even those contributors (e.g., Socarides, 1966; Arlow, 1980) who employed the vocabulary of drives did so in the context of childhood trauma. Most others (e.g., Horney, 1948; Daniels, 1969; Kohut, 1972; Castelnuovo-Tedesco, 1974; Boris, 1986; Steiner, 1996) emphatically favored the deprivation and/or humiliation hypothesis of the origin of vindictiveness.

In a remarkable paper titled "The Value of Vindictiveness," Horney (1948) noted that while rational outrage at a frustrating event settles soon after it's vented, vindictiveness, in neurotic characters, can become a way of life. Its aims then are to humiliate, to exploit, and to frustrate others. Its means can be varied and include the induction of guilt and inferiority in others, ingratitude, indifference, and active assaults upon others' valued traits and capacities. Horney described three forms of vindictiveness, namely, (i) openly aggressive vindictiveness that is associated with a certain kind of pride in what is construed as one's honesty and straightforwardness; (ii) self-effacing vindictiveness which operates covertly and exploits others' inclinations towards fairness and justice—vindictiveness of this sort evokes the puzzling impression of being done at the person's expense; and (iii) detached vindictiveness that expresses hostility towards others "by not listening, by disregarding their needs, by forgetting their wishes, by making them feel as disturbing intruders, by withholding praise or affection, and by withdrawing psychically or socially" (p. 4). Horney emphasized that vindictiveness, while destructive in intent, serves some positive functions as well. These include its protective power against real and/or imagined hostility from others, its defensive aim against self-destructiveness, and its promise to restore injured pride. The need for vindictive triumph, in Horney's formulation, arose from many sources, the prime variable being a pressure to reverse the thoughtlessness or openly cruel humiliations experienced at the hands of others. The feeling of vitality and even thrill provided by acts of revenge also counters the inner sense of inferiority and shame.

Searles (1956) also underscored the defensive functions of revenge. He noted that vindictiveness can serve as a defense against repressed emotions, especially those of loss, separation, and mourning. According to him, the vindictive person is unable to let go of his attachment to the object that is indifferent to his desire; seeking revenge against that object maintains hope of affecting a change in its attitude.

Socarides (1966) noted that the conscious aim of vengeance is retribution and punishment while the unconscious aim is to cover up disastrous damage to the ego that occurred in early childhood and revived in adulthood. Vengeance can also serve as a defense against guilt whereby the self-directed aggression is turned toward the external world. Socarides observed that the vindictive person is "grudging, unforgiving, remorseless, ruthless, heartless, implacable, inflexible [and] lives for revenge with a single-mindedness of purpose" (p. 405). There is a certain kind of 'pseudo-courageous' attitude here too since the vengeful individual will go to any extreme to hurt his enemies. Such unrelenting aggression is a product of early, mainly oral, frustration. "Damaged fundamentally in the capacity to love, the vengeful person is unable to withstand future states of deprivation and attacks individuals in the environment as if they were representatives of the depriving breast, frustrating mother, absent father, lost penis" (p. 410). Envy plays a big role here and the projection of such envy upon superego figures leads to hatred of powerful and secretly idealized others.

Daniels (1969) emphasized that triumph over hated objects is so important for such an individual that he readily cuts ethical corners and uses any weapon in his 'war.' He strikes first and his pre-emptions betray his paranoia and intense need for control. And, when his victims complain, he accuses them of being hyper-sensitive and weak. Daniels noted that the vindictive person's hostility goes beyond his explicit 'tormentors' since envy plays a great role in his life as well.

> Aside from those who actually "cross him," the vindictive character also perceives as definitely threatening anyone possessing more than he does—materially, intellectually, or psychologically. Bitter envy assails him. Such people must be diminished, reduced to his level; otherwise, his pride suffers and he begins to slide into the depression upon the brink of which he is already standing. Even worse, he begins to be cognizant of the misery of his lot and of his anguished aloneness. He must enter into relation with the envied person and make him miserable too; then he will be less lonely. (pp. 187–188)

Kohut (1972) described the phenomenon of narcissistic rage with great eloquence. He stated that

> narcissistic rage occurs in many forms; they all share, however, a specific psychological flavor which gives them a distinct position within the wide realm of human aggressions. The need for revenge, for righting a wrong, for undoing a hurt of whatever means, and a deeply-anchored, unrelenting compulsion in the pursuit of all these aims which gives no rest to those who have suffered a narcissistic injury—these are features which are characteristic of narcissistic rage in all its forms and which set it apart from other kinds of aggression. (p. 379)

Kohut went on to note that such rage is only mobilized if there is an archaic grandiose self seeking its preservation and regulating the perception of reality. The 'enemy' who incites narcissistic rage is not perceived as a separate individual and an autonomous source of initiative but as a flaw in a narcissistically perceived reality that must be erased and blotted out.

Castelnuovo-Tedesco (1974) termed the triad of entitlement, stealing, and well-rationalized sadomasochism the Monte Cristo complex. Describing the protagonist from Alexandre Dumas's (1802–1870) eponymous novel and adding two clinical cases with similar psychopathology, Castelnuovo-Tedesco proposed that

> The act of stealing, on close examination, proves to have a variety of discernible meanings and functions, all of which are, broadly speaking, restitutive. It serves, first of all, to undo a loss which is subjectively perceived as a theft where the patient has been the victim. Second, it is seen as an opportunity for revenge, for settling a score and giving back measure for measure. It is my impression, in sum, that the impulse to steal and the urge for revenge are really very close to one another. It is also a way of "turning the tables," of taking the initiative and, in secret, converting a passive experience into an active one. It is

> further a way of controlling a frightening and dangerous object and rendering it harmless by reinstating a long lost but cherished sense of omnipotence. Finally, it is a channel for discharge of substantial aggressiveness and greed. (p. 175)

The connection between greed and revenge found further exposition in a paper by Boris (1986). Greed, in his conceptualization, is appetite turned angry and no longer reliant on the actual object. Greed aspires for an idealized object, hence is inconsolable. The next step in the process is the development of spite or the envious nullification of the other's impact and thus, in turn, is followed by seeking revenge. The aim, at this point, is to stimulate greed and envy in the other.

Steiner (1996) elucidated the reverse of this dynamic. He noted that when taking revenge is felt to be too dangerous, grievance is kept under check and becomes a nidus for sadomasochistic retreat. Steiner also noted that the wish for revenge initially represents the pursuit of a just cause but soon gets caught up in destructive motives of diverse, often unrelated origins. Moreover, revenge-seeking serves to protect the split-off good object, which can be kept idealized till the time a bad object is found and destroyed.

In contrast to most of the contributors cited above, Arlow (1980) returned to the oedipal origins of revenge-seeking. He noted that exposure to the primal scene, especially if vivid and frequent, leads to narcissistic mortification and a conviction that one is unloved and unlovable. This trauma gives birth to the wish to wreak vengeance on one or both of the 'betraying' parents. A common manifestation of such a wish is the tendency to criticize and demean parents and parental surrogates. More striking are the scenarios where taking of revenge occurs in sophisticated enactments or reversals of the primal scene.

> In some instances, the individual brings about a repetition of the primal scene in which he casts himself in the role of witness, often enough interrupting and causing distress to a couple making love. Relatively underemphasized, however, are those vengeful repetitions of the primal scene in which the individual causes others to be witness to his sexual activities. The unconscious import of this behavior is to make the betraying parents experience the sense of humiliation, exclusion, and betrayal that the child experienced at the time of the original trauma, except that in this repetition the role of the parent may be assigned to somebody else—spouse, child, lover, etc. (Arlow, 1980, p. 523)

Having covered the multi-faceted descriptive and psychoanalytic literature on revenge, I am now in a position to offer a composite profile of phenomena that exist in this realm.

AN ATTEMPT AT SYNTHESIS

What becomes clear from this review is that many diverse phenomena are subsumed under the term 'revenge.' It appears in the vastly different contexts of repressed, disguised, and symbolically represented unconscious fantasies as well as of overtly destructive and violent acts towards others. Confusion also rises from the term 'revenge' being employed for a single act of retaliation triggered by hurtful or violating action by someone in external reality and also for the character trait of vindictiveness. Well-justified, rational, and limited acts of retribution also get lumped here. The fact is that such 'good enough revenge' is very different from vindictiveness. 'Good enough revenge' meets the following criteria: (i) it is a onetime occurrence, (ii) more of it is in fantasy and less in action, (iii) it avoids self-destructiveness and masochism, and (iv) it takes socially productive forms (e.g., writing a significant book to prove the 'enemy' wrong) or carries the potential of initiating (or resuming) a meaningful dialogue between the victim and the perpetrator.[1] In contrast, vindictiveness is chronic, boundless, consuming, and, often, self-destructive besides being grievously harmful to the real or imagined enemy. People who are given to vindictiveness continue to harbor resentment towards their offenders for months, years, and often for their entire life. They are prone to sustained hatred and can disregard all limits in their pursuit of real or imagined offenders. Western literature contains many such characters. *The Merchant of Venice*'s Shylock (Shakespeare, 1596), with his literal-minded insistence upon extracting 'a pound of flesh' in lieu of his unpaid debt, and *Wuthering Heights*'s Heathcliff (Brontë, 1847), with his bitter rants against the woman by whom he feels betrayed, are two outstanding examples. Towering above these is the character of Captain Ahab in Melville's *Moby Dick* (1851). His hunger for revenge against the whale that bit off his leg drives him to such 'demonic' revenge-seeking that it ultimately destroys his own self.

The two forms of retaliation (i.e., 'good enough revenge' and vindictiveness) stand on opposite poles of the wide spectrum of socioclinical phenomena involved here (see Table 1.1).

Psychodynamically too, the spectrum of revenge is wide. The phenomena related to revenge seem—like all other psychic phenomena—multiply determined. Although a background of severe childhood frustration does play a major role in it, the dynamics of revenge and vindictiveness exceed it. It comprises variables emanating from all three sources: defect, discharge, and defense. Moreover, the role of these variables and the degree of their contribution to the overt behavior differs from case to case. *From the perspective of defect*, the truly vengeful individual gives evidence of lacking empathy with his victim. Desperately wishing to inflict pain upon the 'enemy,' he nonetheless cannot empathize with the latter's suffering. The 'narrow-mind-

Table 1.1. The Spectrum of Revenge

Variables	Good-Enough Revenge	Vindictiveness
Object	External	Internal
Emotion	Rage	Hate
Frequency	Once	Chronic
Scope	Limited	Unlimited
Cognition	Contextual	Narrowed
Ethics	Intact	Compromised
Narcissism	Regained	Regained
Pleasure	Yes	Yes
Masochism	No	Yes
Sublimation	Maybe	No
Consequence	Constructive	Destructive
Time	Heals	Makes No Change

edness' (Brenman, 1985) that frequently accompanies vengeful actions is also in part due to defects of 'mentalization' (Fonagy and Target, 1997) although defensive curtailment of cognitive functions also contributes to it. *From the perspective of discharge*, revenge gives vent, in a more or less aim-inhibited manner, to primitive sadism. Drive components from oral and anal phases are frequently evident in the form of biting sarcasm and defilement of the enemy's life. Hostility felt as a result of humiliating exposure to primal scene and due to other, more severe trauma also finds discharge in acts of revenge. While sexual acts (e.g., rape, incest) can be used as methods of revenge, it is the satisfaction of destructive aims that is primarily sought and enjoyed. *From the perspective of defense*, revenge constitutes the ego's attempt to reverse humiliating passivity into triumphant activity, to restore traumatically depleted narcissism, and to extrude a malevolent 'interject' (Bollas, 1999), that is, an object that has been violently inserted into the self. Revenge, insofar as it carries the hope—mostly unrealistic—of permanently erasing the trauma one has suffered, also acts as a preserver of the good internal object and a defense against sadness and mourning.

TECHNICAL IMPLICATIONS

The theme of revenge appears frequently in the course of intensive treatments. Individuals who seek psychoanalysis or long-term psychoanalytic psychotherapy often have significant childhood trauma in their background and this makes many of them prone to seek revenge against those who have hurt them (usually, though not invariably, the parents), their substitutes, or the world at large. Needless to add, such scenarios are sooner or later created in the transference-countertransference axis as well. Clinical work can thus become quite bloody. The following guidelines might help negotiate the way through such hard to tread ground.

First, the patient must be allowed to bring out his grievances and, for quite some time, repeat them as if each rendition is their first exposure to daylight. Balint (1968) emphasizes that in the treatment of deeply traumatized individuals the analytic process "must not be hurried by interpretations, however correct, since they may be felt as undue interference, as an attempt at devaluing the justification of their complaint and thus, instead of speeding up, they will slow down the therapeutic processes" (p. 182). To point out discrepancies and contradictions in the patient's story, to bring up the defensive nature of his idealizations and devaluations, and to analyze the potentially masochistic aspects of his outrage are tasks that must be left for much later.

Second, during this early phase, the analyst's activity should remain restricted to empathic remarks, gentle exploratory comments, and what Killingmo (1989) has termed 'affirmative interventions.' The psychological essence of such interventions is constituted by four elements: (i) the element of existence, (ii) the element of relating, (iii) the element of worth, and (iv) the element of validity. As a result, affirmative interventions are empathic comments that render plausibility, context-based validity, and historical meaningfulness to the patient's experience. Such remarks are not aimed at revealing meanings; they are directed at establishing the existence of meaning. On a pragmatic level, they consist of objectifying (e.g., you have felt very hurt by this person and are, therefore, very angry with him), justifying (e.g., no wonder you are upset since what this person has done to you felt so unfair and unjust), and contextualizing (e.g., you experienced his behavior as especially discriminating since you have indeed been treated with prejudice before) elements.

Third, if the revenge fantasies of the patient and their associated hostile affects are close to consciousness, the work can move on, after a while, from affirmative to unmasking and interpretative interventions. The analyst must now explore, in a straightforward manner, the scope of revenge fantasies, the dramatis personae in the theatre of vengefulness, the presence or absence of guilt, and of the actual and imagined reasons why the revenge the patient so desperately seeks has not been taken and/or how it has, at least partly, been acted out. Clearly such work has to occur in a piecemeal fashion and with continued attention to the analysis of defenses and resistances that crop up in this investigative path. Establishing hermeneutic linkages along the axes outlined above gradually would lead to the patient's entertaining healthy forms of 'getting even' and also to responsibility, remorse, and even some forgiveness.

Fourth, if the revenge fantasies have been turned upon the self and the clinical picture is mostly masochistic, the analyst must help the patient see, via a moment-to-moment microanalysis of his associations, how the centrifugal pull of masochism operates. Of course, the analyst's comments themselves might be utilized by the patient for self-castigating purposes ("So it is all my fault?"). This has to be watched for and pointed out. Closely associated is such patient's tendency to develop a 'negative therapeutic reaction' (Freud, 1923; see Akhtar, 2009, for a fuller definition), that is, symptomatic worsening instead of improvement as a consequence of a correct interpretation of his or her malady. In dealing with such occurrences, the analyst must weigh which variable (e.g., unconscious guilt, envious attack on the analyst's goodness, clinging to masochistic pleasure) is the most active, most palatable, and, hence, most interpretable at a given moment. The need for 'tact' (Loewenstein, 1951; Poland, 1975) on the analyst's part cannot be overemphasized in this context.

Fifth, in both types of patients (i.e., overtly sadistic and secretly masochistic and overtly masochistic and secretly sadistic), a modicum of limit-setting might become unavoidable. Apt in this context is Hoffer's (1985) reminder that departures from analytic neutrality are permissible when the analyst, the patient, or someone weak and vulnerable in the latter's life is at risk of being harmed. However, the concept of harm must not be restricted to physical harm; violent projections, tenacious false accusations, screaming, and even consistently deploying metaphors of life and death (e.g., "I am drowning and you are just standing on the shore") aimed at rendering the analyst humiliated and helpless have to be 'prohibited' sooner or later. The analyst must remind himself that there is a long-held tradition, ranging from Freud's (cited in Alexander and French, 1946) injunction to phobics that they face their feared object, through Ferenczi's (1921) 'active technique' and Kolansky and Eisner's (1974) 'spoiling' of preoedipal gratifications, to Amati-Mehler and Argentieri's (1989) rupturing of pathologic hope and Akhtar's (2013b) 'refusal to listen to certain kinds of material.' The analyst must realize that analytic patience, waiting, and tolerance are not there to be idealized by him or to be abused by the patient. Limit-setting is often a necessary step in forcing the enacted material into thought and thus making it subject to exploration and interpretation.

Sixth, in conjunction with attempting interpretative resolution, the analyst—especially when working with tenaciously sadomasochistic patients—must assist the patient's ego in creating choices. Such choices might involve the degree and form of revenge that can be taken safely, the people with whom it should and should not be taken, but most importantly, whether it is essential to take revenge after all. The last-mentioned can lead to the analysis of depressive anxieties underlying the 'optimism of revenge,' which, in turn, might require some auxiliary ego support and gentle reminders of the love and support that *is* available to the patient and is underutilized by him. This can make mourning bearable.

Seventh, while the foregoing paves the way to forgiveness and it is 'good' if that does occur, the analyst must not uphold manic ideals for himself and the patient. He must be able to accept that some injuries might not be forgivable, especially if there is no admission of wrongdoing and apology from the perpetrator. In such cases, analytic work should focus upon why the patient cannot forgive himself for being unforgiving and to help the patient find more productive ways of dealing with the unmetabolized residues of his childhood trauma.

Finally, the management of countertransference forms an extremely important dimension in the treatment of severely sadomasochistic patients. This is especially so because the patients' desire for revenge (regardless of whether it is overtly sadistic or masochistic) sooner or later gets activated in the transference relationship. The analyst is then mocked, devalued, ignored, and actively or passively thwarted. The patient might act out in his or her actual life in order to hurt the analyst (Hull et al, 1989) or directly assault the analyst's mind, personality, or technique (Kernberg, 1984, 1992). All this puts a great burden on the analyst and creates many countertransference risks. The first such risk is that of masochistic surrender on the analyst's part. This evolves from the analyst's desperate attempt to show that he is different from the patient's bad internal objects, that he is unerringly tolerant, and that he never retaliates. Such forced 'disidentification with the aggressor' (Gabbard, 1997), rationalized by the analyst as a necessary accommodation to the patient's psychopathology, is actually anti-therapeutic since it delays or bypasses the analysis of negative transference. It also carries the risk of conveying to the patient that he or she can get away with unfettered hostility and destructiveness; this, in turn, fuels the patient's deep desire for omnipotence.

A second countertransference pitfall is constituted by the analyst's inability to contain the aggression mobilized by violent projections of bad objects into him. When this happens, the analyst finds himself losing control, raising his voice, becoming sarcastic, unduly rigid in sticking to 'rules,' and getting into heated arguments about trivial matters. This is hardly helpful since the patient perceives and utilizes such behaviors as proof that the world is bad, that no one understands him, and that therapeutic interventions are not invitations to think about oneself but sadistic assaults upon his views of internal and external reality.

A third risk is for the analyst to turn didactic, even moralizing. He might find himself appealing to the patient's sense of rationality and reason. Here Kohut's (1972) reminder must be heeded: "The transformation of narcissistic rage is not achieved directly—e.g. via appeals to the patient's ego, to increase its control over the angry impulses—but is brought about indirectly, secondary to gradual transformation of the matrix of narcissism from which the rage arose" (p. 388).

All these risks emanate from the failed containment of the patient's projected hostility. Under ideal circumstances such pitfalls can be avoided. However, in day-to-day clinical work with vengeful patients, enactments of either type often become unavoidable. The analyst's task then involves a post-hoc analysis (and self-analysis) of such interactions and repair of the disruption caused by them (Wolf, 1988; Akhtar, 2011).

CONCLUDING REMARKS

In this contribution, I have provided a wide-ranging survey of the phenomenological, dynamic, literary, and clinical aspects of revenge. My scope has been broad and our theoretical stance multi-faceted. Throughout my discourse, I have paid attention to all 'four psychologies of psychoanalysis' (Pine, 1988), that is, drive, ego, object relations, and self. My understanding of the various phenomena related to revenge and vindictiveness and my technical recommendations to deal with them have been similarly broad-based. Two areas have, however, eluded my attention so far. These pertain to the impact of gender and the culture at large upon the revenge motif in the human psychic life.

First, there is the variable of gender. Are there differences in the frequency, form, and extent of revenge fantasies and acts in the two sexes? The answer seems far from clear. To be sure, literary and movie protagonists of revenge are more often male but the meaning of this remains ambiguous. Does it simply reflect the male preponderance among the main characters in fiction and movies regardless of their themes? Does it embody an anxious avoidance of depicting and encountering female rage and vindictiveness? Shakespeare's declaration that "hell hath no fury greater than a woman scorned" comes to mind in this context. So does Euripides's *Medea*, who killed her two sons as revenge against her husband, who had left her for another woman. And then, there is Miss Havisham, from Dickens's (1861) *Great Expectations*, who, rejected by a man, seeks revenge on all men by grooming her protégée, Estella, to become the ultimate heartbreaker. So there does not seem to be a shortage of enraged and vindictive feelings in women. However, since men in general are more outwardly aggressive, the prevalence of revenge-related violent acts might be greater in them. In women, this rage might be more disguised or turned inward, resulting in a silently resentful paranoid-masochistic picture. Early literature of descriptive psychiatry (Kraeplin, 1905, 1921; Bleuler, 1908) lends some support to this idea but how far have the societal changes over the last century, especially those resulting from the feminist movement, altered such conceptualizations remains unclear.

This brings up the issue of culture. It is my impression that it harbors very mixed feelings about taking revenge. That revenge is justifiable, even godly, is clearly spelled out in the much-revered citation from the New Testament: "Vengeance is mine; I will repay, saith the Lord" (Romans 12:19) and, before it, the harsh Old Testament's (Exodus 21:24, Deuteronomy 19:21) *Lex Talionis* (the talion principle) dictating that one should extract a tooth for a tooth and an eye for an eye. Moral sanctions of such sort fuel the hardwired reflex to retaliate that is our evolutionary legacy.[2] The desire for revenge is thus normalized, even exalted. We accord respect and awe to the vindictive hero in fiction and popular cinema. Captain Ahab from Melville's *Moby Dick* (1851), and the Count of Monte Cristo from Dumas's eponymous novel (1844) mobilize much sympathy and admiration in readers around the globe. And the same is true of the avenging movie characters, ranging from the Dirty Harry series of the 1970s to the 'Angry Young Man' movies of Bollywood cinema (Akhtar and Choksi, 2005). The audience simply laps it all up. It seems as if these books and celluloid dramas afford an abreactive conduit for ubiquitous fantasies of getting even and settling the score. Revenge seems to be 'hot' and well-accepted in all cultures.

At the same time, children are discouraged from 'tit-for-tat' thinking. Vindictiveness is frowned upon. Revenge-seeking is deemed immature and the ideal of forgiveness is upheld by religious and noble men (see the lives of Gandhi, Martin Luther King, Jr., and Nelson Mandela). Parallel to the mesmerizing tales of revenge, there exist moving and poignant narratives of forgiveness especially in the traditions of Christianity.

Putting such diverse perspectives together leads one to conclude that society holds ambivalent attitudes about revenge. Consciously, it strives toward responding to injury by forgiving the enemy. Unconsciously, it seeks to redress the trauma by taking revenge. Vicarious enjoyment of 'well-justified' revenge in the safety of fiction and movies then becomes a compromise formation for this conflict of our culture. Some tension between the correctness of forgiving and seeking revenge nonetheless remains. Moss (1986) declares the two as competing attempts at reconciliation with the traumatizing figures of the Oedipus complex. While the System conscious might tilt in favor of one or the other strategy, both persist unaltered in the System unconscious. There, they are represented as self-object pairs involved in the two respective scenarios of revenge and forgiveness. According to Moss, this fiction of symmetry "lies at the base of the civilization-wide proclivity toward the pursuit of revenge and forgiveness as strategies to obliterate the effects of trauma" (p. 209). The implication is clear: the wish to settle a score never entirely leaves the human heart.[3] And, this might not be bad. Elsewhere, I have observed that

> some revenge is actually good for the victim. It puts the victim's hitherto passive ego in an active position. This imparts a sense of mastery and enhances self-esteem. Revenge (in reality or fantasy), allowing the victim to taste the pleasure of sadism, also changes the libido-aggression balance in the self-object relationship. The victim no longer remains innocent and the perpetrator no longer the sole cruel party. Now, both seem to have been hurt and to have caused hurt. This shift lays the groundwork for empathy with the enemy and reduces hatred. (Akhtar, 2002, p. 179)

A good way to conclude this discourse is therefore to remind oneself of Nietzsche's remark that "a small revenge is humaner than no revenge at all" (1905, p. 71) and Heine's (cited in Freud, 1930, p. 110) witticism that "one must, it is true, forgive one's enemies—but not before they've been hanged."

NOTES

1. Laura Blumenfeld's (2003) book, *Revenge*, reports her encounter with the Palestinian militant who had shot and wounded her father, a New York rabbi. One of her goals was to see if she could make her father human in the gunman's eyes, since terrorism is not so much about killing people as about dehumanizing them to make a political point. In effect, she sought to 'punish' the terrorist by showing his victim's humanity. Her unusual form of revenge led to the Palestinian man's apologizing to her father and her father's forgiving him.
2. The deterrence function of revenge is what leads evolutionary theorists (Pinker, 2011; Barash and Lipton, 2011) to regard revenge as a part of our evolved human nature. "The necessity of revenge and punishment, from such vantage point, are necessary for the emergence and sustenance of cooperation. It prevents the cooperator from being exploited" (J. Anderson Thomson, Jr., personal communication, June 8, 2013).
3. The idea that the wish for revenge might be ubiquitous does not sit well with everyone. The rejecting response to the movie *Inglourious Basterds* (2009, directed by Quentin Tarantino) by many Jewish people is a case in point. The movie depicted the fictional scenario of Jewish violence against the Nazis and thus challenged the apparent absence of revenge fantasies among Jews. In contrast, the movie *Django Unchained* (2012), showing a freed black slave taking revenge against his white tormentors, was received with relative equanimity by the African American community. The socio-historical reasons that might contribute to this differential response remain unclear.

Chapter Two

Green Wounds

Revenge as Preserver of the Self

Kerry Kelly Novick

Despite the pervasiveness of the theme of revenge in the religions and literatures of all cultures from time immemorial, this topic has been relatively little studied by psychoanalysts. Others in this volume will describe in more detail the history of our theoretical ideas. I will focus here on the story of one child in analysis (here I will call him Ali) and what I have learned from him about how threads of revenge can be central in development and personality functioning. I will describe how I became interested in this topic and how my interest lay dormant until it was revived by my work with Ali and the invitation to speak at the 2013 Mahler symposium "The Wounded Self: Narcissism, Rage, and Revenge."

When I was a senior in college, before my ambition to become a psychoanalyst was more than one possible alternative, I wrote my honors thesis in Comparative Literature on "Revenge in 16th- and 17th-Century Drama." Unable to unearth my original document and find out from the source, I have nevertheless reflected on why I might have chosen that focus. I recall that I discerned in those plays two aspects of revenge that fascinated me. One concerned the inter-generational tensions and dynamics of maternal betrayal, uncertainty about the self, and oedipal confusion and conflict. The other implicated the burning drive to reverse wrongs, to redress grievances, to make the world feel right.

With those themes in mind, I turn now to the clinical story I want to share, where I hope to illustrate how Ali played out deep and important conflicts at every stage of development, turning himself into a weapon of destruction in order both to create and protect a sense of self, and revenge himself on his parents for their impossible demands. With the benefit of hindsight and the spur of the symposium's topic, I will describe some of the clinical interactions with Ali and his parents and the formulations I am beginning to make about how he came to be the person I first met when he came for evaluation just before his tenth birthday.

Ali's parents are complex people, who love their children without owning the full range of their other feelings; they initially appeared to have no realistic awareness of their psychological impact for good or ill. I like them, along with feeling frustration at their pathology. I think they each, for their own reasons, have unconsciously harbored massive hostility to this child. We could conceptualize Ali as a target for what Shengold has called "soul murder" (1989) or what Jack Novick and I, following Wurmser (1994), have called "soul blindness" (Novick, J. and Novick, K. K., 2005).

In a sense the whole treatment has hinged on the technical challenge of addressing the derivatives of these unconscious feelings in his mother's and father's parenting and their resultants in Ali. Ali has been the target of opposing externalizations from each parent, and a tool in their relationship; he has identified with those externalizations and with each parent in desperate efforts to retain attachment and defend against his own rage. But the center could not hold, with diametrically different visions of Ali imposed on him and acceptance via internalization the price for connection.

Children, in their actual dependence on grown-ups, are always vulnerable to feeling helpless. Anna Freud described helplessness as the basic anxiety underlying all others in the classic developmental sequence of anxieties (S. Freud, 1926; Sandler et al, 1980; Sandler and A. Freud, 1983). One of Sigmund Freud's most important and revolutionary insights, one we struggle to keep sight of still, was that trauma results from an *internal* experience of actual or potential helplessness, when the ego is overwhelmed from inside or outside (Freud and Breuer 1893, 1895). Modern developmental research offers us an over-arching framework of self-regulation as the biopsychosocial task of our minds, bodies and brains (National Research Council, and Institute of Medicine, 2000). In an effort to combine that perspective with the general psychology offered in psychoanalytic understanding of normal and pathological development, Jack Novick and I have suggested a model of two systems of self-regulation. We have characterized a person's responses at any age to the challenges of developmental tasks, and the consequent threat of helplessness to master them, as open- or closed-system modes of self-regulation (Novick, J. and Novick, K. K., 2002).

What poses the greatest danger of helplessness? I think it is a threat to the integrity of the self, to narcissism in its original psychoanalytic sense of love of self, in contrast to a diagnosis of a pathological preoccupation with self. An assault on one's core identity threatens trauma and evokes deep fears of annihilation, obliteration, non-being. Under such circumstances, a person has no choice but to find some way, any way, to survive, to retain agency and existential identity. Deep and intense rage in reaction to the assault on the self fuels the effort to find a solution.

One solution is the developmentally layered construction of a sadomasochistic character organized around omnipotent beliefs in the right and power to exact revenge from those responsible for rendering the person helpless, what Jack Novick and I have described as closed-system functioning. "Look how you have made me suffer!" is the litany and justification for sadism, envy, vindictiveness, selfishness, lack of empathy, and all the other nasty qualities of those obsessed with the need and desire for revenge. Antisocial tendencies to selfishly exploit others appear related to the pathologic narcissistic personalities of children and adults who feel entitled to perform vengeful actions (Kernberg, 1975). I hope to illustrate how Ali has been, until recently, a living embodiment and instrument of revenge against both his parents. His identity was formed around that mission, which then trapped him in paralyzed incapacity to move forward.

THE CASE OF ALI

Ali's father, a highly successful and secularized immigrant businessman from a Middle Eastern country, married Ali's mother, a woman more intelligent than her achievements reflect, somewhat later than average. I gather that their original relationship held a lot of sadomasochistic sexual excitement for them both, which has not meshed well with the necessary evolution of their marriage and family roles. Mr. T misses the good old days, before his wife was "angry," as he describes her newfound assertion. Mrs. T is torn between her strivings for autonomy and pride and her desperate need to please and mollify everyone around her, fixing anyone's distress with whatever it takes.

The family lives a good hour's drive away from my office, which has been a factor in our history together and has shaped some of the technical parameters of this analysis. The Ts first consulted me for one session when Ali was just over two, because they were alarmed by his intractable temper outbursts; aggression toward his baby brother, only thirteen months younger; and his volatility. I made various recommendations for management changes and referred them to a more local colleague for ongoing parent work. They came back for consultation when he was six-and-three-fourths and again right before his tenth birthday, because they were unhappy with the results from various therapies undertaken since he was four.

As I was very aware of the implications of their repeated failures and dissatisfactions in settling into and making effective any treatments with some colleagues I knew to be generally skilled and humane, the Ts and I decided that I should evaluate Ali and help them come to a definite treatment plan. At nearly ten years of age, he was still hitting, spitting, biting, yelling, and tantrumming as he had at two—something needed to be done. To his physical repertoire, he had added sadistic sarcasm and teasing, consistently and habitually abusing his younger brother and parents. At the same time, he was intensely anxious, panicky when away from his mother, managing tenuously at school.

Mrs. T had converted to her husband's religion of Islam at the time of her marriage. She wanted children and "had a plan" that she would have little girls. Ali was four weeks overdue, and Mrs. T joked that she wouldn't let him be born until the issue of circumcision had been dealt with, since she had never realistically considered she would have a boy. After an emergency C-section, Mrs. T held Ali in her arms night and day for the next three months. She was frantic that "they" would hurt her baby. Eventually her family intervened and persuaded her to go along with the circumcision.[1] From then on, I think Ali was perceived as a damaged boy/girl. Within a month, she conceived a second child, making a condition that he not be circumcised, which Mr. T went along with. Abdullah, thirteen months younger, who actually has plenty of other troubles of his own, has been a boyish and socially successful child, constantly compared by his parents to Ali, who was friendless.

Ali was hypersensitive to loud sounds and bright lights in infancy, talked and mastered toileting early, and was reading before two. Mrs. T nursed both boys until Ali was three. Some time later, he seemed drawn to dress-up clothes and his mother's scarves. After Ali's first rage-filled therapy with a child analyst ended at six-and-a-half, he soon insisted on wearing only girl's clothes. Mrs. T found a therapist who charged the family $35,000 per month and advised that Ali should be allowed to express his "true self." Mother pressured the school to accept Ali's daily attendance through second and third grade in skirts, dresses, barrettes, and all accessories. When his continuing aggressive behavior took them back to a different child analyst at the end of second grade, that doctor said not to bother about the clothes, but focus on the other issues.

Eventually Mr. T couldn't stand it and did Internet research to find himself a "gender identity specialist" in another state, whom he consulted by phone. That doctor advised immediate cessation of all the "girlie stuff," and both parents went along with that advice, clearing Ali's closets and room. Recently, Ali told his father that he knows he is a boy and is glad of it, but that he does sometimes miss the girlie stuff. Mrs. T told me that she still cries every month when her period reminds her that she has not conceived a girl. Her sons see this and know how she feels.

In one of our evaluation sessions, when Ali was quite silent, I pointed out to him that his parents had been telling me about some of the troubles, and how he had seen a number of therapists, but that I had not heard much from him about what he thought about himself and what he might want for himself from therapy. I took out a piece of paper, put his name at the top, divided it into two columns, and wrote "Strengths" above one and "Goals?" above the other. I then listed "smart, healthy, funny, tough, strong" (all of which seemed true to me) under strengths, and "be strong and happy" under goals. Ali reached across the table and crossed out both his name and the "Strengths" heading at the top of my page. I said, "If you don't like my list, how about making your own?" He headed his page "Someone," and noted "I hate Kerry." Then, under "Strengths," Ali wrote "nothing"; under his heading "Weaknesses" he wrote "everything." Ali's deep sense of emptiness, of having nothing to offer but his simmering rage and consequent impulsiveness alternating with inhibition, was palpable.

It was clear from the assessment that Ali needed an analysis, and I thought he actually had the capacities. I attempted several more local referrals, but one or the other of the parents found fault with everyone suggested. Eventually, with internal trepidation, I agreed to take Ali into analysis that included regular parent work, with an explicit long-term commitment by all that I was the end of the line, that there would be no more changing. If this treatment foundered, it would mean that something very different would have to be tried.

Ali started four times per week analysis with me in the summer he turned ten. Because of the distance, we planned that he would come for one double and two single sessions, and his parents would meet with me weekly. Although Ali's style and presentation was to play mindlessly, often emptying the session of any content or affect, blankly deflecting any efforts to make a story, or to attribute characteristics or feelings to anyone (people, toys, puppets, animals), or include his daily life, and so forth, we nevertheless began to develop a connection and his behavior showed some significant improvement almost immediately.

To give a flavor of some early interactions—this was a really good day, with some actual content—we were at the table, where he was making tickets to a magic horror show he was going to devise, with a mummy in a sarcophagus. He incidentally mentioned that he had "made" his mother turn over the broom closet to him to be his sarcophagus, where he could retreat for "private time." I asked one question too many for his taste and Ali snarled at me, "Shut your hole, woman! Shut up!" I demurred and he grabbed a piece of paper and wrote on it "Shut up—you're a crazy old cook!" I noted mildly that I thought he meant "kook," that it was spelled with a "k." I agreed that I was old and said the "crazy" was probably a matter of opinion. By this time he was laughing and we proceeded with our tickets.

Ali's verbal aggression to me was fairly easily dealt with at this point by calmness, being literal, appreciating his wit, and refusing to let it pass. I could verbalize his transparent defensive wishes for superpowers and desperate efforts to boss others, and make explicit hypotheses about the feelings that might lie behind such intense needs to control. Ali never acknowledged these interventions, but his behavior improved at home and school. His parents were getting better at moderating their reactions and were working hard on firming up their prohibitions of Ali's unremitting physically and verbally sadistic attacks on his brother, Abdullah, thirteen months younger.

At a conference with Ali's teachers at his very unstructured, progressive private school, I did my best to give them permission and support to make demands of him, rather than let him avoid work with the rationalization of being understanding of his troubles. I have continued to be in intermittent touch with Ali's school; the teachers and principal see me as an ally and support when they feel daunted.

At that time in the treatment, I often felt fairly hopeless and helpless in sessions, where Ali persisted in emptying content and feelings from the interaction. I soldiered on in making something of the crumbs of material, doing my best to read Ali's face and tones, verbalizing feelings and making connections, however sparse. My puzzlement centered on my sense of his lack of desire, drive, and aims. He was a youngster who seemed to want to obliterate himself, to have no reality, no presence, no agency, no oomph. It felt as if I had to supply the idea of a person with autonomous wishes and a push for progressive development.

But his apparently deliberate vacantness also carried palpable hostility. My attempts to make some meaning of his demeanor and behavior were met with his obdurate efforts to obliterate my functions, indeed my very self. When Ali desperately insisted that I "had" to play mindless, pleasureless, repetitive games of hurling different superpowers at each other verbally, he conveyed his desperate sense of entitlement to being emperor of the world.

Finally, I realized that this was the central issue. Ali, like everyone does, had constructed his identity to meet important basic needs of safety, attachment, defense, and gratification. Children have no choice but to adapt to the circumstances in which they find themselves, doing the best they can even in adverse conditions to make sense of their experience and survive physically and psychologically. It was my job to understand how he experienced his needs, what he thought the parameters were, the accommodations he felt he had to make to meet his fundamental needs, and what our points of entry were to effect any changes. But this formulation might tend to characterize Ali only as the passive victim of his parents' various psychological agendas.

What matters in the discussion here is for us to grasp his seizing of the initiative in avenging his parents' attempts at soul murder by developing what we would describe as his neurotic symptoms and character pathology. For Ali, these were his desperate efforts to preserve his very self. Why was this such a life-and-death struggle? And why did it have the hallmark qualities of rage, resentment, vindictiveness, and meanness that signal the presence of revenge motives? How did it work to revenge himself on his parents?

Ali constructed a creature who was neither boy nor girl, not a baby or a big boy, not like anyone else in his family; he met no one's expectations, and disappointed everyone's hopes in order to avenge himself.

The Ts and I continued to work on setting limits, establishing boundaries, sharing responsibility, reality consequences, ego strengths, self-control, social skills, family roles, and more. This period brought further revelations of underlying issues. Mrs. T had been raped as an adolescent. She struggled with panicky ambivalence about men and their aggression; her attitudes to Ali were further over-determined by this history. She had left her own therapy at her husband's demand, which had originally worried me. Interestingly, the loss of an opportunity to split her transferences and to sequester her pathology into parenting proved constructive. She was shocked, but also relieved when I interpreted the possible connections among her experiences at the hands of men, her fears of male aggression, the circumcision issues, and Ali's gender conflicts.[2]

In parallel, Mr. T's habit of treating Ali as if he were fragile could be connected to his parents' attitudes to him and his older brother. I learned about Mr. T's deadbeat older brother, an occasional drug addict who cannot support himself without subsidy and a house from the successful Mr. T. The paternal grandmother favors Mr. T's older brother; Mr. T said she "couldn't give a shit about me, but I worry that I'll feel guilty when she passes if I cut her off." He could take seriously the parallels between the way he described his brother and the issues of responsibility we were engaging with for Ali, and vowed to try to make sure that Ali does not turn into someone like his older brother. These were the early steps toward Mr. T achieving the insight that he unconsciously strove for Ali to be like the older brother.

Both parents were more successful than their families of origin, and struggled with guilt over the unconscious aggressive meanings this carried for them. Mrs. T was compulsively generous to her parents and siblings, often sacrificing her own children's needs and time to the demands of extended family members. Despite the reality of cultural traditions supporting such care for a wider family circle, each parent carried this far beyond the usual.

The parent work was and is central to this case, both in terms of pathogenesis and hopes for change (Novick, K.K. and Novick, J., 2005, 2013). As time went by and I learned ever more about the parents and their issues, the resonances in Ali's psyche were increasingly clear. There was no way this child could satisfy either parent. He was in a classic double-bind situation. If he pursued his masculine identity, his mother would recoil from him in horror and disgust. If he fulfilled his mother's wishes for a girl-child, his father would reject him. How could he retain some sense of self? Who should he be? Who could he be? What could he do with the rage and terror of obliteration that came with the impossible psychic demands from his antipathetic parents? I think that he devised serial strategies of revenge in the effort to resolve these questions.

Ali's first solution was to be a very demanding, needy, clinging, angry, aggressive, acting-out, effeminate boy. It was a pretty effective plan for a four- to five-year-old. His mother felt indispensable; she approved, with enjoyment, of his interest in adornment and frills, and his lack of engagement in sports or activities of any kind. The power of her continuing unconscious need to turn Ali into a girl was demonstrated a couple of years ago when she claimed she just couldn't find any boy's cardigans for his new school clothes, so had bought him some in the girls' department, which of course buttoned the wrong way and looked feminine. In a parent session with her, I went online and immediately found six options for boys at national children's clothing sites. Mrs. T needed literal demonstrations like this to acknowledge her investment, but, to her credit, she bravely took responsibility for her issues and never acted out the same way twice once it was pointed out.

Of course, such wardrobe choices infuriated Mr. T. His unconscious wish to equate Ali with his loser brother was gratified by Ali's lack of social success with peers; this provided Mr. T with a chronic reproach to his wife, which fueled their sadomasochistic interactions. Disappointed, sarcastic comments to Ali and invidious comparison with Abdullah's relative social success ensured ongoing friction and spiteful interchanges between Ali and his dad. Then, Mr. T would feel wounded and bewildered that his son seemed neither to like nor respect him.

Along with deepening understanding of the family dynamics from the ongoing parent meetings, the work with Ali continued. My experience of sessions with him continued the skimpiness and impoverishment of content and feelings, which reflected how little of himself Ali felt safe to let be visible. I was able to continue caring for him, enjoying the flashes of curiosity and acuity that he let fall. It was clear to us both that, most of the time, we respected each other's intellects and a certain base level of reality, no matter how often Ali rejected my skeptical worldview in favor of his wishful, omnipotent thinking. He was preoccupied with magic, ghosts, werewolves, poltergeists, spells, and superpowers. His older schoolchild solution incorporated a reliance on magical thinking and omnipotent control of his objects, which continued to get reality validation, necessary for any closed-system, omnipotent adaptation, from both parents. Work in the analysis continued to address these issues.

We started Ali's fifth grade year with good feelings in Ali, his parents, and me about continued progress. He was more contained, often more relaxed, and I think felt more in charge of his destiny. He brought books and treasures to show me, discussed his snacks and reading, and occasionally described incidents at school. Companionable times around his homework assignments and his occasional admission that I actually knew a lot of stuff came more often. After one-and-a-half years of analysis, the Ts and I had a hopeful discussion about seeing Ali into middle school the following fall and then being in a position to assess when it might be time for a pause or termination of treatment. We knew that there was a lot of work still to do to reach that point. Then there was a dramatic change. The T family and I were both out of town for the late winter vacation. On their return, Ali's behavior deteriorated drastically, for no immediately discernible reason. Mr. T was deeply discouraged and wanted to quit the treatment. For the Ts and for myself, I wrote up a long and detailed progress report, organized around different areas of Ali's personality, in my head derived from the metapsychological profile, Anna Freud's developmental lines and general characteristics of the ego, two systems of self-regulation, and various emotional muscles from Jack Novick's and my recent work (Novick, K. K. and Novick, J., 2010, 2011). This raises a question of technique—I don't think child analysts generally write such reports, or at least don't share them with parents, but we can ask ourselves why not. I found it helpful and it focused the Ts in a very constructive way, giving the father especially a more comprehensive picture. After meeting with me to discuss the report, the Ts stopped blaming each other so much, pulled together and recommitted to the treatment and to their more regular joint attendance. Mr. T had trouble sticking to the schedule, because of his many regular work trips, but joined in by phone or Skype whenever he could.

One spring evening during a parent session, Mr. T received a cell phone call from Ali, who was attending a baseball game with the family of a classmate. Ali (then eleven-and-a-half) was whining on the phone that he was bored and wanted his dad to come get him; he wanted to be home. Dad told him he would call back shortly and we discussed the situation. Ali called four times in the next ten minutes, upping the ante, screaming and yelling that his dad "had" to come. Mr. T was desperately distressed, wanting to fly to Ali's side, then thinking that maybe they could pick him up and go out for a nice dinner together. The reality was that they were an hour-and-a-half away from the ballpark and in the middle of an expensive professional meeting with me. Mrs. T and I managed to help Mr. T see what message he would be giving Ali if the boy's distress turned everything upside down and became the only priority. This incident, among others, began to illuminate the father's vulnerability and enmeshment more clearly.

Over time, the parents were haltingly developing slightly sturdier responses; common sense and reality were increasingly part of Ali's daily life. While this firming of parental backbone was going on, Ali's behavior only grew worse again. This worried me. I began to sense that changes in the reality parameters of Ali's life threatened his earlier vengeful solutions, what Jack Novick and I would refer to as his "closed-system adaptations." The family dynamic was shifting.

Here is a technical and theoretical challenge for us—if the *raison d'etre* of a person's life is revenge, what happens when the terms change? There is an analogy to the dangers we face when we analyze obsessional defenses against psychotic thinking—if we take something that feels necessary away, it can leave the person prey to traumatic dissolution (Blum, 1981). What do we offer patients as alternatives to meet crucial basic psychological needs? It feels critical to simultaneously analyze old defensive patterns while generating new options. We have discussed this challenge in terms of differential techniques related to both closed- and open-system functioning (Novick, J. and Novick, K.K., 2000, 2003). The reality base of the open system of self-regulation has to be a continuing thread throughout any treatment.

Ali's sessions at this point alternated between hostile, stubborn, sullen silence and shrieking, cursing orders with abusive epithets in response to *any* frustration, disagreement, reality statement, or questioning of his plans. He pushed his face close to mine, threatening to spit, and breathing on me. He would bring his fist within inches, or casually kick out while passing me to fetch something. Occasionally, when his fist looked about to connect, I grasped it in my hand and firmly reminded him that physical threats were not allowed; he usually backed down. One day Ali lost control entirely, trying to hit and kick—by this time, he was nearly my height, although only two-thirds of my weight, and a very weak child (still unable to ride a two-wheeler). I restrained him, sitting next to him on the couch so that he couldn't butt me, holding his wrists crossed over his chest, hooking my ankle over his to prevent kicking. His body eventually calmed and he assured me he would be able to keep us both safe. This happened a few times over about two weeks.

I was alarmed by this rapid escalation. At the same time, Ali was always reachable. The fact that he seemed panicky at meltdown moments was paradoxically reassuring, because it gave them meaning. But it was also an unsustainable situation and he was scaring himself. Note here that I was never frightened by him—more annoyed and sad, plus physically tired. His parents and I talked about the possibility that he would not be able to manage in outpatient treatment and might need a therapeutic school and a more comprehensive treatment program. I also talked to Ali about how sad it seemed that he was setting himself up to realize his own worst nightmare, that is, having to leave his parents. I said that I could see how he felt trapped between not knowing how to be his own person with them or without them, and how frightened he was of his connection to me, since it had come to represent a different set of possibilities. Perhaps his panic came from the fear that his old ways would be taken away and he would be left with nothing, not even the self he had been so used to all these years. He listened intently when I said that I wondered if he still felt that his angry self was the only viable person to be.

But one day it was just too much for me; I had had enough and I told him midway through a flailing tantrum that he was fired. He looked at me in shock, shaking his head in disbelief when I ushered him right out of the office and to his startled mother's car. His parents and I told him that he would have to *earn* back his treatment. Looking back, it feels significant that I used the word "fired." I think I felt underneath that Ali was not doing his job, that he had externalized his ego functions and capacity for self-control on to me; he was expecting me to have all the emotional muscles, so that he didn't have to do his share of the work. Being externalized upon is assaultive in itself; my action handed back the responsibility to Ali, functioning as a refusal any longer to accept the externalization and labeling the aggression accurately. In doing so, I felt relieved, as if I were finally being honest with him about the reality that he had options.

The Ts and I continued with parent work through the summer, in regular sessions, phone calls, and frequent e-mails. The level of auxiliary ego support the Ts needed was prodigious, now that the vessel for externalization that Ali's treatment had provided was not available. As long as he was attending his sessions, they had been able to pay lip service to the parent work, enforcing the ideas intermittently, but preconsciously shunting responsibility to me. Ali's behavior again improved markedly and he made the transition into middle school without overt crisis. The Ts and I talked about his behavioral improvement and their simultaneous impression of poignant, underlying sadness and self-hate, as well as his continuing social isolation. I suggested that they talk with Ali about their pleasure in his growing capacity to feel good and strong managing his behavior better. They could ask him whether he wanted to work on the inside feelings and could suggest that therapy was the ideal place to do that, if he felt ready and wanted it. They were expecting an argument, a rejection, or a tantrum. What Ali said was simply, "Yes, I want to talk to Kerry."

We planned two sessions for Ali to come see me to discuss the situation. We caught up a bit during the first and talked quietly and seriously about what a hard time we had earlier. As we set our agenda for the second meeting, to think about what to work on, the time was up. Ali went toward the door, came back and threw his arms around me, to my complete surprise. "See you next time," he said. The next time we started talking about what there was to work on and Ali suggested that we each make a list and then compare them. Fascinatingly, our lists were almost the same. They each included aspects of developing a more reality-based, gratifying sense of himself as a person able to feel good from mastering challenges, rather than from getting back at others. We agreed that these were important things that could actually be helped and changed by therapy.

Two years have elapsed since then. Ali's inching progress into tentative peer relationships has reassured his father, and the terms of the parents' disagreements have been clarified and improved. A noteworthy sign of internal change in Ali has been his taking full charge of his schoolwork and homework; his assignments get done and in on time and his grades are now commensurate with his intelligence. He is able to go on overnight school trips without panicky phone calls home. He even occasionally has fun with his brother. More active pursuits in sports or just playing outside have begun to enter the picture. In his sessions, Ali now often brings significant material on purpose—a far cry from the early days. I have heard about disputes among kids at school, issues with his cousins, campaigns with his parents. When I speak to less conscious links, patterns, and conflicts, Ali is willing to listen and elaborate on the material. We are beginning to look at the delicate issues around his sexuality and gender identity and their connection to his impossible task to satisfy both parents in order to meet his own basic needs.

SOME REFLECTIONS AND CONCLUSION

I called this chapter "Green Wounds" on the basis of something Francis Bacon said in 1625 (Bartleby.com, 2001). "This is certain, that a man that studieth revenge keeps his own wounds green, which otherwise would heal and do well." For me, this describes the role of revenge in keeping intact a self-representation that included Ali's belief in nihilistic power to destroy his self and others throughout his early years. But it also kept his wounds from healing, as he tried to freeze time in an omnipotent defense against the risk of the developmental tasks that progression poses. By watching baby television shows, demanding his own menu, clinging to his mother, refusing to opt for a definitive gender identity, procrastinating about schoolwork, avoiding the challenge of peer games and pursuits, and so forth, Ali believed he could maintain a bubble of need-gratification, a narcissistic Garden of Eden in which his mother would be solely preoccupied with him and all his needs would be met without effort.[3]

But let's note that Bacon uses the active verb "studieth." Ali *chose* this path, perhaps first in earliest childhood because nothing else seemed available in light of his parents' diametrically opposed visions for him. Later, however, when his treatment and parental changes offered him an alternative, he retreated in panic from the unknown. His terrible anguish and fear at the prospect of having his old empty self taken away, at losing the sense of power he derived from rageful vindictive attacks on everyone, drove him to destroy the hopeful alternative connection we had been forging in his analysis. He erected a catastrophic resistance that I could not withstand. His violence was *really* unbearable and unacceptable. When Ali began to attack me, it represented a progression of sorts. Instead of turning his aggression on himself, in an omnipotent, closed-system, sadomasochistic scenario of victimization, he invoked a passive-to-active defense, finally engaged in an interpersonal struggle with meaning for us both. He was actively attacking elements of *my* basic identity—the important idea to me that I am a helping person, willing and able to commit to engaging with someone, no matter how lost he seems.

When I fired him, I think he heard that I did not see him as solely a helpless and passive victim or only as a raging instrument of revenge. He seemed to get the idea that I really thought he had a choice. He was not helplessly and forever in the grip of revenge, but had the option and the tools to go beyond that. My drawing a line in reality directly contradicted the omnipotent defensive character structure predicated in his vengeful identity formation.

Our reunion was deeply reparative for us both. "See you next time" has come to symbolize for me the idea that the reality of time has entered the equation, that Ali imagines a future for himself that he can shape. Instead of following Hamlet's description that "all occasions do inform against me, And spur my dull revenge!" (Shakespeare, 1602, Hamlet, 4.4.35–6), Ali is increasingly able to differentiate when something is actually aimed at him and when it is the other person's problem.

I look forward to Ali's future as his own person. He now has a choice; sometimes he slips back into Hamlet's position, but he is often now capable of pulling himself together—he has a sense that there is a person inside who can do that and he values how it feels to be capable. I have hope that he will "heal and do well."

NOTES

1. It seemed very unusual the first time I encountered it, but I have subsequently seen numerous examples of mothers who showed similar near-psychotic reactions to circumcision, with consequent grave impact on their relationship to their babies.
2. In line with the model of parent work described in "Working with Parents Makes Therapy Work" (Novick, K. K. and Novick, J., 2005), I made full use of the psychoanalytic technical repertoire in relation to the impact of dynamic and unconscious factors on the Ts' parenting.
3. It is noteworthy that LaFarge (2006) describes clinical phenomena in her case in very similar terms, while using different theoretical concepts to articulate her understanding. There seems to be marked convergence in the literature on the experience of treating vengeful patients and the ways they relate to themselves and their analysts.

Chapter Three

Revenge and Reparation

Thoughts About the Treatment of a Boy and His Family

Barbara Shapiro

I am delighted to have the opportunity to discuss Mrs. Novick's riveting presentation about a complex patient, family, and therapeutic process. Reading her contribution, and perusing the literature regarding revenge, has made me realize how frequently I have missed various aspects of revenge and its henchmen in my own work and supervision. Despite the fact that revenge, in all its variations, is deeply embedded in human nature and culture, the psychoanalytic literature is relatively sparse. We have missed a part of human nature that has been a major theme for writers, artists, filmmakers, and storytellers over the centuries. Revenge themes repeatedly emerge in creative and religious endeavors, such as Greek plays, Eastern and Western literary classics, mythologies and folk stories of multiple cultures, fairy tales, religious writings, opera, artistic masterpieces, movies, and children's literature (Beattie, 2005; Rosen, 2007; Berke, 2012). Wanting to get back at someone who has hurt or humiliated you is normal and natural. Revenge is rooted in our need for fairness and justice. Children of all ages are keenly aware of what they think is fair. Recent observational research on morality reveals that babies as young as three to six months of age demonstrate nonverbal understanding of fairness, justice, kindness, and meanness (Bloom, 2010; Hamlin et al, 2011; Hamlin, 2013); the same is true of some primates (de Waal, 2013).

Families and societies need just and effective consequences for hurtful actions—a law of the house or of the land—to avoid random vigilante-style justice and idiosyncratic revenge. Families that for the most part are kind and respectful and that have reasonable and relatively consistent limits and expectations provide a structure in which children generally don't need an extreme of revenge dynamics. The same is true in larger groups and societies. We are all profoundly shaped by the culture(s) in which we develop and live our lives (Akhtar, 1999; Siassi, 2006; Tronick, 2007). Societies, cultures, communities, and micro-cultures differ in the acceptability of vengefulness and revenge, both in degree and in form. In general, most societies based on 'an eye for an eye and a tooth for a tooth' limit the scope of revenge to that which is perceived within that society to be equivalent to the hurt. Also the revenge is episodic and does not take over the life of the individual (Rosen, 2007). Of course, there are cultures, just as there are individuals, in which revenge becomes a primary and chronic motivator for action (Beattie, 2005; Siassi, 2006).

We all have our vengeful fantasies and acts. The question is the degree to which the desire for revenge takes over psychic function, the self, and relationships. There is a big difference between a child who is sporadically vengeful, and a child like 'Ali,' from Mrs. Novick's chapter. Ali's rage and revenge were intense and ongoing. As powerful organizers of his developing self and character, his rage and vengefulness posed a significant threat to the present and future well-being of himself and others.

Revenge, in moderation, serves a function in the competitions and rivalries of human relationships, from childhood on; that sort of revenge that is short-lived and episodic. Malignant revenge takes over the person. It has momentum; it is self-organizing and self-reinforcing. Eventually, it takes on a life of its own. Its henchmen are malignant narcissism, envy, self-righteousness, and omnipotence. Eventually self-righteousness and omnipotence nullify guilt, and revenge becomes ego syntonic as it deflects feelings of weakness, sadness, helplessness, and loss (Rosen, 2007).

The form of revenge differs with psychic structure, age, executive function, degree of sadomasochism and malignant envy, family dynamics, and social/cultural forces. Revenge stays within bounds when it is integrated with compassion, love, gratitude, kindness, respect, and the ability to acknowledge and repair hurtful words or acts (Gabbard, 1996; Tronick and Weinburg, 1997; Akhtar, 2012; Berke, 2012). When the capacities for repair, compassion, and kindness are impaired, the stage is set for revenge to become malignant.

We are not born chronically vengeful. Certainly, some babies have more innate aggression, and/or more innate vulnerabilities. However, an overabundance of revenge usually rests on a bed of varying combinations of hurt, abuse, shame, humiliation, parental hostility, hatred, and neglect. All or some of these factors may be transgenerational, and result in narcissistic injury and developmental trauma in the infant and growing child (Gabbard, 1996). The child feels, and is, helpless. She experiences helpless rage, feels herself to be worthless, nothing, bad. She hates others and herself. This often starts early in life, in the non-verbal sphere, and then stays there, dissociated. Early traumas and neglect can then be compounded later by destructive family dynamics, ongoing trauma, and community and societal dysfunction. The infant may show avoidance or freezing behaviors. By the beginning of the second year of life, one can see the child ragefully attacking herself and others, alternating with sulking, hostile withdrawals. Other times the child is terrified, regressed, and fragmented (Fraiberg, 1982). She becomes envious of others who have the power, and power and control become the currency of human relationships. If trauma has not entirely stripped the child of self-agency and aggression, she develops a compensation of omnipotence. The core self is hollow, hated. Narcissistic rage and omnipotence protect against terrible sadness and fragmentation, self-annihilation. Revenge provides proof of power and the pride of forcing a primal justice. Self-righteousness dissipates shame and guilt; narcissism becomes malignant; rage becomes hatred; envy becomes destructive malevolence; and revenge provides agency, mission, power, and meaning. And we all need agency, a sense of control, and meaning. If there has been familial trauma, without rescuers, the stage is set for mistrusting everyone—paranoia. There is disgust with one's self, which becomes subsumed into a disgust with the world (Horowitz, 2007). All this takes place in the crucible of the family, community, and society, in which transgenerational and interpersonal identifications, dynamics, and traumas may feed the rage and revenge (Siassi, 2006).

It is important to see the strength as well as the vulnerability in Ali's rageful attacks and vengefulness. We must remember that rage and revenge are strong responses, employing aggression and self-agency. In contrast, other children and adults who have experienced significant trauma may be cowed into a selfless compliance, a conviction of total unworthiness, and a concomitant erosion of self-agency. And rage and revenge (in fantasy or act) is also stronger than resentment, in which helpless rage is subsumed into an obsequious compliant reaction formation (Beattie, 2005). Hatred and revenge are as relational as love. We take revenge on a person or a group of people. When all we can think about is getting revenge on someone, we are tied—attached—to that person, in an intense internalized object relationship (Rosen, 2007). We are besotted with hatred, obsessed with contempt. We lovingly fall in hate, and we don't let go (LaFarge, 2006). This could be viewed as a version of Fairbairn's concept regarding the exciting-rejecting object (Fairbairn, 1952, 1963; Beattie, 2005; Rosen, 2007).

At what age does one first see actual revenge? Certainly there is a developmental line. Revenge requires some executive function and some degree of mentalization. Mentalization has to be sufficient to have a degree of understanding the other person's mind, as well as the effect on the other person of the vengeful act. Let me give an example from my practice. A traumatized mid-latency-aged boy, whom I will call L, regularly attacked me, physically and verbally, with a meanness of spirit. Gradually, the physical and verbal attacks disappeared, and the rage and sadomasochism were expressed and worked through with puppets and other play. One day, I was unavoidably late for L's appointment—I had not been late before. I walked past his father, who was in the waiting room, and the father told me L was in the bathroom. I asked him to tell L that I would be in my office with my door open. In a few minutes, L appeared at the door, holding something behind him. He had an evil smirk on his face. Before I could get up from my chair, L went to the shelf where I always kept my coffee cup, with coffee in it (he knew this), and opened the paper towels which he had held behind his back. Inside the paper towels rested a medium-sized nicely formed bowel movement. Before I could move, L put the bowel movement into my coffee cup. His initial attacks were impulsive and out of control. They were also mean—a sort of proto-revenge. But the bowel movement in the coffee cup was a plotted and well-executed revenge for my being late. He knew that I valued the coffee cup and enjoyed drinking coffee, so in this instance mentalization, executive function, and non-compassionate empathy were intact.

Revenge can be active, attacking, aimed toward someone, or withdrawing, passive, turning away from someone. Active vengeful attacks are obvious. We may not recognize withdrawing actions as vengeful. Sulking is one example. The child or adult in a deep and lasting sulk achieves considerable power and revenge (Berke, 2012). Think how hard it is to ignore a loved one who is mired in an obvious and petulant sulk. We might pretend to ignore the sulk, but really it fills our minds and the relationship. A deep and prolonged sulk is highly effective in controlling the minds of others. It takes over, sometimes to the point of erasing the selfhood of others. Pride makes it difficult for the sulker to give up, give in, and forgive (Steiner, 1996). The children's book *Spinky Sulks,* describes this phenomenon beautifully (Steig, 1988). Other examples of withdrawn and passive revenge include the silent treatment, cutting someone dead, gas-lighting, leaving abruptly, and hanging up on someone. Also, in some instances, suicide, masochism, self-defeating acts, and depriving someone of the pleasure of your success achieve vengeful purposes.

Revenge is on a spectrum of hot to cold. Hot revenge is, well, hot. It doesn't involve much executive function. It is immediate, stormy, impulsive, and poorly planned. Cold revenge is carefully planned, and executed so as to have the pleasure of getting back at someone without being caught. This requires a high level of executive function. Rould Dahl describes this in his children's books, such as *Matilda,* and Dav Pilkey in his *Captain Underpants* children's book series (Dahl, 2004; Pilkey, 2013 as one example). Another more extreme example is Poe's (1846) story *The Cask of Amontillado*, in which the revenger coldly and carefully plots the painful demise of the man he hates. The narrator of the story says:

> The thousand injuries of Fortunato I had borne as I best could; but when he ventured upon insult, I vowed revenge. You, who so well know the nature of my soul, will not suppose, however, that I gave utterance to a threat. At length I would be avenged; this was a point definitely settled—but the very definiteness with which it was resolved, precluded the idea of risk. I must not only punish, but punish with impunity. A wrong is unredressed when retribution overtakes its redresser. It is equally unredressed when the avenger fails to make himself felt as such to him who has done the wrong. (310)

This sort of totally cold revenge described by Poe requires a quite high level of executive function, along with a lack of or dissociation of conflict, guilt, or the sort of moral masochism that would involve getting caught as punishment. The plotting of the murderous revenge is entirely ego syntonic. Young children are not capable of this degree of coldness. The capacity for this sort of revenge would likely first be seen in mid to late latency, and perfected in adolescence and adulthood.

Finally, malignant revenge is sticky. It has a life of its own. It keeps its wounds green, and itself interferes with healing. This makes the therapeutic work very slow and difficult, and prone to negative therapeutic reactions. Slowly, gently, the underlying worthlessness, sadness, losses, envy have to be unveiled and integrated without increasing shame and humiliation. It is difficult to give up chronic vengefulness toward a particular person or group without a terrible loss of pride (Steiner, 1996).

Let us turn to Ali as an illustration of the development and treatment of malignant vengefulness. Ali was born into a family with malevolent ghosts and intergenerational trauma on both sides. The parents, as Mrs. Novick puts it, were loving but 'soul blind' (Novick, 2013). His traumatized mother, who wanted only girl babies, held him in her arms for the first three months of his life, protecting him, in her perception, from her husband and his family. This unbearable tension in the mother and the family would have been felt by the infant. When Ali was four months old, his mother became pregnant. It is not easy to have a baby and be pregnant, and then to have two babies only thirteen months apart. Also, the mother now had two boys, and she wanted girls. From Ali's point of view, it is not easy for a thirteen-month-old to understand and bear the presence of another baby even in the best of circumstances. The brother was not circumcised, and this was an emotionally and culturally pivotal issue with the parents. Ali's aggression toward his brother is understandable from many perspectives.

When Ali was only two years old, the parents sought help because of his intense temper outbursts and unremitting aggression toward his brother. Transgenerational traumata had left their marks on the next generation. Ali's developing sense of self and his object relationships, both real and internalized, and his identifications, were deeply affected. This is the soil of hurt, rage, envy, shame, and helplessness, in which rage took root and grew, choking out development of other spheres with a resulting relative emptiness of the self. The ghosts of hostility, spite, and revenge weighed heavily in this family. At the same time, Ali got away with murder, and his parents catered to his wishes, as there were no age appropriate limits or expectations. The lack of limits further fed compensatory omnipotence, which grew wildly.

Ali was caught in a war in which his core self, especially gender identity and role, became a focus of parental dispute. His mother wanted him to be a girl, rejected his boy self, and bought girls' sweaters even when Ali did not request them. His father wanted Ali to be a boy, and rejected his girl self. Ali's parents were trapped by their ghosts, and Ali was trapped in the middle of ghastly ghostly wars. He became the tool by which his parents unwittingly took their revenge on one another. Ali requested girlish things, but it is not clear how strongly this came from Ali, how much was to please his mother and meet her vision of him, and how much was to oppose and take revenge on his father. Additionally, his previous therapists disagreed about how to handle his gender identity and role behavior. One, found by the mother, advised letting Ali express himself. Another, found by the father, advised taking away and forbidding all girlish activities. The parents had their allies. The system was split, polarized, at war. How terribly confusing for everyone. One can see how making sense of Ali's own gender identity and Ali's own gender expression is now a sensitive and difficult area for therapeutic work. This was not a naturally developing girly boy (Corbett, 2009). Meanwhile the actual child was not seen, heard, or known. He could, however, force others to see him and make his story known by utilizing attacking and vengeful behaviors. One can see how revenge, in certain forms, serves the important function of making one's story known.

The family dynamics had the characteristics of schismogenesis, described by anthropologist Gregory Bateson (1972), in which people or groups dynamically respond to attacks with counterattacks, distortions, and ever increasing polarization. The word itself, of Greek derivation, literally means the creation of division. This dynamic process gathers its own momentum, perceived differences are destructively magnified and fortified, and oppositional positions spin out of control. Clearly communication, understanding, and 'agreeing to disagree' are rendered impossible. This dynamic in Ali's family, teamed with other intrapsychic and family dynamics, fed the wounded green monster of revenge, begetting more revenge. Everyone, parents and children, actively participated in a sadomasochistic drama. By the age of ten, when Ali and his family started treatment with Mrs. Novick, he had eight to nine years of experience in terrorizing others physically and verbally. At the same time, he was terrified, and full of self-loathing. Certainly he had strengths: he was very bright, witty, and capable of love and attachment. And the parents, although psychologically deaf, loved him, and had consistently sought treatment for his problems.

After treatment started, Ali improved. His initial mindless, empty, inhibited play, along with his need to control and his vengefulness, are consistent with what we often see in a traumatized child. But he and Mrs. Novick were able to connect, which means that Ali was able to connect. And the parents also connected with Mrs. Novick in a therapeutic alliance. Eventually as a result of Mrs. Novick's work with the parents, they placed more limits on Ali's behavior, introducing some rule of law and justice. Then a year and a half later, all hell broke loose. Ali again became physically and verbally attacking, and had to be physically restrained in the sessions. The parents wanted to quit. This was a negative therapeutic reaction which could have turned into a total impasse.

What are some of the factors that were operative in producing and then resolving this negative therapeutic reaction?

- *First*, there was a break in the treatment, which had been going well. As we all know well, demons tend to rush in during breaks.
- *Second*, the family was on vacation, and sometimes the worst times in troubled families happen during those vacation times. We don't know what happened there.
- *Third*, Ali was approaching adolescence, and was also transitioning to middle school. One can wonder if perhaps his testosterone levels were starting to rise.
- *Fourth*, the parents had talked with Mrs. Novick about termination at some point. Did Ali know or sense this, or overhear his parents talking? Did he try to keep treatment going by regressing to terrorism?
- *Fifth*, Mrs. Novick had to physically restrain Ali. Perhaps this physical contact further reinforced the dynamic of dominating and being dominated—a sadomasochistic solution, perhaps with erotic and sensual components. Was this too exciting and terrifying? Did the restraint feed Ali's internalized representation of Mrs. Novick as an exciting/rejecting object (Fairbairn, 1952, 1963)?
- *Sixth*, presumably an important factor in Ali's previous improvement was that the parents were better able to set limits and expectations as a result of their work with Mrs. Novick. Now Ali was exploding with rage and revenge. It seems that his very sense of self was threatened. The omnipotence was compensatory. Without omnipotence, who was he? And who was most responsible for this change? Mrs. Novick was the one encouraging his parents to set realistic limits, and of course Ali would have known this. So perhaps he took revenge in a desperate attempt to reestablish his control and dominance.

I assume Mrs. Novick helped the parents establish compassion and kindness along with limits, and reparations as consequences for destruction. Compassion, kindness, gratitude, and reparation counterbalance malignant narcissism and revenge. However, malignant narcissism and envy often hate goodness, kindness, and support. The very goodness weakens compensations and defenses against sadness, pain, helplessness, and loss, and evokes further envy and revenge. In this world, one either controls or is controlled. Looking at this another way, the parents and Mrs. Novick probably preferred the 'good' Ali to the 'bad' Ali. But his envious, contemptuous self may have felt scorned, under attack, and abandoned. Did he fight for the life and recognition of that powerful aspect of his self? And then one day Mrs. Novick had it. She 'fired' Ali. And it worked. How often do we do that openly? Over time, Ali's behavior subsequently improved. He eventually came back to the analysis. This was his choice. He gave Mrs. Novick a hug (love and gratitude, and reparation for both of them). And the analysis was restarted, with a different feel.

What factors and actions helped resolve this looming impasse? I am curious about Mrs. Novick's feelings and thoughts before, during, and after 'firing' Ali. Something shifted in her, and in the transference-countertransference matrix. It was clear that something had to give. Was this in part a counter-revenge? Was it an enactment that enabled Ali and his family to shift their internal and familial dynamics? Enactments, even when they don't ever reach the level of conscious awareness, can be powerful forces for positive as well as negative change.

How about the progress report that Mrs. Novick wrote when the parents wanted to quit? Perhaps this move gave the parents a concrete and coherent narrative which they could hold and read at home. These were parents who seemed prone to repress, dissociate, disagree, distort, and project, probably during the parental sessions, and in their memory of the sessions, and in discussions with one another of what was said. The report could have helped to correct those distortions, provide narrative meaning, and also would have been tangible evidence of Mrs. Novick's thoughtfulness and of the therapeutic alliance.

The parent work was now in earnest. We learn that the parents had participated before in the parental work, but now they had to work on and change their parenting 'for real.' Ali did not have Mrs. Novick to absorb and contain his tumultuous feelings in the analytic sessions. The parents started to see Ali's self-hatred and sadness. This showed psychic change in both Ali and his parents. Ali was feeling the vulnerability beneath the omnipotence and revenge and his parents were seeing it and hearing it. I think this was made possible by the previous year-and-a-half of work before Ali got fired. Perhaps then the firing opened up a system that was closing, creating a developmental nodal point, and then transformation. Things shifted. Perhaps the whole system, including the analysis, the analyst, the patient, and the parents, had become a closed system—stuck (Novick, J. and Novick, K. K., 2003). A closed system would have been a breeding ground for malignant never-ending revenge to keep its wounds green. When a system is stuck, inflexible, and closed, someone or some thing has to introduce a change. Otherwise, in a different story, Captain Ahab is pulled to his death, linked to the dying Moby Dick with a harpoon, taking everyone with him (except for Ishmael) (Melville, 1851).

Mrs. Novick took a stance in reality. She showed Ali that she believed in his strengths and his ability to make a choice. She gave him control over a choice, a choice of *HIS* treatment, his actions. She also put a stop to the continued intense sadomasochism in the analysis. We want our patients to express themselves, but sometimes the intensity and power of enacted sadomasochism in this sort of patient is itself tremendously exciting, and reinforces the same solution again and again. This could apply to Ali intrapsychically, and/or to the parental and family dynamics, identifications, and projections. I think the good analytic work of the first year-and-a-half laid the foundation for the resolution of the impasse. Ali loved Mrs. Novick. By the time of the impasse, Ali had internalized new loving relational schemas, good self and object representations. These new representations were present, side by side with the grandiose and hateful/hated representations and relational schemas (Gabbard, 1996). But although these loving and hating schemas were present, they were perhaps still somewhat split off, dissociated, from one another. However, it was now possible for Ali to make a choice, intrapsychically and developmentally, as he now had internalized loving as well as hateful relational schemas. Mrs. Novick changed the rules. Her show of adult power could have been both feared but also longed for. Most children do not really want to feel like and be regarded as monsters. We become monsters when that becomes our total and inflexible identity, as exemplified in the children's book *The Odious Ogre* (Juster, 2010).

The family work was pivotal. And the work Mrs. Novick did, I think, illustrates the kind of work that is required in these terribly traumatized families. Mrs. Novick commented that the mother left her analysis on her husband's command, and the good thing was that this took away the opportunity to split her transferences and to sequester her pathology into her parenting. I think this is absolutely right on. This sequestering of pathology when the parents are in their own treatment is not an unusual problem in working with children. Collaboration between the analysts involved can be helpful here. All analysts involved with individuals in a family system have to be sensitive to how malevolent ghosts can escape the analyses and become expressed and dissociated in various family relationships. But we must also open our minds to the idea that the analyst working with children, especially in traumatized families, needs to utilize considerable ongoing psychodynamic work with the parents—exploring, clarifying, interpreting, being a new developmental object—as well as the more usual supportive and educational work with the parents (Novick, J. and Novick, K. K., 2005). This is essential, transformative work. It is my impression that Mrs. Novick did this sort of work beautifully, and that this work was necessary to go beyond what otherwise could have been an unresolvable impasse.

Chapter Four

"As the Twig Is Bent, So Grows the Tree"[1]

Reparation, Rage, and Resynthesis

Daniel M. A. Freeman

When Freud set out on an inward voyage of discovery he began with the perspective of a middle-aged European father, scientist, and physician. The self-analytic search and analytic experiences he shepherded in others were inwardly directed re-awakenings, seeking to relive and reprocess early incompletely or unsatisfactorily resolved conflicts and developmental issues. He reached backward in time like an archaeologist, digging progressively deeper into forgotten layers of the unrememberable and yet unforgettable past. He was intrigued by the similarity between his own triadic conflicts and those symbolically portrayed in one section of the Greek story of Oedipus. But it was harder, in self-analysis, to reach even further back into the more deeply repressed earlier dyadic experiences of ambivalence to understand the fantasies portrayed in the initial pre-'oedipal' infanticidal portion of the Greek myth. Freud was aware that there were earlier phases, but he was not able at first to fully conceptualize and formulate preoedipal development. Later, in his 1931 paper "Female Sexuality," he recognized that there had been an underlying antecedent developmental layer, an earlier preoedipal dyadic crisis that was crucial in a girl's development. He compared this to realizing that there had been an earlier Minoan-Mycenaean civilization that had preceded and had laid the foundation for the later Hellenic civilization of Greece.

Innovators often face a challenge when trying to find ways to share and explain novel insights or ideas, and communicate about a new discovery as yet unnamed. In order to discuss concepts for which there had been no words, Freud turned to metaphors and analogies. Speaking to a classically educated European audience in the early twentieth century, he chose stories of Moses, Oedipus, and Narcissus from Greek and biblical mythology, with which his audience was familiar. Some metaphors or analogies may turn out to be inexact and perhaps need further clarification. Stretching the meaning of a pre-existing concept may inadvertently result in connotations that become overextended when taken out of their original context. The words 'narcissism' and 'narcissistic' can have confusing, sometimes contradictory, meanings. They can refer to positive building blocks of self-esteem and of being esteemed by others, or they can refer to disordered personality development leading to psychopathology. Miscommunication can occur. An analyst once made a mistake of referring to an analysand as having a narcissistic personality disorder. This was perceived as an insult by a group of professionals who admired this person as their leader. This was unfortunate, since Freud had specifically pointed out that healthy narcissism is an essential ingredient of the personality of any effective group leader (1921).

Salman Akhtar has more than twenty different entries in his *Comprehensive Dictionary of Psychoanalysis* (2009) concerning different ways in which Narcissus's name has been utilized. Similarly, two other words in our title, 'rage' and 'revenge,' can have potentially misleading constructive or destructive connotations in different contexts.[2]

CLARIFYING WORDS: REFINING AMBIGUITIES

Several of the words in our title may have either positive or negative implications, depending on whether the emotions contribute to and stimulate constructive maturational progress or become negatively entrenched and destructive. Spitz (1965) referred to the early stages of ontogenesis as a quest into uncharted waters, casting bridges outward into the darkness and void, toward unseen distant shores. Growth is a voyage of striving, exploring, searching for patterns and meaning. An evolving self seeks to find a way forward, beyond the unknown, reaching to achieve integration and mastery. An infant moves along a pathway of ontogenesis through a puzzling world of sometimes gratifying and sometimes unsettling surprises. Crises may lead to deflation, rage, and sometimes impulses toward revenge. These create a need for reorganization, which may lead in a new direction. Sometimes people are able to develop a 'work-around,' like a tree's roots or branches bending around an obstacle. Sometimes, however, one hits a dead end. We may have to go back to wherever everything went astray, reorganize, and head in a new direction.

How can we refer to turning points or nodal points where a person's life, worldview, and game plan have hit a wall or a dead end? Unmasterable crises may initially lead to panic, outrage, or impulses for revenge. However, after one has refocused, such crises may lead to the discovery of alternative pathways for adaptation. Ideally in a best-case scenario, one may be able to bend in a new direction allowing development to continue. However, if an obstacle cannot be circumvented or if one bends too far, one may get 'broken.' If a person finds himself or herself 'up against a wall,' he or she may be forced to go back to a critical turning point and start over.

Painful external traumata and painful internal needs cause infants and children to cry out in an appeal for rescue. In their emergency need to escape from anguish, they try to use whatever motoric actions they have available, thrashing around in case there is some way they can initiate an escape from distress. They latch onto whatever has seemed to offer comfort in the past, and become attached to those who are responsive. If children experience recurrent crises for which no responsive rescuer provides adequate relief, they may fall back onto primitive coping or adaptive efforts, attempting to do the best they can under circumstances for which they have no adequate resources. These efforts may become maladaptive. They may distort, derail, or detour development in an ultimately disabling direction.

In psychoanalysis and psychotherapy, we help children and adults enter into a process of reliving and re-experiencing critical turning points where things had become derailed in the past, opening opportunities to discover a way back on course and ways to resume moving forward.

CONCEPTUALIZING CHANGE: DISRUPTIONS OF FLOW AND EXPERIMENTING TO REORGANIZE

When young children are unable to remove dangers, have their wishes gratified, or adequately cope with fears or rage in real-life interchanges, they generate imaginative hypotheses in creative transitional fantasy. Later they may actualize their fantasies in play with dolls and toys. During latency and preadolescence they often experiment with hypothetical ways to integrate their feelings and fantasies by enacting them in interpersonal play and in dramatizations with peers. Their transition into an extrafamilial world of latency occurs at a crossroads when children are distancing from dangerous intrafamilial wishes, fears, and fantasies. Their intrapsychic and interpersonal reorganization allows triadic intrafamilial conflicts to cool and to become 'latent.'

Two terms proposed by Anthony Wallace, chairman of the Department of Anthropology at the University of Pennsylvania in the 1960s, might stimulate our thoughts in trying to find words to describe the intrapsychic and interpersonal reorganizations that occur at several points as a child moves through what Erik Erikson (1950) described as a series of epigenetic stages.

Wallace (1961) suggested the terms 'mazeway resynthesis' and 'revitalization' to describe processes of reconsidering and reformulating that one goes through in charting a new modus operandi, moving in a new developmental direction. Such processes occur in individuals, groups, and cultures as a whole. People review, regressively re-experience previous critical turning points, deconstruct previous ideas, and set off in a new direction. In psychoanalysis and psychotherapy, we help people on this introspective voyage of review, rediscovery, and reformulation.

Latency is a phase of exploring and resynthesizing intrapsychic and interpersonal pathways in a novel extrafamilial world. Wallace suggested that this process can be compared to searching, finding, and mapping one's way through a sometimes confusing (or even seemingly inscrutable) obstacle course or maze, a partly unpredictable system of dynamically interrelated potential pathways and surprises. Unforeseen blind alleys may lead, at times, to exasperated frustration and a need to back up, reconsider, and grope one's way in unfamiliar uncharted territory. After retracing and experimenting, one gradually updates his or her mental 'map' of possibly fruitful pathways, leading to synthesis of a new integrated dynamic system—one's personal 'mazeway' or game plan. It reflects values, attitudes, and beliefs which 'make sense' of a confusing world. Each individual's personal mazeway continues to evolve in response to changing circumstances at subsequent stages of life.

We will consider psychoanalyses of a ten-year-old boy whose development was altered by a major traumatic change at age six months, and of a young woman in her mid-twenties whose development was detoured by traumatic events at age two. In one case, the disruption led to the persistence of ego splitting and the development of both borderline and neurotic defenses; in the other case, neurotic defenses.

CHRIS

Chris was a ten-year-old boy eager for help because of severe emotional discomfort. He had symptoms of separation anxiety, rocking and playing a 'twirling' game since his first year of life, and obsessional symptoms dating back to age six. Chris was afraid of being disliked because of his internal feelings of aggression, had difficulty sleeping, was afraid of being left alone, had a frequent need to urinate when away from home, and episodic nausea and vomiting. His parents described Chris as very intelligent and having a great 'adult' sense of humor. He was a prolific writer of poetry and novels, and interested in paleontology. In spite of intellectual achievements in these areas, he was doing poorly in school and had no peer relationships, nor interest in age appropriate activities. He had become very involved with ventriloquism during the previous year and was spending much of his time interacting in play with his dummy. At first, Chris's parents resisted the idea of getting him a dummy for fear it would only encourage a tendency to play with dolls. But when Chris started to make origami 'mouths' by folding up pieces of paper and showed persistent interest in and proficiency with ventriloquism, his parents provided him with a dummy. Chris also had an intense interest in monster movies and was particularly intrigued with the story of Dr. Jekyll and Mr. Hyde. An important part of Chris's life centered around his adaptive use of splitting in his hobby as a ventriloquist. It kept severe neurotic and characterological problems in reasonable ego-syntonic balance and became an important factor in his psychoanalysis.

Chris had had a very close intimate symbiotic interaction with his mother during his first six months of life. She perceived him as a loveable, affectionate, cuddleable infant, "just what you would want a baby to be," in contrast to sharply negative feelings that she felt toward her six-year-older daughter. Chris's mother was attuned to any sign of distress when Chris was an infant and held him whenever he cried. However, when Chris was six months old, his father developed acute anxiety attacks, fainting spells, and a 'cardiac neurosis' in response to seemingly unfounded accusations by Chris's mother. This led to the parents taking a spur-of-the-moment one-week vacation on the recommendation of his father's physician. The children were unfortunately left with angry, unwilling, disgruntled grandparents who resented having to suddenly care for the children and were very angry that they were not relieved by the other set of grandparents as they had been promised. Chris had severe separation anxiety during his parents' absence. When they returned, Chris initially showed a common reaction of no initial outward sign of recognition, merely staring at his parents without coming to them. His mother felt totally rejected. She abruptly and resentfully withdrew completely from her previously intimate relationship with Chris. Henceforth, she would set Chris up at arm's length in his playpen in front of a television set, to be amused by images on the television screen and by spinning the wheels on his toys.

His mother's depression and withdrawal that had been triggered by what she perceived as Chris's rejection of her after her absence continued through Chris's first two years of life. Her depression was further increased when she thought that Chris was weaning himself at nine months when he pushed his bottle away. She was not aware of her own need for Chris to precociously control his impulses and to prematurely individuate. This was evident, however, in the contrast between the way she had handled weaning in her daughter and her opposite response in the case of her son. She had attempted to start to wean his sister at the same age, but when she saw that her daughter put her thumb in her mouth Chris's mother had continued his sister on the bottle for three more years. When, on a single occasion Chris pushed the bottle away, his mother "just didn't bother giving it to him again." As Chris's mother became more depressed, she clung to her daughter, with paranoid feelings toward both her husband and her son.

Chris became acutely distressed, and began thumb sucking, head banging, and rocking at eight months. He became preoccupied for long intervals with watching spinning wheels and causing objects to spin, in what he later called his 'game.' His mother reported that he would sit, seemingly endlessly preoccupied with any wheel he could spin or any object like a pencil that he could twist back and forth rapidly in his hand to create a blur. This was accompanied by loud spitting noises. His parents noted that he sought to cuddle less. Chris would simultaneously clutch his blanket with the same hand as the thumb in his mouth, rock up on his haunches, and bang his head against the end of the crib. Within the blurred image of the spinning object, he would fantasize an image that he said was a face (and later identified as also being a breast). This head banging and spinning appeared to be directly related to his mother's withdrawal.

Chris seemed to have an addictive need for this game at times. His father became somewhat concerned about this, but his mother perceived Chris as being 'happy and content,' 'amusing himself,' and as being a 'good child.' She kept Chris supplied with toys with wheels whenever he sat in the playpen or whenever she took him out with her away from home. Chris showed acute separation anxiety whenever she left the room or took him out with her, but he found relief in his 'game.' His intense separation anxiety, later accompanied by urinary frequency and polyuria, persisted. Chris was still frequently playing the game in his preteens when he started in psychoanalysis. It diminished, along with his defensive use of splitting in ventriloquism, during the course of the analysis.

In the blur of the spinning object, Chris would visualize an image of the face of the split-off projected bad introjection and he would have primitive violent fantasies of inflicting sadistic destructive tortures on it. Later in his analysis, he described this as biting a breast. At the same time, he would chew on a thread (originally, on his transitional blanket) while emitting loud spitting and explosive noises, enacting his introjective-expulsive conflict. He attempted to deal with his premature abrupt separation from his mother by a precocious attempt at differentiation and premature individuation, using splitting and projection to deal with aggression in a massive effort at impulse control. The defensive use of primitive splitting served adaptively to permit him to remain relatively stable. His mother was not able to tolerate any expression of aggression, and Chris's game helped him to deflect the aggression and to meet her need that he precociously individuate.

Later in his analysis, Chris told me of a remarkable vivid memory that seemed to him to be awesomely real but that he could not understand. He remembered that it had occurred on his first birthday. He, his sister, and his mother were standing in their living room, but it was eerie because his father was not there and all of their furniture was gone! There was nothing in the living room. They were about to go out into a storm. Looking out the living room window he could see an image that he could not understand, but it seemed to look like a Nabisco symbol. He recalled that for some reason this image was referred to by his parents as a 'hotel.' Chris felt he was going out into a hurricane. When I asked Chris's parents about this memory (which Chris had never mentioned to them) they were totally astonished. Yes, it was true that on Chris's first birthday, his father wasn't there, and all of their furniture was gone—because they were moving to a different home that day. The image that Chris described of a 'Nabisco' symbol outside the living room window was also exactly correct. The view outside that window was of the triangular end of a gabled roof with a television antenna on top, very similar to the image that the Nabisco Company used as its trademark at that time. His parents used to refer to that home outside the window as a motel because it had a rapid turnover of occupants. Chris had never mentioned this memory to his parents, but it had vividly stuck in his mind as one of the critical eerie turning points in his life, on his first birthday. All of the details of the memory were correct.

A further change occurred when Chris learned to walk at twelve to thirteen months. His mother perceived this as his 'becoming a real person.' His six-year-older sister reacted antagonistically to Chris's newfound mobility and the parents became more emotionally involved with appeasing her than with Chris, manifestly to reassure her that she was still loved and wanted. Again Chris was pushed toward precocious individuation and was ignored. Both parents frantically and unsuccessfully sought to contain the daughter's aggression by showering her with gifts. Chris sought to gain attention by falling down, a precursor of his later defense of being a 'schnook,' hurting himself and drawing attention to his failures as the only way to get his parents to respond. The sister remained uncontrollable and sadistic towards Chris and the parents continued to be preoccupied with her.

In Chris's second and third years, his mother was unable to adequately relate with Chris when she was alone with him, when his father was at work and his sister away at school. Television served as his babysitter from age one except in the afternoons, when his mother would take him to a local store that had toys and children to play with there. She was not adequately available as a protective shield or an auxiliary ego for 'refueling' during his practicing subphase and not able to tolerate the cycles of warding off and clinging and the coercive intensity of his rapprochement (Mahler et al, 1975). Chris's experiences in the practicing and rapprochement subphases underscored his reliance on his own resources for channeling aggressive impulses, mastery, and control. He continued to enjoy and find comfort in his spinning game and fantasies, which in subsequent years helped him to write stories that he described as 'books.'

At age three, Chris would periodically assume the name Tim and exhibit a change from his usual character. When he was Tim, he would answer only to that name and would become a model child, conforming to his mother's ideals, seeming to assume the characteristics of a 'good self' in relation to a 'good mother.' This change would persist for hours or days, was taken very seriously by both Chris and his parents, and had the quality of more than a childish caprice. The parents felt they had no alternative but to go along with this since Chris made it very real. 'Tim' had been the name of the boy in the book that his mother read to Chris when he sat on the potty while she toilet trained him. From age three and a half, Chris gave evidence of intellectual precocity and extreme sensitivity to the activities of adults. His use of splitting mechanisms similar to those later used in his ventriloquism could be traced back to at least age three. He developed a fascination and preoccupation with monsters and robots while simultaneously being afraid of them, asking for larger and more frightening robots while simultaneously being afraid to leave them unattended in his room and needing to lock them in his closet at night.

In kindergarten at age four, his teacher described him as very insecure, having difficulty adjusting to new situations, and avoiding sports. Chris worried about adult things such as war and world conditions. At times, he threatened other children with magic potions with which he said he would 'change' them. He developed a fascination with bears. On the one hand, he 'became' a bear himself in a Halloween costume that he continued to wear for months. On the other hand, he craved the companionship of and felt sorry for a plush toy bear that had a very sad face. His parents described Chris as more frequently wearing the bear costume than not. When he was in the costume, he would not talk to them since bears do not talk. Thus, he split off and projected negative introjections onto proxies he could control, exemplified by frightening robots, and he evidenced alternating ego states in his change to Tim and becoming a bear.

At age five in first grade, Chris was not able to keep up with class work, cried easily, and spent much time running back and forth to the bathroom to wash his hands and flush the toilet. He had difficulty falling asleep after struggling with simple homework. At six, he developed further symptoms of obsessional neurosis, wondering whether he had turned off lights, guilt about having kicked the dog, worrying about how much he loved the dog, and very frequent hand washing after handling the dog. He was afraid he would turn into a girl because he did girls' things and put on his sister's clothes when she was not at home. His schoolwork deteriorated and he developed compulsive swallowing and burping. He was evaluated by psychological testing and treated in intermittent play therapy that directed Chris to vent hostility toward his sister by hitting dolls.

At age nine, he was referred for psychoanalysis because his symptoms were intensifying and changing. He had not become part of his latency or preadolescent peer group and was asking for more intensive help. His parents noted a similarity between the intensity of his preoccupation with monsters and robots in earlier childhood and his preoccupation with pet bats and ventriloquist dummies at this stage. As in the earlier instances, the sudden emergence of his preoccupation with having a pet bat was accompanied by fear, in this case fear of the dark. Chris had polyuria and frequency whenever he went out with the family, was afraid they would get angry about his frequent need to urinate, and was afraid to go into a new bathroom alone when away from home without reassurance his parents would not leave while he was in the bathroom. He said he was afraid of losing his mind and that when he thought the word 'kill,' his hand would move. He feared he would destroy my desk if he accidentally touched or kicked it.

Chris's rapprochement conflict was re-aroused when he felt he was being pressured by his parents to individuate and become a man. He complained bitterly that the more mature he behaved, the less attention he got. His sister, who was constantly having aggressive explosions, got her demands met. He sought to grow up so that he could escape from his mother's attempts to manipulate and control him. He would get angry at me if I did not do things for him and yet furious if I did. Chris was both proud and threatened if I underscored one of his observations or insights. He complained frequently of inability to handle things, fearing that if I would think him too capable or too healthy, I would end his analysis and put him out. Chris was eager for help because of the distress caused by his obsessional ideas and his fear of being disliked because of his aggression. He spoke of Jekyll and Hyde feelings, jealous feelings toward rivals and fears he would do something destructive or be abandoned because of his aggression. He frequently sought to play the role of Mr. Hyde, as when he formerly played being 'bear,' and would split off and project onto his dummy, William, thoughts and feelings that he was afraid to express. He said, "William can be anything I want him to be, friend or enemy. I have power over something . . . because I don't have many friends." Chris was aware of his use of the dummy alternately as a proxy onto whom to project split-off impulses he could not tolerate and as an object, imaginary companion, or peer with whom he could relate.

Chris alternated between a need to keep William separate and an opposite need to reassure himself that it was Chris himself, not the dummy, who was in control. Chris was aware that William was expressing Chris's own dangerous feelings, while he sought at the same time to demonstrate that it was the dummy, not he himself, who was speaking. In his need to reassure himself that the dummy was not real, Chris alternated between a tender, warm, relationship with William and dropping him on the floor. At times, Chris expressed confusion about the actual state of being of the dummy. "Somehow I have trouble mastering this guy! I felt he was going to come alive, but I got over that. I was told that I shouldn't think it'll come alive." Speaking of his need to see William as a friend, Chris started off saying, "It's interesting to transport life into another be . . . ," but continued, " . . . into a toy." He went on, "It's not just a doll. It's a friend. I've kept it in its place. It's not human. It's a doll. Every time I want to be sure I know this, I hit it over the head. I know I don't hurt it. It's just damaged. At times I say, 'That thing's no more human than a dead rat!'" Once, when Chris thought one of his dummies was actually suddenly coming to life, he impulsively choked it, but then worried about whether it was against the law to prevent something from coming to life.

Chris was aware of a Jekyll and Hyde contending inside himself and of his split personality and sadomasochistic conflict. "Every time I think of 'kill,' my hand moves . . . like a killer instinct in my subconscious. If I grow up, I don't want to kill too much. I don't want to be a criminal and kill! That's why I'm worried." In another session, he said that William had a split personality. He then took William's head apart from his body. The dummy turned its sarcasm and belittling (that formerly had been directed at Chris) towards me for the first time. Chris threw both the dummy and himself on the floor several times, at first apparently to punish himself, but then to reassure himself that William could not break and that stunt falls could not hurt him.

William started to criticize and be aggressive like a bully towards me, as he had formerly been towards Chris, in ways that Chris was only later able to directly do himself. William started to reveal Chris's jealousy towards girls and treated Chris as a girl. Chris allowed the dummy to express his jealousy towards me and his wish to be close to me. Dealing with each issue in his own split relationship with the dummy and in the dummy's relationship with me facilitated Chris's subsequent ability to start dealing with them more directly by using obsessional neurotic rather than splitting mechanisms. An element of submission and fulfillment of a passive sadomasochistic wish was evident in Chris's relationship to the often dominating and belittling dummy, even as he simultaneously and vicariously gratified his own assertive and aggressive impulses through the dummy. He hinted at and used William to help him express his jealousy of girls. He then started to want to get a female dummy, and sought help to become a man. He sat down his sixteen-year-old sister, who had intimidated him for years, and assertively 'gave her hell' for the first time.

Chris extended the tender relationship between himself and the dummy to a desire on William's part to come close to me. William then served as a vehicle for a developing friendship with a boy who had formerly bullied him at school. This boy became interested in ventriloquism, got a dummy, and asked Chris to bring William to school so they could talk with each other, leading to a growing friendship. Ventriloquism altered all of Chris's peer relationships as he was now less a 'brain' trying to impress other kids. In a session when transference feelings toward me became intense (as manifested by hyperactivity, restlessness, and feelings that he wanted to scream), Chris fell back on his splitting defense and allowed William to treat him as a girl. The dummy said, "You don't want to make out with me?!" Chris replied, "No! You're a boy. You're not a girl!" William said, "Dorothea! Dorothea!" Chris responded, "William! William!" William suggested that maybe the analyst, too, was a girl. "Maybe he would be interested in my cousin, Mabel. His glasses are plastic, her hair is plastic. Maybe he is my cousin Mabel." Later, William started to directly express Chris's positive transference feelings, singing, "Dr. Sauerkraut, I love you! If only I knew who Dr. Sauerkraut was, I'd marry him or her. If it's a girl or a boy!" Chris's pregnancy fantasies were illustrated by a wish to have a baby-sized dummy and then remaking of one of his dummies into a baby. Chris had an awareness that "actually this is just a very sensible way of talking to yourself, through a dummy. Sometimes it's hard to believe it's me! Ventriloquism has a magic all its own." At the same time, a strong sense of peer bond developed between Chris and his dummy. Despite getting several other dummies Chris remained primarily attached to William.

Chris showed evidence of identifying with his father, with me, with a fictional hero of his own most recent novelette, the ego ideal aspects of William, and young entertainers towards whom he had previously felt obsessively jealous. He gradually found it less necessary to use William as an intermediary and was able to acknowledge William's aggression as his own. He began to call attention to the fact that he was becoming less proficient as a ventriloquist, pointing out that his lips were now moving. During this period he would alternately throw the dummy on the floor or do stunt falls, throwing himself onto the floor. I interpreted that neither he nor the dummy was destroyed or damaged, but Chris was disappointed by my failure to intervene to rescue him. Chris's aggression appeared directly in the transference as he began to direct hostile and competitive attitudes more openly, mainly in checker games. As William's role decreased, Chris began to express more libidinal material directly to me, varying between submissive homosexual strivings and competitive heterosexual attitudes. William now seemed to have more of a quality of a third person rather than the previously dissociated split-off quality. Chris began to report better peer relationships as evidenced by his interest in age appropriate activities and receiving invitations to coed parties.

Toward the end of the first year of the analysis, Chris thought of getting a new dummy to replace William. A violent dialogue was exchanged between Chris and William when Chris announced he was going to get a fancier, more expensive dummy. As Chris anticipated giving up William, he thought about the burial and wondered if he would miss William. He thought that if he put William in a sufficiently secure box, William would be preserved, so that if he was ever needed again Chris could dig him up. "I'm not going to be rash. I'm not going to bury him tonight. After a month or two, if William's personality isn't there, just me, I'll bury him. I'll bury him in a little black box with an epitaph. It may be the best for all of us, a period of adjustment." The epitaph was: "I'm not the best ventriloquist in the world. I may move my lips quite a bit but it still doesn't mean I wouldn't fall in love with my dummy."

The new dummy arrived and was only transiently a character in the analysis. He was very proper, polite, and compliant—the antithesis of William. Following the 'burial' of William, Chris experienced an actual mourning reaction with periods of self-recrimination, depression, agitation, and concern about his ability to function without William. Chris reported a fantasy about a pregnant woman who would keep her baby inside her and the baby would be able to talk in utero. Concurrently for several years, Chris had also been rewriting and revising what he called a novelette about a Super Hero becoming merged with his evil Arch Meany opponent. The novelette, which portrayed images of rage and revenge in more raw, violent form, was being revised and completed during this same period. It reflected the vicissitudes and ultimate resolution of the violent rage of Jekyll-and-Hyde-like characters and of their impulses for revenge toward one another. Chris brought this book into his analytic sessions as he was completing it. The following is a brief portion of the final chapter concerning the ultimate merger of the Jekyll-and-Hyde-like figures into a single being:

> We were thrown into a gondola type car, which the apes and monkey fastened to the ceiling by a chain. Arch Meany brought himself up to the chain and used a fantastic karate chop to break the chain! Below us was not a welcome sight. He called it "the mechanical mess." Giant wheels, chains, wires, machines, smog, oil, smelly stuff, and two huge gears—one made the other turn. We were dangling right above it. It was directly under us! We would be crushed into leather and the gondola would be tin! Only "The Super Hero of Them All" could save us now! We need him! Urgently! Arch Meany backed up his aim . . . and swung. The chain cut and we began to fall toward the huge towering wheel! Through a tube on the side of the wall came a swoop, dive, ballet dance and a great catch of the gondola, which Super Hero flung to a ledge which was safety!
>
> We crawled out of the car and up onto the floor above the ledge to see Super Hero and Arch Meany clasping each other. Meany gave Super Hero another karate chop like the first that sent him to the guardrail. The apes and monkey kept hitting Super Hero or Arch Meany, they really didn't know. There was nothing we could do. We watch. And then at last, an eye popping sight. They both went over the rail! Super Hero fell on the wheel first and Arch Meany fell on him, and looked around to see the huge wheel coming straight at

> his entire body. He tried to wake up the unconscious Super Hero. But he got up too late. It was too late to move! The scene below was covered up by one of the huge wheels. All that was heard were two voices screaming in terror, then silence. A fifteen minute silence. No one knew what happened. No trace was ever found. They may be alive and well. Ya neva know!

The healing of Chris's primitive ego splitting, as reflected in the fusion of Super Hero and Arch Meany and in Chris's being able to set aside ventriloquism and his relationship with his dummy, was the major turning point in Chris's analysis. It was a point of major intrapsychic reorganization and beginning of resynthesis, allowing him to begin to deal with residual hitherto-unresolved issues of narcissistic injury, rage, and revenge at each of his oral, anal, and phallic libidinal levels. As these changes were occurring in his analysis, Chris's real life became more object-oriented but also temporarily chaotic. Within a period of two weeks, he broke his glasses and had fears of his eyeball being popped out. He complained of severe pain in his leg, for which no physical cause could be found. In anticipation of a skiing weekend with his family, he reported a fantasy about a boy being lost in the cold. While on the skiing trip, he intentionally skied into his mother, who had already fallen and injured herself. He then went out alone and got lost in the snow. He told me he did this because he felt his father did not punish him severely enough for skiing into his mother. The following weekend he actually broke his leg while skiing.

With the burial and subsequent internalization of William, and the destruction and merging of the Super Hero and Arch Meany, Chris's previously split-off identification systems were internalized. The attempt at introjection and metabolism of the bad objects presented an enormous task of resynthesis and reorganization. Chris experienced a reworking of his rapprochement crisis. He turned directly to me for help and used me in the transference in the coercive manipulative manner that Mahler described concerning rapprochement children's attempts to coerce their mothers, which Chris had previously been unable to do with his mother. A second theme of the analysis was characteristic of more typical neurotic oedipally derived material. Chris's growing interest in girls alternated with intense castration anxiety and regression to anal sadomasochistic fantasies. While he had a cast on his broken leg, he could be more interested in girls and active in boy-girl parties. But with the removal of the cast, he became more inhibited. Periods of resistance were frequent and intense, reproducing in the transference Chris's manipulating his parents into trying to extract information or trying to coerce work from him, only to then frustrate them by outwitting or charming them. Chris described how he derived pleasure from getting adults into a state of utter frustration to the point where they would do what he called the 'Hitler dance' (referring to Charlie Chaplin's portrayal of Hitler in the movie *The*

Great Dictator). This was a foot-stomping rage with facial and physical expressions resembling someone experiencing urinary urgency, related to Chris's own experience and his former use of urinary frequency to coerce and manipulate his parents. Intense arguments and rage reactions that used to occur between Chris and his dummy were transferred and now took place between Chris and me. His chief complaint was that I was not being sufficiently protective against the dangers that he felt from without and within. Primitive, violent, vengeful and retributive, oral cannibalistic, poisoning, spanking, anal penetrating, and negative oedipal fantasies emerged, but it was noteworthy that despite the primitiveness of this material there was no further regression to borderline phenomenology.

Chris returned to oedipal-level competitive fantasies and moved toward heterosexual object relationships. Everything became focused into the transference. His material was typically neurotic without further primary process coloration or elaborate symbols or fantasies, as he moved through oedipal resolution without further evidence of a sadomasochistic perverse erotic focus and preoccupation. There was a gradual decathexis of primary objects as he progressed through early adolescent stages of object removal and his shift toward peer relationships. By middle school, he reported excellent relationships with peers, became typically preoccupied with mid-adolescent issues of girlfriends, began to date, and developed an intense relationship with a girlfriend.

DISCUSSION: CHRIS

After Chris had been idolized by his mother as a perfect child in his symbiotic phase during his first six months, he was suddenly abandoned by her transformation into what Andre Green (1980) has described as a present but unresponsive 'dead mother.' Since his father was only intermittently available, Chris did not always have a stable object to help him to mediate between good and bad sides of his self-object universe while he was differentiating and individuating. He reached toward the primordia of autonomy and individuation, trying to find ways to feel safer within creative transitional fantasy by creating an external spinning blur to be his sustaining object when his father was absent. Images of a caregiving father were able to pinch-hit, at least in part, when his father was away. The images emotionally refueled Chris, and the relationship with his father helped Chris to bridge gaps in basic trust and safety and dispel feelings of panic and rage.

Chris imaginatively projected both good and bad images onto the controllable spinning blur, creating interactions within his transitional fantasies. Within these fantasies, Chris started to sort out 'good' and 'bad' self-images from 'good' and 'bad' object representations. It is noteworthy that Chris did develop a degree of what we might refer to as paternal-object constancy, as evidenced by the fact that Chris's concern about his father's absence on his first birthday became so vividly etched into his memory from that very early age.

Biting on his blanket, spitting, and banging his head during his game also channeled Chris's rage and impulses toward revenge. A distant, zombified 'dead mother' was always present in the background. The stories that Chris wrote in mid- to late childhood often included a zombie or a 'Krankenstein' monster. Strengths gained in Chris's first six months of life augmented by his father's subsequent support contributed to Chris's resiliency and perseverant active striving. Split-off destructive impulses and sadistic rage were directed into (a) biting on his transitional blanket in the spinning game as he would bang his head against the end of his crib, (b) violent and reparative fantasies in childhood solitary fantasy play, (c) persevering attempts to create restitutive enactments in fictional dramas and in written stories, and ultimately (d) ventriloquism and the transference. Both the biting, persevering, never-give-up child and a retained transitional fantasy of the good parent were condensed in his relationship with his ventriloquist dummy. His integration of good and bad introjects and the healing of his original ego split were partial, so that ego splitting and neurotic defenses came to exist side by side as has been described by Kernberg (1970) for the intermediate level of character organization. In the course of the analysis the persisting pathological split in Chris's ego healed. Splitting subsequently became a regressive defense in the service of the ego and marked changes in ego structure and functioning occurred.

Chris had to be a scriptwriter, director, producer, actor, and often his own audience as well. He re-created good and bad 'mothers' and 'selves' when he became 'Tim,' the cooperative potty-training boy, and when he became the mute 'bear.' He concretized these interactions in written stories. In his struggle to reorient, resynthesize, and enter into a post-oedipal process of intrapsychic reorganization, he had to first complete a healing of his ego split, which had colored, skewed, and distorted his oedipal experience. In the early portion of Chris's latency, he needed to move away from interactions within his family before he was ready to fully enter into interpersonal interactions with peers. William offered him the opportunity to have 'someone' imaginary to interact with (just as his spinning blur had filled this role earlier), but someone that Chris could control within a scripted dialogue that would not veer off in unpredictable directions like interacting with other latency children could. William then served as a bridge helping Chris to develop real relationships with latency and preadolescent peers.

Chris wondered about and recognized the unreality of playing with a doll, and he experienced distress at feeling such a confusing compulsive need to continue to play this unreal pretend ritual game. Trying to figure this out,

Chris had written and rewritten his novelette several times over a period of years. He feared, at the time of trying to distance from destructive rage and retaliatory fears of his triadic family conflict and move toward latency, that he might be destroyed between gears, ground up and crushed between triadic fantasies and violent revenge impulses. At times when Chris was unready/unable to deal directly with and to express dangerous rage and revenge impulses, his Arch-Meany would squirt 'boring juice' on others so that they would not be aware of what Chris was thinking. The final healing of the split between Super Hero and Arch Meany was the culmination of Chris's introspective search to achieve self and object constancy, and to synthesize stable internal self and object representations.

RUTH

Ruth was a young married teacher who came for psychoanalysis in her early twenties. She was an only child who had been born with congenital strabismus (an external deviation of her right eye). She also had had severe eczema during her infancy, which had led to her arms being restrained to prevent her from scratching. She sought assistance for dystonic feelings of "Hate! Hate! Hate!" and impulses toward revenge. She said she had felt "like a bull in a china shop" since early childhood.

Just before she turned two, Ruth's father was drafted into the armed services during wartime. She and her mother moved to live with Ruth's maternal grandparents in another community. Her mother was an outgoing, sociable, well-liked, eager to please, conscientious 'tiger mom' and an elementary school teacher. Ruth always felt that she was a disappointment to her mother because she was not as pretty and not as sociable. At age two, shortly after their move to her grandparents' home, Ruth was hospitalized to correct her strabismus. Occurring at the peak of her rapprochement crisis and just having left her familiar surroundings, Ruth was alone in a ward with many upset young children, in the care of strangers, without her parents being allowed to stay. Her eyes were bandaged and her arms were restrained, replicating the earlier restraint when she had eczema. From the perspective of a two-year-old, it seemed as though she had been totally abandoned. Ruth's memory of that hospitalization (and subsequent unsuccessful operative attempts to correct her strabismus) was of feeling terrified and desperately struggling to get free. She had what she later described as a 'half-crazed feeling' of panic as she awoke, remembered wanting to bite the men who were bandaging her eyes, and wanting to take revenge on her mother for having left her. Her recollection was that after the operations, she would move her eyes about violently inside the bandages. Doctors concluded that her sutures may apparently have become pulled out, making the operations unsuccessful.

When her mother picked Ruth up to take her home from the operation, her mother recalled Ruth being affectively flat. All that Ruth could say was that she wanted to go home to her pet dog. Ruth vividly recalled her own feeling, "Get away from me! I hate you all!" When her mother took her back for a follow-up visit, Ruth could not express her feelings in words. She simply grabbed hold of her shoes, which had been taken from her when she had been hospitalized. Throughout childhood, she had fears of abandonment and not being allowed to cry out in anxiety and rage. Her integration of self-representations and object-representations was disrupted, and she did not attain stable libidinal self- and object-constancy.

Living with her mother in her maternal grandparents' home for the next two years, through her rapprochement subphase and into her early genital phase, Ruth was an only grandchild, pampered and spoiled by her grandfather. Ruth's mother was strict, wanting Ruth to behave properly and do what she was told. Ruth recalled that on many occasions her mother would suddenly decide it was time for Ruth to go to bed and would put Ruth in her crib. Ruth would protest and cry, not wanting to be left in a crib alone again. Her memory was of desperately wanting to be with people. Undoubtedly this had been sensitized by the hospital experience. Her grandfather would repeatedly 'rescue' Ruth and take her out of the crib, but her mother would become frustrated and angry about being undercut. At one point, Ruth's mother tried giving Ruth a huge Sears mail-order catalogue to rip up in the crib, saying, "Spare me your RAGE!" Expressions of either anxiety or anger were unacceptable. Ruth's grandfather became, in effect, an 'oedipal father' for Ruth between ages two and four.

One important memory from this period was of Ruth's pet chicken. One day, the pet chicken was decapitated and served for dinner. Ruth realized what had happened, and was extremely upset, but could say nothing. Her mother got Ruth to speak by asking, "Where is your pet chickee?" Ruth felt obliged to answer. She replied, "In my mouth." "I knew where it was! They couldn't fool me!" From that moment forward, as best as we could later reconstruct, Ruth continuously deviated her lower jaw to the right (the same side as her deviant right eye) in a conversion reaction that resulted in her bite being 'off,' with her tongue often rubbing against her teeth or being bitten, and her facial appearance being altered by a second deviation.

When Ruth was four, her father received a medical discharge from the armed services for psychophysiological gastrointestinal problems, and found a job in another community. Just as Ruth and her parents were leaving her grandparents' home to move to the new community, Ruth's grandfather suddenly died of a heart attack. Ruth's father was preoccupied with his own illnesses, which continued to cause problems, and he largely ignored Ruth.

Her mother was preoccupied with her work as a primary school teacher and with caring for her sickly husband. Ruth's mother reportedly regarded Ruth's father as a weakling and hypochondriac, and Ruth feared a similar reaction if she complained, got sick, or did not perform up to her mother's standards. Ruth felt that her father had first dethroned and then had rejected her, and she talked about her sadness at never having been able to develop a positive relationship with him. She had a couple of oedipal dreams of sitting in her father's lap and of her father promising "to take me to Paris, where I would learn to dance." But . . . "I was a distant daughter. I've never been close to anybody in my whole life." Ruth felt abandoned by her mother, "pushed to the side of the bed, desperately trying to hold on." On one single occasion Ruth threw a tantrum, but never again. Just after their move away from her grandparents' home when she was four, Ruth was outside playing with older children when her mother interrupted, wanting Ruth to come inside for a nap. Ruth threw a tantrum saying, "I don't WANT to!!" On this one single occasion, Ruth did not use her more common response of saying, "I can't!" "That was the only time she ever spanked me!" Ruth recalled that her mother then felt "badly, worried, guilty," and that her mother would subsequently "bring it up from time to time, like she was trying to resolve that." But Ruth always feared that her mother would be very harsh if she got her angry.

Ruth constantly tried to live up to her mother's expectations and live up to the highest standards of what Ruth called her mother's "Women's Club." She feared being disliked. "I needed to punish myself in order to be fixed and get another chance to be good, without 'I WON'T.' In her early teens, Ruth was taken back to the hospital three times. She recollected, "I even asked for the fourth chance. I needed to be fixed." In peer play during latency and preadolescence, Ruth had what she described as an inferiority complex and felt that she was possessive, demanding, deceptive, and manipulative. She sought to be a leader and take control as an author and playwright, scripting and directing her peers in dramas; but she would freeze when she herself was put up on stage to perform, whether reciting a poem, dancing in a tutu, or playing a violin. A key memory from childhood was the image of the ballerina in 'The Red Shoes' ballet who, when dancing in the red shoes, was hit by a train. For a while, in her analysis, Ruth used a Scheherazade defense, trying to present a multitude of dreams in order to indefinitely postpone ultimate 'penetration and castration' in the transference.

Ruth defended against the rage of the frightened angry child inside her by sadomasochistic, moral masochistic, and obsessive compulsive manipulative and self-punitive defenses. "Magicians are devious. They use devious ways of making you believe something. That's exactly what I did with people. Standing on a platform above everybody, trying to manipulate them." She contrasted the precocious development of rigid impulse controls and restriction of autonomy that were demanded by her mother with the spoiling and channeling of aggression into fantasies of omnipotence fostered by her grandparents. Intermittently, Ruth had recurrent thoughts of "HATE! HATE! HATE!" The anger was kept inside but she felt like a bull in a china shop. She had an image of herself as a 'wild Indian.' She would ask, "Why don't you preach to me? Tell me I'm not doing myself any good!" She blurted out, "You won't fight and my husband won't fight! You guys aren't any fun at all!" But then, "I don't know why I said that." She remembered her outrage at her father when he would get angry at her for little things such as using his comb. She felt, "The nerve! Where do you get off? How demeaning to have to put up with this! Spare me your rage!" Ruth imagined that she had in fact succeeded in getting me to fight with her. "I did drag you into my fighting! You just don't want to admit it!" She had been seeking to fight because there were sexual things she did not want to tell me and she was not going to let me 'undress' her. "I have a strong desire not to be cooperative . . . feeling that I might as well explode and blow this analysis up! I was angry at my mother in childhood just the way I'm angry at you right now! I have that feeling, a feeling that 'I'll get to him! . . . I won't!' I hate to be prodded! I have such a desire to lock my mouth and not say a word! And now I'm fighting back. I'm not doing a thing! And I must be driving my mother wild!" . . . "I'll go along without challenging you because I can't. You have the upper hand. But if I go to my grave, I'm always going to have a certain amount of belief in myself and you can't destroy it!"

Ruth realized that her punishments had been self-imposed "because the fact of the matter is that my mother wasn't into punishments. She's not a punishing person in reality. In my head, I started to see her that way because I thought that's why she sent me to the hospital. But she didn't talk in that language. Somewhere along the line, I decided I needed to be punished. 'Punishment' isn't her word, it's my word! I got to be quite a punisher of myself." "I want to be a wildflower. I've had this thing about wildflowers lately. The word 'wildflower' keeps going through my mind. I get euphoric when I think about wildflowers. I think maybe I was a wildflower when I was a child before I froze." Ruth dreamt she was a man who was hogging an elevator and keeping everyone outside waiting while he was masturbating, with the elevator neither going up nor down. She wanted me to open up the secret things that were on her mind. She dreamt of twins, representing residual unintegrated good and bad components of her self-representation as she was reworking her rapprochement resolution. As more conflicts were handled autoplastically, superego conflicts were portrayed in dreams as struggles between two figures, both of whom were recognized as parts of herself.

Ruth felt she was like one of her aunts, who alternated between dependent demandingness, and compliance, on the one hand, and defensively distanced separateness, on the other hand. These represented persisting unresolved aspects of rapprochement ambi-tendency contributing to the interpersonally coercive aspects of her sadomasochistic behavior. She felt she had isolated herself in a protective shell but now wanted to come out of the shell and take a chance. She wanted to find a way to reach out and relate yet maintain her autonomy and identity. "If you can't touch the people around you, you're just an actor on a stage. You're pretty safe up on the stage away from all the people, but I would rather come down off the stage. I don't want to be an actress any more. But to get off the stage, I would have to be myself. But I don't know who that is." She started to cry: "I think there's something good in me. Wouldn't it be something if it turned out that just as I'm capable of great hate as I'm capable of great love? What a surprise that would be! Then I wouldn't have to act any more. Who would think a caterpillar can change into a butterfly?"

She recognized her soap-opera tendency to play a melodramatic role of the wronged and violated innocent outraged by external contaminating evil. Coming down off the stage meant acknowledging the bad side as a part of her self, letting go of the cloak of immaculate chastity and purity, and acknowledging responsibility for taming and neutralizing her aggressive and sexual impulses. It meant taking off all masks and giving up being a ballerina or Scheherazade so that the thousand-and-one nights of beautiful dreams would come to an end. She looked forward with anticipation to being a flower that would bloom or a butterfly that would emerge from the cocoon. However, there was still considerable narcissistic deficit, incestuous oedipal contamination, and feeling of vulnerability, requiring that she continue to posture as a butterfly. "Pretend, pretend, pretend! But pretend will only go so far. Pretend will not tell the truth! That's all I've done my whole life. I'm all pretended out! I can't pretend any more. Maybe I'm working at changing the story I made up about myself. You have to have freedom to change the story! About my whole outlook on life. It's scary to change. It's YOUR 'STORY,' woven into your being! Hard to change. My instinct tells me to wonder. I guess at some point, you have to have some confidence in yourself. I have to go into my own self and think. I don't know how I can live my life without questioning." This was a crucial point in Ruth's 'mazeway resynthesis' and revitalization.

"I was left out. That's when I started to throw a quiet temper tantrum. It all went inside. That little girl became possessed by demons! I feel I've gone all the way back to when that happened. I know how it happened!" For several months, Ruth alternated between being negativistic, manipulative, sarcastic, and fighting in one session and being all 'sweetness and light' in the next. "I do want to have an effect on you! If I'm having a tantrum, the least you can do is let it have an effect on you, or what good are they?!" She realized that the only way she had been able to get her parents' attention was by creating crises or by subtly manipulating their guilt and making them anxious about her. She had to make them fret or worry about her, "Like draining them, sucking their attention right out of them. They couldn't turn their back on a moping child." She could only conceive of relationships in terms of a victor and a loser with a bitter fight unto the end. "It's like a captain going down with his ship, not giving up, grim struggle. I've been fighting this battle for a long time. You wouldn't expect me to give up now!" Again she started punishing herself and expected me to punish her: "I'm sucking up punishment like a sponge sucks up water! I just can't seem to get enough. I need one of those things monks use to flail themselves!"

Ruth was feeling positive and more individuated feelings, yet she would regress periodically to intense sadomasochistic struggle. A fantasy emerged of being like a flowering bulb that would go through a long cold winter but then bloom as a flower in the spring. She imagined lining up her parents in front of a firing squad for having pushed her out into the cold during childhood. She was determined that no one would ever frustrate her again. If they would try, it would be "Off with their heads!" She recalled her childhood struggle over bringing together and neutralizing good and bad feelings and integrating self and object images: "It brings to mind my eyes and my eye operations. I have a feeling for needing to fuse something, like fusing with your eyes, bringing two images together to make one. If I could only get rid of that dark, angry, watchful eye!"

DISCUSSION: RUTH

Ruth sought relief from dystonic vengeful feelings and assistance in trying to restructure herself and her relationships with people. The twig of her emotional development had become bent and Ruth's defensive work-around, developed in an attempt to conform and to compensate, had become increasingly dysfunctional. She felt she had reached the end of a blind alley. Ruth's life had not become broken but her maturation had become distorted and detoured. She needed to go back, find herself, and find a new direction. Ruth was fortunate to have had a committed good mother of symbiosis and the early phases of separation-individuation (Mahler et al, 1975), albeit that her mother was somewhat overcontrolling, which (along with Ruth's eczema restraints) may have already had some impact on Ruth's practicing subphase and on her developing a sense of autonomy as opposed to shame and doubt (Erikson, 1950). But then, to Ruth's astonishment and terror, Ruth suddenly found herself forcibly immobilized, blindfolded, and abandoned during her rapprochement subphase. Her entire world suddenly inexplicably disappeared. Ruth's mother was preoccupied with a need to 'fix' Ruth so that she would look pretty and be well socialized, but not attuned to Ruth's perspective during Ruth's hospitalization or afterward when they were living in Ruth's maternal grandparents' home.

The startling disappearance of Ruth's entire 'world' and disruption of her sense of safety and trust occurred at age two, when Ruth was at what might seem to have been a more 'mature' stage of development than was the case for Chris. But during this particular stage, which Mahler referred to as the rapprochement subphase of separation-individuation, there is an inherently greatly increased sensitivity to separation anxiety. At this stage, children suddenly become alarmed if their mother seems to have disappeared when they urgently need to reunite for reassurance in order to emotionally 'refuel' (Mahler et al, 1975). Ruth was blindfolded and restrained so that she could neither see nor move, and no recognizable person responded to her cries. She experienced a total absence of anything she could recognize or relate to—mother, father, home, transitional object, or even possibility of calling out to be heard—and no possibility of the reunion for the emotional refueling that is essential for children at that stage. Like Chris, she was frozen and could not at first respond emotionally when her mother finally did appear. Severed from the world, totally restrained, with no one responding to her pleas for help and her need to emotionally refuel, Ruth was bursting with rage but had to keep it inside. When her mother did ultimately return, Ruth's memory was of feeling rage and "Hate, hate, hate!" She could only express an urgent wish to go home to reunite with her pet dog. Ruth would cry but suppressed her rage, and only once dared to say, "No!" When forced to verbally acknowledge that what she was chewing on in her mouth was her pet chicken, Ruth's jaw became deformed. Then, just as her family was moving away from her supportive grandfather's home, he suddenly died. Each of these upheavals necessitated a fundamental intrapsychic reorganization or resynthesis.

I have presented only the initial portion of Ruth's psychoanalytic work that helped her get back on track toward healthy intrapsychic and interpersonal development. Ultimately she became a sensitive elementary school teacher and a loving caretaker for her elderly relatives in their old age. She rejoiced in children's autonomous optimistic searches for what was inspiring to them and their free-spirited, free-thinking autonomous constructive determination to question and to challenge.

CONCLUSION: RESYNTHESES

Major intrapsychic reorganizations occur at nodal points when one's world has suddenly changed or one's ways of relating with the world no longer seem to be working. Crises may startle and precipitate panic or violent impulses, or they may stimulate exploration and contribute to a new adaptive integration. It may be possible to bend and find an alternate work-around pathway, or one may need to go back, rethink, and significantly reorganize.

The myths of many cultures portray pivotal points of emotional reorganization as turning points in a voyage that embarks in a new direction. Oedipus's encounters with both Laius and the Sphinx are said to have occurred at crossroad intersections. Adam and Eve's departure from Eden, Abraham's departure from Ur toward Canaan, and Moses's travels from the burning bush to Pharaoh's palace and then across the Red Sea to Mount Sinai each portray a voyage toward a new destination.

An infant or young child attempting to relieve pain is forced to utilize whatever adaptive or defensive mechanisms are available at his or her as yet immature stage of life. However, emergency reactive or compensatory efforts may lean too far in a particular direction distorting development. Pivotal turning points may later need to be re-experienced and reprocessed in the transference in order to synthesize an adaptive integration that facilitates healthy development.

Both Chris and Ruth were hurt and angry, biting but persevering, wounded but trying, 'never give up' children. Throughout childhood, pain energized their efforts and they continued wondering, trying to get a perspective on conflicting experiences of their selves and forces within. In mid-childhood both were writers and enactors of dramatizations in creative fantasy play. Ruth tried to enact a role of a perfect daughter at arm's length from her feelings of rage. But she felt endangered in a pretend role, and simply wanted to again become close to others and to become real. Ultimately, she became a warm teacher, supportive of students' excitement in learning and discovering, and a warm caretaker for her mother and an aunt in their old age. Chris initially alternated between enacting split-apart aggressive and compliant roles and tried to integrate these in written stories. In mid-childhood, he alternately 'became' the aggressive figure (bear) or the compliant figure (Tim). Later, he became an interlocutor interacting with a safely controllable actualization of a fantasized friend (his ventriloquism dummy). This helped Chris experiment as he was trying to reach toward relationships with peers for the first time. With the resolution of his borderline splitting and preoedipal conflicts, he developed real relationships, and he progressed in a healthy way through latency, preadolescence, and adolescence. Reworking their crises in the transference allowed Ruth and Chris to adaptively reintegrate and resume their development.

NOTES

1. Alexander Pope (1734).
2. Similar problems have resulted from metaphoric misapplication of words such as 'oedipal,' 'phallic,' and 'castration' when referring to women. Kulish and Holtzman (1998) suggested that the Greek story of Persephone might provide a more suitable example than the story of Oedipus in describing a girl's development. But why limit ourselves to references from Hellenic or biblical mythology? As early as 1931, a Japanese psychoanalyst, Heisaku Kosawa,

explained to Freud that mid-childhood triangulation interactions are completely different in non-Western families and mythologies. It may also be of interest to note that, even within Western cultures, during the millennium preceding Hellenic culture, the 'supreme deities' of Mycenae and of most Mediterranean and Near Eastern cultures (and even the Pharaohs in Egypt) were not men, but rather women (Stone, 1976)! Schiller (2012) has proposed that a 'labial' conceptual framework might be more suited to describing female sexual subjectivity than male-centric words such as 'phallic,' 'oedipal,' and 'castration.' It is important to seek ways to express our ideas simply and clearly. Considering the rapidly changing structure of families in our own culture during the past century, the cross-cultural diversity in other societies in a rapidly shrinking multicultural world, and the importance of clarity in communicating with colleagues of other mental health and social science disciplines, it may be worthwhile to explore whether there are ways to clarify how we express some of these ideas. For examples of developmental studies of child-rearing and family dynamics in some preliterate cultures (Apache, Eskimo, and West African Anyi) during the first half of the twentieth century, and how this shaped their channeling of narcissism, rage, and revenge, please refer to references in the bibliography by E. F. Foulks, P.A. Freeman, D. M. A. Freeman, and P. Parin.

REFERENCES

Akhtar, S. (2009). *Comprehensive Dictionary of Psychoanalysis*. London, UK: Karnac Books.

Erikson, E. (1950). *Childhood and Society*. New York, NY: W.W. Norton, 1963.

Foulks, E. F., Freeman, D. M. A., and Freeman, P. A. (1978). Pre-oedipal dynamics in a case of Eskimo arctic hysteria. *Psychoanalytic Study of Society* 8: 41–69.

Freeman, D.M.A. (1968). Adolescent crises of the Kiowa-Apache Indian male. In: *Minority Group Adolescents in the United States*, ed. E. Brody, pp. 157–204. Baltimore, MD: Williams and Wilkins.

———. (1989). Contributions of crosscultural studies to clinical theory and practice: the work of Paul Parin. *Psychoanalytic Study of Society* 14: 281–299.

Freeman, D. M. A., Foulks, E. F., and Freeman, P. A. (1976). Ghost sickness and superego development in the Kiowa Apache male. *Psychoanalytic Study of Society* 7: 123–171.

———. (1978). Child development and arctic hysteria in the North Alaskan Eskimo male. *Journal of Psychological Anthropology* 1: 203–210.

Freeman, P. A. (1971). Kiowa Apache concepts and attitudes toward the child. *Papers in Anthropology* 12: 90–160.

Freud, S. (1921). Group psychology and the analysis of the ego. *Standard Edition* 18: 65–143.

———. (1931). Female sexuality. *Standard Edition* 21: 223–243.

Green, A. (1980). The dead mother. In: *Life Narcissism, Death Narcissism*, transl. A. Weller, pp. 185–221. London, UK: Free Association.

Kernberg, O. (1967). Borderline personality organization. *Journal of the American Psychoanalytic Association* 4: 641–685.

———. (1970). A psychoanalytic classification of character pathology. *Journal of the American Psychoanalytic Association* 18: 800–822.

Kosawa, H. (1931). Two kinds of guilt feelings—the Ajase complex. *Japanese Journal of Psychoanalysis* 1: 5–9, 1954.

Kulish, N., Holtzman, D. (1998). Persephone, the loss of virginity, and the female oedipal complex. *International Journal of Psychoanalysis* 79: 57–71.

Mahler, M., Pine, F., and Bergman, A. (1975). *The Psychological Birth of the Human Infant*. New York, NY: Basic Books.

Parin, P., Morgenthaler, F., and Parin-Matthey, G. (1980). *Fear Thy Neighbor as Thyself: Psychoanalysis and Society Among the Anyi of West Africa*. Chicago, IL: University of Chicago Press.

Pope, A. (1734). *Epistle to Cobham*. Published anonymously.

Schiller, B.M. (2012). Representing female desire within a labial framework of sexuality. *Journal of the American Psychoanalytic Association* 60: 1161–1197.
Stone, M. (1976). *When God Was a Woman*. New York, NY: Dorset Press.
Wallace, A. (1961). *Culture and Personality*. New York, NY: Random House.

Chapter Five

Revenge and Reparation

Loss and Restitution

Frederick Fisher

In "Inhibitions, Symptoms, and Anxiety," Freud (1926) described a developmental sequence in response to danger situations: loss of the object, loss of the object's love, fear of body mutilation, and dread of the prohibiting, punitive superego. Freud's timetable for experiencing the loss of the object and the object's love has been revised based on numerous developmental studies including Tronick's (1989) still-face paradigm, Stern (1985), and Beebe et al (2012). Recent studies reported by Vivona (2012) have confirmed the infant's perception in utero of the mother's voice, creating the potential for an affective bond between infant and mother upon entering the extra-uterine world.

Margaret Mahler's work (1975) emphasizes the role of the object in drive theory. Her parent-child research provides us with a language, a developmental map, delineating such concepts as symbiosis, hatching, practicing, rapprochement, and rapprochement crisis. In normal early development, the child protects against the loss of the object and the object's love in two basic ways. Internalization constructs a mental representation of the object that leads to libidinal object constancy by age two and a half to three years. This means the object is no longer need satisfying but loved regardless of the degree of frustration. Externally, there is the creation of the transitional object as described by Winnicott (1953), the early amorphous and the later, more structured form. When the three-year-old leaves for pre-school, he takes mother with him in his head as well as in his knapsack as the beloved "blankie."

Having a cohesive self-representation is crucial in balancing the developmental tracks of separation and individuation. Separation is the ability to disengage from the nurturing figure, and individuation, the evolution of discrete mental processes such as memory, cognition, and perception. A six-year-old boy with atypical development told me that if he left his home, he would melt. Aspects of the self can also be seen in transitional phenomena such as the transitional object, the imaginary companion, the false self, and the double. In his presentation, Dr. Freeman has provided us with a wealth of examples of these concepts giving us the theoretical underpinning that helped him to understand and treat Chris, age ten.

CHRIS

At six months, Chris was the idealized child who appeared to have a secure attachment to Mother. I say "appeared" because their interaction resembled Stern's (1985) concept of overattunement, described as a form of "psychic hovering that is usually accompanied by physical hovering." Stern considers that this form of attunement approximates in the external world what Mahler has called the internal symbiotic state, creating the illusion of a dual unity. Then, Mother's sudden paranoid accusations resulted in her turning against Father, who, in response, became symptomatic with anxiety attacks. An impulsive decision to heal their rift by abruptly going on a weeklong vacation eventually resulted in Chris feeling the emotional loss of both parents. His caretakers could not fill the enormous emotional vacuum that resulted from the separation. Upon her return, Mother did not encounter a joyful, receptive, six-month-old. With contained affect, he searched for his pre-vacation mother. Mother's response was withdrawal and, ultimately, rejection. Chris searched for the mother that left, but the one that reappeared was significantly altered. Chris fell from paradise. One could infer that as he was emerging from the symbiotic phase and hatching, Mother disappeared. He attempted to re-create the once warm, receptive, ever-present mother by mechanically recreating her face via the spinning game. Based on our understanding of internal object representation and the concept of splitting, this projection also became the persecutory image that had deserted him. This image became the focus of his aggression in order to protect the outside mother.

Mahler (1952) reported that in extreme cases, during hatching or early practicing, the self and object representations remain fused, hindering further individuation. She called this condition "early symbiotic psychosis," a syndrome describing the psychotic child's inability to tolerate separation from the mother by seeking permanence in the illusion of dual unity. When a mother attempts to separate or the child perceives separation, the child responds with terror. With loss, separation, or neglect during this crucial time, the mental representation of the symbiotic object can become fixed to the early representation of the self in varying degrees, thereby shaping development. Mahler's concept of symbiosis is crucial in understanding all the phases of normal separation-individuation.

In the practicing phase, the child's perception of union with the nurturing figure persists, creating a sense that "the world is my oyster." With rapprochement, at about two years, the child is beginning to have a dim sense of separation. In response to this, parents endure their child's sleep disturbances, renewal of stranger anxiety, the wish to share the parental bed, an intense need to maintain sameness, and an alternating darting away/clinging pattern of behavior. Many parents view this as a regression, but these behaviors confirm a growing awareness in the child of the reality that child and parents are separate creatures. Mahler referred to this phase as the rapprochement crisis leading to the quest to find an optimal distance from the nurturing figure. At this critical point, the child may believe that safety is only achieved by the presence of the nurturing figure. If the parent/child triad reinforces this belief, then the illusion is maintained that safety can only be achieved by the presence of the real object with diminishing reliance on the intra-psychic representations. Failure of the parent/child triad to resolve the rapprochement crisis can lead to subsequent escalation of developmental issues manifesting as the pre-school, kindergarten, and college dropout or the fearful child who avoids sleepovers and overnight camp. At times, the child may fear going to the second floor of the home unless accompanied by a family member. An eleven-year-old boy refused to attend birthday parties without his mother being present. Mother told me he was "shy" and the other boys were rough, but as he approached puberty, sharing the parental bed became uncomfortable for all.

The theory of internal object representation involves splitting into a good and bad object, providing a dual protection. Not only is there bonding with and protection of the good image but also the avoidance of the bad image as dangerous. Splitting is an early process of internalization prior to the ego's ability to utilize repression as a defense. According to Sarnoff (1970), repression is manifested by the appearance of a symbol, the phobic object, starting around two years of age. The phobic object as a repressed, displaced wish protects the loved object from aggressive impulses. For symbol formation to occur, ego function must include memory, image retention, spontaneous recall, language skill, and the capacity to delay action. As a result of this maturation, repression is achievable. In normal development, the pattern of splitting diminishes and is replaced by a broader range of defense. But, as we shall see in Chris's development, splitting mechanisms play a major defensive role.

At this point, the usual developmental path is a fusion of good and bad object representations into one loved object with faults. The predominant use of splitting is seen in some pathological states such as the borderline personality disorder but, to a lesser degree, can also be seen in normal development for adaptive or defensive purposes. A young man believed that he was cared for early in life, up to age three years, by his aunt and mother. Years later, he was informed that, after his birth, his mother suffered post-partum depression and became an alcoholic. The "mother" that cared for him during the day was his sober mother and the "aunt" that cared for him in the evening was actually his inebriated mother who became verbally and physically abusive throughout the evening.

As her depression deepened, Chris's mother prematurely weaned him, mistaking his pushing away the bottle as rejecting his need for her. She withdrew from him, substituting TV and toys, non-interactive objects. The dyadic misalignment manifested at nine months when Chris made himself an object for self-stimulation by rocking and head banging. Chris began to display some of the significant symptoms described by Spitz (1965) in his study of children who, in the latter half of their first year, were impacted by depressed and psychotic mothers. Rochlin (1953, 1961) declared that for children attempting to preserve the self, the object cannot be totally lost. The actual object might be renounced but a substitute, usually an inanimate object, replaces it. Rochlin's clinical example is a four-month-old child, abandoned much like Chris, who by two years preferred to relate to his mother's fur coat while secreted in a closet.

However, in Chris's case, he shows inherent resilience in his continued struggle to connect to his mother despite his self-stimulation and connection to inanimate objects. Chris's hatching and exploring the world in the practicing phase was fraught with danger. The role of his father is poignantly revealed by the recovered memory trace of his first birthday party when his father was absent. This memory may represent a telescoping of multiple memories of his father's absence or unavailability. Father seemed to be accepting of the mother's view of Chris as the "good child" and did not intervene with rough-and-tumble play, supportive interactions, or become, as Abelin (1971) described, a force in the pre-oedipal triad. As Diamond (1997) and Herzog (2001) have reported, the presence of the father shapes the boy's concept of masculinity and the mother's admiration reinforces it. Without this developmental preparation, gender constancy is unstable and entrance into the phallic-narcissistic phase is tenuous. In these children, the oedipal phase can be characterized by an oscillating gender identification and regression to anal- or phallic-inhibited patterns. The late practicing phase, usually heralded by bipedal discovery and mastery, was rewarded instead with maternal attention when Chris fell down and later when he hurt himself. Chris had separation anxiety when his mother left the room, as well as generalized anxiety when she took him out with her to encounter the world. This situation reminded me of Mahler (1975) citing Anthony's description of the child who not only has nowhere to go, but is afraid to get anywhere. Unable to find comfort in exploring the world as many children do in the practicing phase,

Chris failed to achieve an optimal distance from his alternately encapsulating/distant mother in order to create a rudimentary cohesive self.

During his rapprochement crisis, Mother was unable to relate to him and could not be a regulator of his motoric or affective outpourings. Chris was unable to establish, once again, an optimal distance from Mother. Instead, when his parents took a second vacation when he was two and a half, Chris experienced "organismic distress" with separation issues so severe that the parents decided not to leave him alone again and withdrew him from school. These decisions may have reinforced the concept that the world is a dangerous place and that only the actual presence of Mother would protect him. With his aggression directed towards the bad internal mother in his spinning game, the good external mother was preserved. Her attention was his reward when he was pathetic, defective, and infantile. Manifestations of splitting as a projected double became evident from about three years in the form of "Tim," whose compliance met the expectations and therefore the love of Mother. This also served the defensive purpose of victory over his struggle with aggression. Another double, the silent boy in the bear costume, achieved mastery over his world with contained aggression: for example, "I can be a powerful but harmless bear." This Jekyll and Hyde theme recurred throughout his development. The use of the double is common in world literature. Conrad's (2004) *Heart of Darkness and The Secret Sharer* is an example of encountering a good double. Poe's (1951) "William Wilson" is an example of the persecutory double. In Chris's case, there is a use of multiple doubles.

Mother's preference for his older sister may have contributed to the creation of a cross-gendered double to compete for Mother's love on a level playing field. This may also have served as a defense against expressing closeness towards Mother as an oedipal-aged boy. He felt safer in the disguise of a girl. Coates (1991) describes gender identity disorder in some boys as being an attachment disorder manifesting around age two years. This is another example of fusion of self and object with a more focused loss of reality testing in regard to gender. Dynamically they have a mother forever by becoming the mother via an identification of being. Think Norman Bates in *Psycho* (1960) by Alfred Hitchcock. Chris's passivity as a defense against his aggressive impulses led to an avoidance of peers and peer-related activities such as sports. He sought mastery over others through magic potions instead of the give-and-take of meaningful interaction. Living in the world of black and white splitting with obsessive struggles and gender confusion made entrance into early latency a challenge for Chris. While evidence of his intelligence was clear, he was unable to approach his classwork successfully because anxiety disrupted his cognitive functioning.

Chris's symptoms intensified as his journey through latency became more tortuous. Archaic pre-oedipal fears (fear of the dark and abandonment) co-mingled with castration anxiety. The onset of polyuria resulted in penis checking, a reassurance against castration. As a ventriloquist, he evoked a proxy, another double theme, and defended against his increased pre-pubertal difficulty with aggression and sexuality. Wangh (1962) defines a proxy as "a person other than oneself who is used to experience feelings, exercise functions, and execute actions in one's own stead" (452–53). Lipton (1983) describes ventriloquism, seen in latency-aged children, usually boys, as serving either a conflict-free or defensive function. Chris's struggle between good and evil is manifested when William, the dummy, would say things that Chris was unable to speak. At times Chris's hold on reality was tenuous and he required reassurance that William was "just a doll." Would his dummy come alive? Recall Chris's earlier fascination with monsters and robots and how he would lock them in his closet at night lest they come alive. In Freud's "The Uncanny" (1919), he describes the dread of the inanimate becoming alive as well as the encountering of a double. How many young children have nightmares after seeing *The Nutcracker*? Chris's hold on reality, his sense of identity, and his ability to control his impulses appeared to weaken under the pressure of pending puberty.

As the analysis deepened, Chris used the dummy to express his conflict over the wish to be close to the analyst. Here again we see cross-gender fantasies with the dummy viewing Chris as a girl in competition for the analyst's affections. The interpretative work helped Chris use fewer splitting mechanisms and deal more directly with his feelings toward the analyst. Prepubescent conflicts then emerged as Chris feared losing the analyst, replicating his childhood fear of losing his mother to his sister. Envy of the female (having a baby) and jealousy (the oedipal victor can only be a girl) became the focus of the work as manifestations of an evolving transference neurosis. During his early adolescence, Chris was able to consolidate his gender identity, form positive male peer relationships (via the dummy), attend boy-girl parties, and identify with his father and analyst. However, oscillation between the wish to grow up or remain dependent surfaced, fueld further by his pubescent awareness of the complexities of male–female interaction. The infantile wishes were again re-created and examined in a safe place, the office, as his fear of alienating and losing the analyst was linked to his early sudden abandonment. Chris began to feel greater comfort in claiming aggression as his own, not attributing it to a proxy. Therapeutic progress manifested as he expressed a competitive heterosexual attitude towards the analyst alternating with submissive homoerotic wishes. The burial of William was experienced as mourning the death of an aspect of himself. He was in the process of becoming, like Pinocchio, a real boy.

Chris's resilience is impressive. His ongoing cognitive functioning, memory, and sense of humor were crucial for his developmental progress. He was able to maintain an ongoing relationship with his mother during his pubertal struggle. His shift to storytelling represents a more integrated functioning of the ego, especially the synthetic function. This aspect of his creativity provided greater opportunity for insight and pleasure in mastery. He was able to establish a therapeutic alliance and tolerate painful reconstructions during this phase of treatment. The final chapter of the story of Super Hero and Arch Meany's demise represents a literary merging and eventual destruction of these two aspects of the self but an ego consolidation for Chris. Tausk's (1933) paper on the influencing machine describes the projection of paranoid ideation on elaborate machinery that controls the individual's thoughts, body, or commands them to commit sexual acts. Rather than "the devil made me do it," "the machine made me do it." Several non-psychotic early adolescent boys have reported such ideas to me. The gears in Chris's complex machinery where Super Hero and Arch Meany fall on top of each other and fuse in death may represent a birth-in-death fantasy, resulting in his liberation. Characteristic of Chris, where there is progression, there is regression. The loss of these projected idealized/de-idealized figures resulted in a return to his fears of abandonment. Again, the weak, defective, infantile boy returned to an earlier adolescent phase where he found himself defenseless against his internal world. The skiing trip has elements of all the danger situations: loss of the object (lost alone in the cold), loss of the object's love (skiing into Mother), fear of body mutilation (popped-out eyeballs), and dread of the punitive superego (getting lost in the snow because Father did not punish him sufficiently). Chris's struggle with separation-individuation issues may follow him through the major life cycle events of his life. Leaving for college may present a significant challenge in terms of both separation and consolidation of his gender identity. However, his ability to utilize the analytic work created a multicolored world rather than a black and white reality, establishing the potential for a more reality-oriented relationship with his parents and peers.

RUTH

The body ego is formed by the infant's earliest somatic sensations coupled with the infant's interaction with the nurturing figure. What of the formation of Ruth's early body ego? Writers such as Schechter (1972) and Spitz (1951) describe complications in body self-representation as a result of dermatologic pathology. Raw, painful, or bloody skin can be hyper- or hypocathected, forming distorted or displaced self-representation. Mothers of children with infantile eczema often avoid touching their children, resulting in a stunted kinesthetic bonding. The child may be viewed as fragile and easily damaged, which conveys a sense of imperfection to the child. Ruth felt she was never pretty enough for Mother or herself.

What of the impact on the process of separation-individuation when a young child is immobilized? During her first year of life, Ruth had severe eczema requiring her hands be tied to prevent scratching when she slept. At two years, Ruth underwent a surgical procedure to correct a strabismus that again required immobilization, reviving memories of earlier restraint for treatment of her severe eczema. Mahler (1975) emphasizes that free movement contributes to the integration of body image resulting in a sense of body ownership. One of my adult patients discovered that she had worn a nighttime bar-brace from eight to eighteen months. A significant theme in the analysis was "don't tie me down," resulting in fleeting object relationships and a poor sense of body boundaries. She did not appreciate her early history until the full extent of her immobilization was reconstructed in the analysis.

What terror Ruth must have experienced with the surgical procedure—sightless, restricted, in pain, and no mother to modulate her affective state. In a world of strangers, she could only protect herself by biting when approached or by withdrawing into her inner world. This event significantly influenced her sadistic impulses towards her tormentors. We hear the early theme of revenge toward her mother, whom she blamed for abandoning her. Her self-destructive impulses were directed inward as she attempted to undo the surgery by deliberately moving her eyes. To be wronged unfairly is a common human experience but the wish for revenge tends to diminish with time. However, in Ruth's case, these wrongs did not heal with time. Instead, fantasies of reciprocating the hurt in order to restore her self-esteem became an organizing life pursuit. Pathological vindictiveness, as described by Daniels (1969), evolves when the quest for justice becomes an insatiable force leading to object destruction. When revenge has a sense of right, the quest for vengeance is freed from anxiety or guilt. One is driven to destroy the offending party and often self and object fall together as in Melville's (1851) *Moby Dick*.

Consider Shakespeare's (1592) *Richard III*:

> Cheated of feature by dissembling Nature
> Deform'd, unfinished, sent before my time
> Into this breathing world, scarce half made up . . . (Act I, Scene 1, Line 20)

Freud (1916) describes the impact of defect on Richard III's character development in his paper "The Exceptions." Richard attends to (mother) Nature as the offending source. Children often have the fantasy that their mother gave them the defect as punishment. Ruth's rage towards her perceived defective body, parents, and unseen violators led to unstable self and object representation and subsequent difficulty in establishing an optimal distance. "I have never been close to anyone my whole life." Addressing the persistence of the need for revenge, Steiner (1996) writes that the "relinquishment of a grievance would lead to a collapse and catastrophe and it seems to provide a sense of integration and protection from breakdown" (433).

Mother was intolerant of Ruth's display of anger. For Ruth, the threat of abandonment shaped her as a compliant child predisposed to dissociation. She came to realize that she had masked her inner rage by an outer, false self, and that all through her life she had pretended, like an actress, to be something other than what she was. Feeling inferior to her peers in latency and preadolescence, she later described her superior position as "standing on a platform above everybody, trying to manipulate them." Because she felt inferior, she became enraged toward peers, especially those she perceived as superior. By diminishing others to achieve comfort, her envy destabilized relationships. With the resolution of the rapprochement crisis, the child achieves an optimal distance from the nurturing figure and can safely explore the world. Ruth's failure plagued her and she failed to internalize a stable self-representation. In her dream life, she created a twin, perhaps the wished for, non-defective other that would bring her a sense of stability.

There is a link between disruptive moves and loss. Just before age two years, Ruth experienced the sudden departure of her father when he was drafted and then a move to the maternal grandparents' home. At four years when her father returns, she leaves the maternal grandparents' home and the maternal grandfather, perhaps the only positive figure in her life, dies suddenly, an echo of the earlier loss of her father. In addition, one could consider whether Ruth and her mother had competed for the grandfather's love since he was the only man in the house. Ruth may have feared further abandonment if her mother was jealous of their relationship. The perceived harsh, rejecting, possessive maternal figure can strongly influence the little girl's discomfort with oedipal wishes. How did she understand her grandfather's sudden death? Was it a repeat of the sudden loss of the pre-oedipal father? Father's return was plagued by his medical problems and, with his subsequent distancing, she felt "dethroned" and rejected. How did she take this rejection and to whom could she turn in the family? As analysts, particularly child analysts, we need to understand the family history in order to appreciate the individual dynamics. The perceived rejecting, tiger-mother with such high standards was the only one available to her.

I inferred that Mother, overwhelmed by her daughter's medical conditions as well as multiple stressors, must have transmitted her depression to the child. Ruth stated what a disappointment she must have been, never living up to Mother's or her own standards. Parents of special-needs children struggle with their rage towards the "special child" and often overcompensate with overprotective love or reject the child outright. In the play *Joe Egg* by Nichols (1967), the parents' reaction to a special-needs child is portrayed through an ongoing dialogue of mutual blame. The challenge of raising a child with special needs often divides the parents with accusations and disagreements over parenting issues.

Fearful of abandonment, Ruth identified with her mother by becoming the controlling, manipulative person unable to tolerate affect. "Spare me your rage" became her message to the world, as it was her mother's when Ruth was a child. Although Ruth was able to work, marry, and tolerate the analytic process, she continued to maintain a distant, bellicose stance in order to protect herself against closeness with both husband and analyst. Relationships are viewed in terms of power positions: if not on top, she is vulnerable to assault. Ruth slowly came out of her shell and was able to examine lifelong beliefs. With insight into her punitive superego/masochistic ego, she realized that she, not her mother, imposed her punishments. Associations included her transformation into wildflowers or butterflies, implying metamorphosis into something beautiful. Progress and regression is seen as part of the analytic process. In the analysis, she alternated between a dependent, demanding stance and a defensive, distancing position as an aspect of her unresolved rapprochement phase. Mahler (1952) has described this pattern of alternating action in opposite directions as "ambitendency," connoting a conscious doing and undoing. As development proceeds, that which has been observed as ambitendent behavior becomes internalized as ambivalence.

Ruth's Scheherazade theme is a thinly veiled erotic transference wish, not only to delay being "undressed" but also as a prelude to the analyst falling in love with her after 1,001 stories are told. Unlike the beheaded virgins, she will be special, win the love of the unavailable father figure, and feel beautiful from within and without. Ruth gradually assumed responsibility for "her story," and while her "dark, angry, watchful eye" will not disappear, she was on her way to a more balanced vision of herself and the world.

> *And then it was, that suddenly sweeping his sickle-shaped lower jaw beneath him, Moby Dick had reaped away Ahab's leg, as a mower a blade of grass in the field. . . . Small reason was there to doubt, then, that ever since that almost fatal encounter, Ahab had cherished a wild Vindictiveness against the whale, . . . for that in his frantic morbidness he at last came to identify with him, not only all of his bodily woes, but all his intellectual and spiritual exasperations . . . all evil, to crazy Ahab, were visibly personified in . . . Moby Dick.* (156)

Chapter Six

The Spectrum of Narcissistic Transferences

Otto Kernberg

This presentation explores the different transference developments of a spectrum of severity of narcissistic personality disorders that determines different clinical challenges and technical approaches. It is inspired by the collaborative work of the Personality Disorders Institute at the Weill Cornell Medical College, Department of Psychiatry in recent years. In earlier communications (Kernberg, 1984, 2007) I have outlined the salient clinical characteristics of the narcissistic personality disorder, and shall limit myself here to describe the transference manifestations of this pathology at the various levels of severity of patients' illness, with the corresponding particular psychoanalytic interventions found to be helpful in these cases.

COMMON TRANSFERENCE FEATURES REFLECTING THE PATHOLOGICAL GRANDIOSE SELF

While the clinical characteristics of narcissistic patients may vary widely depending on the degree of severity of the pathology and the regressive features of these patients, there are certain common transference developments that remain constant. They include, first of all, the activation of a dominant transference relationship between a grandiose, entitled, superior self and a depreciated object, reflecting the patient's pathological grandiose self, and a complementary, devalued, inferior, paralyzed counterpart, usually projected onto the therapist but sometimes enacted by the patient himself. This devalued object corresponds to the patient's own devalued, dissociated, projected, or regressed infantile self. In contrast to the typical activation of dissociated internalized relations between aspects of the patient's infantile self and his internalized dissociated object representations (i.e., self-representation, object-representation dyads), here the dyads are constituted by the relation between the pathological grandiose self and devalued self representations.

This particular constellation of grandiose and devalued self, however, may appear in different forms, depending on various associated characterological features. These features, in fact, determine the types of narcissistic personality disorders described in the literature as the 'thick-skinned' and 'thin-skinned' narcissists, the 'syndrome of arrogance,' chronic non-depressive suicidality and parasuicidality, and the development of antisocial behavior.

In addition, patients in the narcissistic spectrum cannot depend on the therapist or analyst. His interventions are discarded, ignored, or distrustfully examined for anything 'new' that the patient thinks he has not heard before. The patient does not feel understood or helped by the therapist's manifestation of interest and concern, and is unable to explore with curiosity what the analyst's comments may evoke in his mind. The patient either talks to himself in the presence of the therapist or to the therapist in order to influence him in the direction the patient desires. As mentioned in earlier work (Kernberg, 1984), this affects the countertransference reaction of the therapist in that it conveys the impression that the therapist really is alone in the room.

These two features, in short, the activation of this particular self-self relationship in the transference, and the patient's incapacity to depend on the therapist, differentiate narcissistic patients at all levels of severity of illness from the usual type of primitive, dissociated object relations activated in the psychoanalytic approach to patients with borderline personality organization. These narcissistic transferences, when dominant, require lengthy and consistent working through. What follows are particular forms these transferences take in different patient constellations, and technical approaches to them that we have found helpful. In describing these constellations in a sequence of degrees of clinical severity, the emergence of predominant infiltration of the grandiose self with aggression in the severe realm of this pathology and the gradually predominant direction of this aggression against the self in the most severe cases will become apparent.

Narcissistic Transferences at a High, Stable Level of Functioning

Standard psychoanalysis is generally indicated for narcissistic patients functioning at a relatively high level, if, and when, some symptomatic difficulties motivate them to enter treatment. The dominant experience of the analyst with this type of narcissist, initially, is as if there were no transference. In fact, the transference is between the pathological grandiose self that denies all dependency and an unimportant outsider, who might be useful as a source of admiration, but is also potentially dangerous. The analyst, in the patient's mind, might replicate the patient's grandiosity, devaluing the patient in the process, or, under the effect of the patient's implicit devaluation of him, crumble and give the patient a sense of wasted time, emptiness, and disappointment in the treatment. It is as if the patient were defending himself against the double danger of either being depreciated by somebody who acts superior to him, or wasting his time and money with a worthless therapist. Efforts to control the analyst, who should be as good as the patient but not better, because this would evoke envy, or worse, devaluation, characterize this transference. This dominant transference may remain stubbornly unchangeable over an extended period of time.

Narcissistic patients may perceive the treatment as a 'cognitive learning': they may be curious about interpretations as meanings that they have to learn and incorporate in order to not have any further need of the analyst, and that typically, once absorbed, tend to be unconsciously devalued, with no felt need for further exploration on the part of the patient. One patient carefully repeated my interpretations to him, 'checking' their correctness or questionable nature. The same patient repeatedly experienced questions emerging in his mind whether this particular session or a segment of a session was 'good' or 'useless.' These patients are forced to carry out omnipotent control of the analyst to keep him within an acceptable range of value for them, and behind this control and distancing are powerful defenses against profound envy and resentment of having to depend on what the analyst presumably has to give and the patient needs.

This dominant relationship between the pathological grandiose self and an outsider to be controlled so that he does not become a replica of the devalued part of the self-concept may oscillate into its opposite, that is, periods of feelings of inferiority, failure, and humiliation on the part of the patient, and his fantasies of the analyst's grandiosity and contemptuous superiority now may dominate the picture. Upon systematic analysis of this transference, the relationship between the pathological grandiose self and the devalued self is gradually dismantled into its components, which are idealized representations of self and others that are enacted and/or projected by the patient.

As the pathological grandiose structure is dismantled we see subtle shifts toward transferences that seem more object related, while, at the same time, they have a more primitive and predominantly paranoid character, as the patient projects grandiose and threatening aspects of significant others of his past onto the analyst. One patient, a mental health professional, whom I was treating in a relatively small town where the entire mental health community was familiar with each other, was spreading derogatory comments about me to a few colleagues, at this point of his analysis. A few weeks later, he heard these same comments repeated by others, became frightened, and 'confessed' them in a session. On exploration of this behavior, it turned out that he had been acting out an identification with his mother, whose chronic feelings of inferiority had motivated her to spread derogatory gossip regarding friends within her social circle. At this time, the patient also became afraid that I might be discussing his case with other colleagues.

The task now becomes to explore the gradual development of periods of rupture of the pathological grandiose self into these component internalized part-object relations and the correspondent unconscious conflicts involved. The treatment, over time, becomes more like that of ordinary borderline patients, in terms of split-off activation of idealized and persecutory relationships. Gradually, the underlying conflicts beneath the defensive structure of the pathological grandiose self may emerge, typically intense primitive aggression linked to feelings of envy, a condensation of pregenital and oedipal conflicts, and the activation of traumatic early experiences against which the pathological grandiose self had become a major defensive structure.

There are patients who generally function quite well in their social and work life, but who are so bereft of an internal world of object relationships that all openness to fantasy and daydreaming seems completely closed. The 'thick-skinned' narcissistic personalities described by Rosenfeld (1987) belong to this group of patients. They live in the concrete reality of their interactions with the analyst, which do not lead to any development of fantasy, desire, fear, or deeper conflict. The patients themselves may state freely that they see no reason why they should develop any particular emotional reaction to a relationship that, after all, follows the principles of a commercial contract where 'one person gets paid to take care of the problems of the other.' A patient assured me that, while I seemed like a nice person, if I died suddenly, he would have no particular feeling about it.

The patient's efforts to carry out free association may be severely distorted by his unwavering need to keep the analytic situation under control. Free associations are so well structured and orderly in sequence that they reveal an intentional effort to direct the analyst's attention in a certain direction, pre-consciously planned by the patient. Or the patient's 'checking' on the meaning of what he is saying while communicating it to the analyst may provide his discourse with an empty, intellectualized quality.

I have found it helpful to analyze the defensive function of this way of associating by focusing on the patient's reactions to the analyst's interpretive interventions. Patients may simply ignore what the analyst says, resuming their monologue after a respectful brief silence, or examine carefully all the implications of the analyst's comments, speculate on their meaning, express their agreement or disagreement, or dismantle the analyst's statement altogether—anything, really, to avoid being impacted by the analyst in a way that is not totally under the patients' control, in an attempt to avoid a humiliating indication of their dependency and, therefore, inferiority to the analyst.

The interpretation of this constellation may allow patients to become aware of their need to control the analytic relationship implied in their style of carrying out free association.

An additional helpful technical approach to these patients may be to analyze in great detail their difficulties outside the transference situation, the details of their difficulties in work, in intimate sexual relations, in their social life, with their families. It is usually not difficult, by sharply focusing on the areas of daily conflicts in their lives, to gradually open up their understanding of aspects of their interactions that are motivated by emotional pressures and deeper fears or desires that can then be linked to similar manifestations that in subtle ways emerge in the transference. The 'microscopic' analysis of extra-transference relations allows for gradual exploration of the transference itself. For example, behind the indifference toward their partners, one may detect the emergence of envy of the other person's capacity for love and friendship, and the freedom to have an interesting daily world of experiences from which the patients are excluded.

The 'indifferent' patient whom I referred to above bitterly resented his wife talking animatedly for hours with her friends by phone, comparing it with his own restrictions and limitations in such interesting interchange with acquaintances. Similarly, behind the admiration and sexual excitement involved in the patients' transitory infatuations, one may discover and highlight for the patient resentment of an exciting, teasing, and withholding other, and its repetition of past similar experiences with significant objects of childhood and infancy. The development of negative therapeutic reactions in the sessions, reflecting unconscious wishes to devalue the treatment following precise moments of envious recognition of the therapist's capacity to help and be interested in them, offers another entrance into this transference development. Above all, these patients' constant need to compare themselves to others, and the fluctuations between triumphant superiority and anxious fear of being devalued, are dominant issues in the extra-transferential relations to be explored, providing a bridge to the later exploration of similar issues in the transference.

Narcissistic Transferences at a Fluctuating, Borderline Level

In our research projects studying the treatment of borderline personality disorders with Transference-Focused Psychotherapy (TFP), we found a significant number of borderline patients with predominant narcissistic transference developments and became more able to identify narcissistic personality disorders functioning at an overt borderline level, as well as patients whose symptoms centered on inordinate arrogance and aggressiveness, in addition to patients with the syndrome of malignant narcissism (Kernberg, 2004, 2007; Clarkin, Yeomans, and Kernberg, 2006).

Cases with severe clinical syndromes may present indications for psychoanalysis or psychoanalytic psychotherapy, but when they appear as descriptively 'borderline,' that is, with a general chaos of behavior patterns and breakdown in social life, work, love, and sex, they may optimally be treated with TFP (Clarkin et al, 2006). This is particularly true when they present prognostically negative features, such as the infiltration of the pathological grandiose self with severe, ego-syntonic aggression towards others or self; chronic suicidal behavior; and, particularly, antisocial behavior.

The contribution of aggression directed against others or self, severe paranoid traits, and antisocial behavior constitutes the syndrome of malignant narcissism. Although malignant narcissism is at the boundary of treatability, TFP may be indicated if a clear framework and structure for the conduct of the treatment can be established and maintained. Within this most severe group of narcissistic patients, we find other typical developments in the transference that correspond to the 'thin-skinned narcissistic personalities' (Rosenfeld, 1987), the 'syndrome of arrogance' (Bion, 1957), or an almost psychotic level of social functioning by patients who have zero tolerance for any 'triangulation' (Britton, 2004). Some of these patients present a severe, chronic self-destructiveness with a significant risk of suicide (Kernberg, 2007). Indications for specific treatments, and complications in the treatment, prognosis, and technique are affected by the variables of the degree of superego integration, antisocial behavior, paranoid tendencies, the ego-syntonic nature of aggression, and chronic manifest self-destructive suicidal and parasuicidal behavior.

These patients are more severely regressed, often fail in analytic treatments, but respond well to TFP. They present both severe infiltration of the pathological grandiose self with aggression and a structural weakness of the pathological grandiose self, so that shifts from states of arrogance, superiority, and contemptuous feelings about the analyst to severe feelings of inferiority, humiliation, depression, self-accusation, and suicidal tendencies may occur frequently and rapidly. Such shifts, sometimes, are motivated by minor sources of triumph or defeat, and their hypersensitivity to any experienced criticism, real or fantasized. Their clinical presentation evinces severe characterological depression or chronic dysthymic reactions, suicidal tendencies, marked identity diffusion—in spite of the pathological grandiose self, reflected in goallessness, uncertainty, and confusion about their life and relations. Ego-syntonic sadistic features are both expressed and projected onto the therapist, who is frequently perceived as a seductive, scheming, and dishonest persecutor. These are patients with rapid changes in the transference developments, extreme frustration for not being able to totally control the therapist in terms of his thinking or behavior, and angry outbursts of total devaluation of the therapist and wishes to interrupt the treatment. Their contemptuous attitude may take the form of accusing the therapist of 'not understanding anything,' projecting onto the therapist the confusion in their own relationships with significant others, along with heightened paranoid tendencies in the transference.

Often these are patients who have been severely traumatized by physical or sexual abuse or gross neglect in their infancy or early childhood. Their unconscious tendency to reactivate these traumatizations in the transference conveys both important information about the past and determines difficulties because of their high acting out potential. These are the patients for whom John Steiner (1993) recommended to interpret 'in the projection,' clarifying their experiences and views of the analyst, rather than interpreting fully their projections into the analyst. This corresponds to an extremely effective technical approach of TFP whereby the therapist points out, at every point, the kind of relationship that the patient's experience is activating in the transference, with attention to how the same relationship tends to get activated, again and again, with role reversals. In the role reversal, the patient experiences himself in the role of the internal object representation, a role that he had previously projected onto the therapist while remaining identified with an aspect of his self. Now, however, the self is projected into the object, the patient can experience what he had previously projected into the object, and the full nature of what had been projected may become available to the patient's subjective experience.

Bion (1957) had described the syndrome of arrogance in severely regressed patients, consisting of 1) an openly aggressive and extremely arrogant behavior toward the therapist; 2) incapacity for any cognitive reflection, so that the patient appears to be 'pseudo stupid;' and 3) an inordinate curiosity about the therapist rather than one's self. It reflects the chronic enactment in the sessions of primitive hatred and envy, but with the particular characteristic that the aggression is acted out without the patient's having any self-reflective awareness of it. The arrogant behavior expresses his combative aggressive needs; the lack of any capacity for cognitive communication with the therapist; the desperate effort not to have to acquire any awareness of the significance of his behavior; and the curiosity, the need to control the therapist to avoid the projected and feared aggression to return in the form of counterattacks from the therapist.

I have found that the best way to manage this syndrome, which presents in some of the most severe types of narcissistic regression, is a combination of interpretation and maintaining firm boundaries of the treatment situation. There need to be very clear limits set regarding how far the patient may express his aggression verbally, without attacking the therapist physically, nor the office, nor invade the therapist's space outside the sessions, so that the attacks are limited to an extent that can be contained in the therapeutic sessions. At the same time, the therapist's focus needs to be on the patient's intolerance to recognize the sadistic pleasure that he obtains from his aggressive behavior. The defense against the fear of recognition of the pleasure in his sadistic behavior, when it is overcome, permits the patient to accept that pleasure without fear of retaliation or guilt, and, by the same token, this tends to reduce the intensity of the aggression, opening the possibility of studying the origins of that reaction in the transference.

One of our patients cut the plants in her therapist's office, abused him verbally in public spaces, but was able, eventually, to acknowledge and explore her pleasure in these attacks as an unconscious identification with a sadistic aunt who had dominated her childhood, and had been extremely physically abusive. The decomposition of the pathological grandiose self into its component internalized object relations—in this case, the activation of the sadistic aunt identification—signals the resolution of the structure of the pathological grandiose self in the course of transference interpretation.

There are patients who function at a much higher level, with much better controls of their behavior inside and outside the sessions, but where the attitudes of contempt, devaluation, depreciatory competition with the therapist go hand in hand with periods of self-contempt, despair, and suicidality under the effects of this self-contempt. These patients usually have strong paranoid tendencies, and tend to justify their contemptuous behavior through intellectual debates with the therapist that are expressed in combatively arrogant attitudes. This same contempt creates severe conflicts at work, in the social sphere, and in intimate relations. With these higher-functioning patients the contemptuous behavior and arrogance is less intense and overwhelming than in the regressed arrogant patients; nonetheless, it is very clear to the analyst that he is being treated contemptuously, and clear to the patient that he is doing that, so that, in the short run, this is open to transference exploration. However, the extended duration of unrelenting contempt may undermine the analyst's positive disposition toward the patient, which, actually, is one of the unconscious objectives of this transference development: both revenge against hated parental images and, at the bottom, a desperate effort to still maintain a good relationship with the analyst and not be abandoned, in spite of this behavior.

In fact, the tolerance of the countertransference may become quite a central issue in such cases; particularly when patients involve third parties, complaining to relatives and to other therapists, requesting consultations to protest about the way they are being treated, it is difficult to maintain a technically neutral stance. It may become necessary in some cases to establish limits to the patient's behavior, geared to permit the indispensable sense of security—physical, emotional, professional, legal—the therapist needs to maintain his position of concerned objectivity. The therapist's capacity to evaluate what enactments and projective identifications are activated in the transference/countertransference developments needs to be protected.

An extreme form of omnipotent control may evolve as part of the intolerance of triangulation (Britton, 2004), in very regressed narcissistic patients. Intolerance of triangulation refers to a particularly severe distortion of internalized object relations, a regression within which the patient cannot tolerate any thoughts that are different from his own. The role of the therapist is to confirm the view of the patient, and to assure the patient of the reality and stability of that shared experience. Any contribution from the therapist that is at variance with the patient's thinking is destabilizing to the patient's grandiose self and carries malignant implications. At the bottom, it is the search for a perfect symbiotic relationship within a dyad that does not tolerate the disruption by a third, excluded object, and, at the same time, represents the fragile omnipotence of a pathological grandiose self that attempts to maintain absolute control over experienced reality. Here, archaic oedipal conflicts, the intolerance of the relation between the parental couple from which the infant feels excluded, surfaces in the transference as the envious resentment of the therapist's relation to an internal object of his own (his independent thinking, his theory, his reflection about what is going on in the relation with the patient), making different perspectives intolerable to the patient.

Efforts by the therapist to bring in views different from that of the patient are experienced as either a total abandonment and rejection or else as a sadistic intrusion, an aggressive effort to control the patient's mind. This situation, originally described by Britton (2004), even may be observed in patients functioning at a relatively high level within the spectrum of narcissistic pathology, where it is revealed in very subtle ways of rejection of the therapist's independent thinking by highly sophisticated maneuvers that reassert the patient's initial views and force the therapist into a temporary emotional retreat. But this condition emerges as well with extremely regressed narcissistic patients, functioning on an overt borderline level, where the patient's experience of reality has such an extremely distorted quality that it is close to psychotic.

In this latter case, the patient may be totally convinced of the realistic nature of an emotional experience within which the patient's behavior may have been extremely inappropriate, and, as mentioned before, practically psychotic in the context of its social surround. Here, any effort of the therapist to probe reality testing may be experienced as an attack, bringing about a rageful effort on the part of the patient to shake off the intrusion.

One patient maintained an almost delusional conviction that a man, who was obviously exploiting her and showed his indifference at every turn, was in love with her. In turn, she treated the therapist who, over an extended period of time, was trying to confront her with her illusions as if he had a totally unrealistic view of reality. This woman functioned remarkably well in other areas of her life. Another patient, with severely overt borderline functioning, created such a disruption at a family funeral that family members escorted him away from the grave. In the subsequent sessions, he raged against the lack of understanding by his family of his intense suffering and developed an extended rage attack at any effort of the therapist to raise the question whether, under the circumstances, the expression of his mourning had acquired characteristics that were, in fact, quite problematic and socially inappropriate.

A technical approach that has been helpful with these conditions is enormous patience and consistence in pointing out to the patient the very fact that any view that is different from his own creates an intense pain, as if the patient, his thinking, his very capacity to deal with reality were questioned, so that the patient has to protect himself against such a dangerous assault. It is a case of the therapist seemingly trying to drive the patient mad. The analyst needs to spell out gradually the nature of the danger that is creating panic in the patient, the fear of a total disqualification of his capacity to think, the fear over total abandonment and loneliness, the fear of the patient's own intense enraged reaction to this dangerous situation, and his fantasies of the sadistic intention of an 'imaginary outsider' who now seems to be committed to destroying the safety of the patient's earlier experience, and the therapist's collusion with such an enemy. By its absence, in these cases, the situation described points to the importance of the 'three-person psychology' that constitutes the basis of a therapeutic relationship, and the resolution of this severe regression marks an important improvement for these patients.

The concept of the 'three-person psychology' refers to the consideration of the therapeutic relationship as determined, at least, by the transference, the countertransference, and the analyst/therapist's position as an 'excluded third party,' that is, that part of the analyst's personality able to explore the transference/countertransference relationship without being immersed in it (Kernberg, 2012). It is a reflection of an internal split in the analyst's ego in relating to the patient that gets 'obliterated,' again and again, in countertransference enactments and in the developments of projective counter-identifications (Grinberg, 1979). Symbolically, this third excluded other represents the oedipal triangulation, in contrast to a dyadic, pre-oedipal relationship (Britton, 2004).

Extreme Non-Depressive Suicidality and Self-Destructiveness

It usually is not difficult to differentiate the chronic suicidal and parasuicidal behavior of severe personality disorders without dominant narcissistic features from that of narcissistic personalities functioning on an overt borderline level. Non-depressive suicidal behavior of borderline personality disorders usually is impulsive, an equivalent or symptom of an acute affect storm, related to a frustrating, enraging, or traumatizing experience, or an effort to influence or control a close family relative or love/hate object. In contrast, chronic suicidal or parasuicidal behavior of narcissistic personality disorders evolves slowly and in a determined way over a period of weeks or months, is prepared and carried out on what impresses an observer as a cool and deliberate plot, quite often in the context of surface behavior that is seemingly friendly and relaxed. Patients with this extreme degree of severity of narcissistic pathology differ from the constellation referred to above, where suicidal behavior is part of severely disturbed, aggressive, and shifting moods with strong depressive features. Here, in contrast, suicidal and parasuicidal behavior, even severe self-mutilation, punctuate a generally stable, seemingly 'normal' behavior.

From a psychodynamic and transferential perspective, this behavior reflects a deep and consistent aggressive devaluation of the external world, a radical devaluation of significant others and the self, a 'negative narcissism,' in Green's terms (1993b), with a patient's profound sense of superiority derived from overcoming all feelings of fear of pain and death, all feelings of needs involving others, and a sense of omnipotence by controlling one's own death as a final, absolute power and freedom. This general transference disposition naturally takes many different forms. The therapist's capacity, within his countertransference reaction, to empathize with this terrible psychological reality of the patient, with that part of the patient identified with a self-murderous grandiose self, may become a crucial aspect of transference interpretation: the therapist is a natural enemy of that internal object, and a major question arises, whether the therapist has any ally in the patient's mind: Is there some way to contact the patient's oppressed, tenuous wish to survive? Highlighting this potential internal conflict in the patient's mind as it becomes activated in the transference, a true struggle between the death drive and the wish to live, is a major therapeutic task in these cases. For example, one of our patients chronically ingested rat poison in order to kill herself. In spite of careful searches carried out during her hospitalization at our service it was not possible to find the source for obtaining the poisonous substance; the patient denied her continuous ingestion of the poison, while the serum prothrombin time gradually increased over days. She already had a history of severe internal hemorrhages that required extensive diagnostic and therapeutic interventions, and, in the middle of all this, she maintained an apparently calm and almost cheerful attitude that belied the extreme gravity of her condition.

There are patients who deny their suicidal intentions and preparations, and convey a sense of triumph in their capacity to shock the unsuspecting therapist with their behavior; other patients may talk freely about their suicidality, while implying that it is beyond their control, and that, for the time being, they are not in touch with that part of them that wishes them to be dead. The implicit attack on family and on the therapist in such behaviors often remains unconscious, but, at times, is accompanied by a sense of sadistic satisfaction and triumph. At the same time, patients may unconsciously bring about situations in which their suicidal behavior would seem to reflect some neglect or insufficient alertness on the part of the therapist, and families may become enraged at what they perceive as the therapist's failure to contain or prevent the patient's behavior. Some patients triumphantly point out that their behavior is not only not under their own control, but not under the therapist's either, and is a reflection of the therapist's impotence and incompetence. We have all seen cases where family members unwittingly collude with the patient to 'blame the therapist,' and it's 'on to the next one.' The patient, a 'serial killer' of therapists, experiences an unconscious sense of triumph at having killed off another therapist.

The combination of severe self-destructive tendencies and antisocial tendencies may be expressed in provocative and litigious behavior, blaming the therapist for not having been attentive to the risk of a severe suicidal attempt by the patient, indirectly exerting an omnipotent control over the therapist by means of induction of paranoid fears and guilt feelings. Here, the aggressively infiltrated pathological grandiose self provides the patient with an illusionary power, not only over the therapist, but over life and death, over pain and suffering, and opens an escape into a 'liberating' death from a world that cannot be controlled.

A related group of patients, on the surface much less severely ill, but, at a deeper level, evincing a relentless determination to destroy all relationships, the efforts of the therapist, and, at the bottom, even their own sense of being alive is reflected in the syndrome of the 'dead mother' described by André Green (1993a). Under these conditions, there is a rejection of any significant relationship out of identification with an internalized imago of a dead mother, frequently derived from the early experiences with a severely depressed, unavailable mother. The patient unconsciously attempts to maintain the relationship with this absent, non-responsive mother, unconsciously enacting the fantasy that in his own emotional death and loss of self, he will be reunited with an idealized mother and protected from any further suffering. To give up one's own existence as an autonomous self, one's own need to depend on anybody else, to devalue completely all representations of significant others would, in the fantasy of these patients, provide definite restfulness, security, and equanimity. These are patients who may, on the surface, attentively listen to the therapist's interpretations, and then react saying, "All this is very interesting, but doesn't touch me at all." Their attitude of 'so what?' in response to interpretations is persistent and unmovable. By the unconscious devaluation of all relationships, what Green calls 'de-objectalization' (Green, 1993b), they obtain the same effect as patients whose repeated severe attempts at self-destruction reflect their dominant motivation in life.

A third group of patients, somewhat less severe in the manifestations of their self-destructiveness, unconsciously attempt to transform all relationships into hostile interactions, into severely sadomasochistic involvements. It is as if the only way in which they can trust that someone cares about them is to provoke an attack from that person. Within the frame of a psychotherapeutic treatment, this need to provoke attachment through hostility may lead to disastrous stalemates and breakdowns. This latter group, at least, still attempts to maintain some kind of relationship with the therapist, in contrast to the 'dead mother' syndrome, in which the destruction of all relationships seems to be the overriding goal. Here, the therapist's interpretive clarification of this consistent attempt to provoke the therapist to attack the patient may open the possibility of modifying this pattern. These cases, in fact, represent the most severe form of negative therapeutic reaction.

Regarding all the most severe cases described, we have found that technical requirements include, first of all, the establishment of realistic conditions under which the treatment can be carried out. The structure of the treatment, as determined through contract setting, must create conditions in which the therapist is protected physically, psychologically, socially, and legally. The involvement of the family in the process of setting up the conditions for the treatment is absolutely essential. During the treatment itself, it may be necessary to maintain ongoing family contacts in order to maintain and reinforce the treatment frame and realistic expectations. In a litigious culture such as the United States, it is particularly important that the therapist be solidly protected from any risk of being involved in threatening lawsuits related to a patient's attempted or completed suicide. If the safety of the therapist cannot be established and maintained, the treatment is not possible.

I believe that it is important that the therapist accept honestly, in his relation with the patient and the patient's family, and in the elaboration of his countertransference, the possibility that the patient may, in fact, commit suicide, and that the treatment may not be able to prevent it. The therapist may have to acknowledge openly, in diagnostic sessions with the patient and the family, that outpatient psychotherapeutic treatment carries a serious and unavoidable risk of suicide, given the patient's severe condition, and yet, still be preferable to the alternative of a long-term, indefinite duration of hospitalization. The fact that here suicide is not predictable by the presence of severe depression, nor preventable because of its deep characterological basis, may have to be made explicit verbally, and at times, in documentation that protects the therapist legally. At the same time, the patient's knowledge that he will not be able to blackmail the therapist with suicidal threats may reduce the secondary gain of this symptom, and limit the patient's sense of omnipotence. The therapist, I repeat, needs to be assured of his own physical, psychological, and legal safety in order to be able to dedicate himself to helping these extremely difficult cases.

In all these cases one must interpret openly and calmly that the patient, while willing to undergo a psychotherapeutic treatment that hopes to bring about improvement of his condition, is, nonetheless, under the sway of powerful and destructive internal forces. An acknowledgment of objective concern (the excluded third) for the patient's self-destructiveness conveys the possibility of discussing destructive impulses openly to assure the patient that one respects the severity and the power of this part of him. The need to protectively dissociate the destructive part of himself from the apparently 'cheerful' participation at other moments in the treatment can be clarified and resolved, and the patient's open acknowledgment of his dominant self-destructive motivation becomes the main issue to be explored in the sessions.

An important related technical requirement is the exploration of the patient's apparent absence of concern over this terrible control that the part of him wishing him to die has over whatever part of him wishes to remain alive, and the reasons for the devaluation and implicit hatred of that part of him that wishes him to be alive. Here the gradual discovery of the dangers of remaining alive, the terrible suffering related to the implied loss of control and superiority that is implied in identification with death, having to experience oneself alone and abandoned, having to face envy toward people not condemned to such self-induced destruction all may emerge, in the context of more specific aspects of the patient's infantile and childhood history. Sometimes, the patient unconsciously hopes for an omnipotent good object that will rescue him from that desperate state, and projects his own omnipotence to an illusional godlike rescuer. This fantasy, in turn, needs to be explored for its potentially self-destructive implications.

In the midst of all these struggles, the patient's attempt to destroy the therapist, spoil his reputation, expose his impotence, blacken his image with his family members needs to be explored as an expression of that part of the patient that, at the bottom, is attempting to destroy himself. The exposure of a sadistic, murderous internal object and the patient's fascination, submission to, and identification with that object, and the savage suppression of his infantile self and aspirations for love, are frightening aspects of the transference. They also may emerge as very disturbing aspects of countertransference developments. This, again, requires a combination of objective security of the therapist and 'space' for working through one's countertransference reactions. The therapist's survival in spite of a patient's consistent unconscious efforts to transform him into a sadistic and devalued object, the tolerance of the feelings of frustration, delusion, envy, triumph, and loneliness dominant in the inter-subjective field are the heavy price for carrying out these treatments, as well as the material on the basis of which understanding may be gained, and both success and failure evolve.

In short, I have presented an approach that reflects the application of psychoanalytic theory of pathology and technique to a broad spectrum of patients, and expands, in my view, the realm of classical psychoanalysis with its extension by a specific type of psychoanalytic psychotherapy.

Chapter Seven

Cautionary Tales

A Private Practitioner's Experience Treating Severe Narcissistic Pathology

Melvin Singer

We live in the Age of Narcissism (Cooper, 1986) that has been digitally enhanced so that even the video games that occupy the minds of our youth are filled with grandiose fantasies of superheroes and super-antiheroes. Moreover, they are now played more often than ever before solipsistically. There are even residential treatment facilities available for those youths who become pathologically addicted. In discussing technical strategies for patients who fall within this continuum of pathological narcissism, we, as sole practitioners, can only describe these strategies as developed not systematically, but by the seat of our pants. Sometimes successful, but more often unsuccessful, as they represent the most challenging of patients who fall at the farthest end of the difficulty continuum. Besides being severely disturbed, they are suicidal, antisocial, and so isolated as to be unable to form the all-too-necessary object-related transference.

These severe, pathologic, narcissistic patients are not just the phallic narcissistic run-of-the-mill male patients or the male and female cases with major narcissistic aspects to their personalities who can form, to varying degrees, object-related transferences and are eminently treatable: these cases present seemingly insurmountable problems. With his team, Kernberg, to his credit, has tackled and developed treatment strategies under the rubric 'Transference-Focused Psychotherapy' (Clarkin, Yeomans, and Kernberg, 2006), which is a systematic, clinical/theoretical approach organized around the immediate direct confrontation and interpretation of dyadic narcissistic transferences. He utilizes his theory of internal object relations with expansion of the classic psychoanalytic technique. This is in contrast to the alternative clinical directions taken by other systems, such as Self Psychology (Kohut and Wolf, 1978).

NARCISSISTIC TRANSFERENCES

These transferences, once decoded, turn out, surprisingly, to consist of dyads that are two sides of the same coin, that is, the pathologic narcissistic self-system—the grandiose self and the devalued, worthless, self. The latter is usually projected onto the therapist or by role reversal where the sides switch. These manifest transference positions are revealed to be the first line of defense against the emergence, in a successful devolution, of the more typical internalized primitive part self and part object representations, as seen in borderline pathology (Kernberg, 1967). Therapeutic focal points emerge in this regression that trend towards paranoid fantasies, severe envy, spoiling of the analyst's work so as not to feel this envy, rageful resentment issues around dependency, self-destructiveness as an escape route, and, in general, a negative therapeutic reaction. All this to avoid facing the excruciating pain of living with their now exposed, inner, lonely, empty, desolate, hate-filled lives. This direct confrontative approach reminds me of Clint Eastwood's portrayal of *Dirty Harry* (1971), who fearlessly walked into the headwinds of danger. Tolerating these therapeutically destructive transference trends requires not patience, courage, and self-protective measures, but, in my experience as a prerequisite for the above, the therapist's capacity for inner sustenance, and a sufficient reservoir of self-esteem to maintain a therapeutically neutral stance to avoid damaging countertransference enactments.

Treating these patients alone in private practice has not allowed me to be as forthright as Kernberg. Sometimes temporarily encapsulating the grandiose self and working on the more neurotic ego-dystonic and dysfunctional aspects of their personality came first, to build up a more realistic, legitimate self-esteem. Only then could I tackle the ego-syntonic grandiose self which had to be made not only ego-dystonic, but seen as a defensive posture against their massive, split-off, low self-esteem.

SOME TECHNICAL GUIDELINES

I am in general agreement with Kernberg's (1967, 1984; Clarkin et al, 2006) recommendations for treatment for these patients. Some recommendations I found especially useful and worthy of being underscored:

- Interpret the patient's ignoring of your comments as an avoidance of dependency and envious feelings.

- Address extra transference issues first in the more fragile thin-skinned narcissists as a bridge towards confronting the transference directly.
- Interpret the transference, in the projection form, in the thin-skinned narcissist by relating it to its roots in the patient's past history, not directly into the transference.
- Interpret the use of arrogance and distain toward the therapist as based on envy and hatred and as an expression of sadistic pleasure, plus an avoidance of positive feelings of attachment.
- Make contact in the non-depressive suicidal patient with that part of his personality that wishes to be alive, in spite of the grandiose, split-off side that wishes to die, to be freed of the need for others, to be omnipotent and triumph over the fear of death.
- Maintain contact with the patient's family as a protective device for the therapist, as well as a therapeutic necessity. But, in my experience, beware of making critical comments towards the family; later on, they could have negative consequences if the patient harms himself or even commits suicide. The family may only be able to resolve their guilt by making recriminating projections onto the therapist.
- That being said, to the non-suicidal side of the patient, always interpret the danger of suicide as a dissociated aspect of his personality and his absence of concern, a denial of it. And to the suicidal aspect of his personality, the hatred of that part that wants to live, and his wish to escape from the pain of aloneness, envy, and loss of superiority. Sometimes there is also the fantasy of uniting with a godlike savior in death.
- Confronting omnipotent control of the analyst as an attempt to 'freeze' the treatment, both to protect the grandiose self and to secure the binary connection because of the patient's intolerance of triangulation. The latter implies that any independent thought would mean the entrance of a third object, which signifies a loss of the dyadic symbiosis and the introduction of an archaic oedipal complex.

Time does not allow me to review Dr. Kernberg's well-known developmental schema organized with internal object relations as a basic framework in conjunction with classic conflict theory and ego psychology. This evolves into self- and object-constancy, the tripartite model, and the classic structural theory. Points of fixation occur along the developmental pathway, one of which presents as split-off unmetabolized units of good and bad self and object, leading to borderline pathology, while a second presents as a grandiose self/devalued self, leading to narcissistic disorders. His basic internalized object relations theory in association with classic conflict theory has allowed him to address the problems of preoedipal pathology with their ego defects, primitive defenses, and drives.

This has proven to have great explanatory power for understanding borderline and narcissistic disorders, as well as elucidating explorations into the psychology of love and hate, the development of affect theory and even delve into the sociocultural realm of our administrative and organizational systems. In the spirit of good science, he has maintained his basic theoretical perspective, which is still evolving and expanding, as evidenced today. He has not muddied his theoretical or clinical waters with deficiency state theory, which is not only good science, but in which he obviously firmly believes. We are truly indebted to him for his major contributions to our field (Kernberg, 1974a, 1974b, 1975, 1976, 1984, 1991, 2000).

INSIGHTS FROM MY OWN CLINICAL EXPERIENCE

In perusing my archival notes from over forty years, certain experiences came to mind as caveats reflecting cautionary tales, while others express agreement, and hopefully others being addendums to the spectrum of cases falling within the realm of pathological narcissism.

- Instead of experiencing boredom from the lack of recognition of one's importance, or even feeling 'not there' in the patients' eyes, or before your very eyes, having your knowledge plundered as if it were the patient's own, another scenario has presented itself. A severely depressed narcissistic female patient was about to be discharged from the hospital. She was bright, sophisticated, charming, and engaging, seemingly attached to her therapist, who had developed a reciprocal attachment. But, on discharge, rather than experiencing any evidence of loss, gratitude, or even rejection, she became cold and indifferent, as if he meant nothing to her or did nothing for her. He didn't even seem to exist in her mind. An emotional cut-off switch was thrown, as all libido was suddenly withdrawn, a force foreclosure rupturing the dyadic envelope. The therapist was left shocked but the wiser for it. Rather than the patient, the therapist was left feeling the loss, rage, and rejection that she couldn't tolerate. A projective identification had taken place. She was saying in nonverbal action language: "You are of no use to me anymore, so you don't exist." The cold veil that came over her was absolutely chilling.
- After a traumatizing rejection, a highly functioning, brilliant woman unleashed a six-month period of arrogance and contempt towards her analyst, as her defensively activated, grandiose self unrelentingly attacked her now-worthless, devalued analyst. No aspect of her analyst was left untarnished as she bashed his character, suits, ties, furniture, paintings, etc. During this period, her self-esteem seemed too fragile to directly confront this hyperbolic transference in this thin-skinned, narcissistic patient. So,

analytic work addressed conflicted areas of her personality that interfered with her successfully functioning and concurrently reinforced her grandiose self. Then, the analysand triumphantly announced that she had purchased the last tickets to Birgit Nilsson's final performance of "Isolde" at the Met. She had the tickets and I couldn't get any. Then, she off-handedly turned the knife, mentioning that Birgit Nilsson was this century's greatest soprano except for a soprano known for singing "Salome" early in the century. Without thinking, I heard myself saying, "You mean Ljuba Welitsch?" (I only knew that bit of trivia from my wife.) A stony cold silence gripped the office. The grandiose self and devalued other were now gone—sent diving underground. Without addressing this event, we continued our work on her dysfunctional areas that successfully strengthened her ego's adaptive capacity and self-esteem. She terminated when her grandiose self was sufficiently stabilized, ostensibly as well to move with her boyfriend to a distant location. Of course, the grandiose self was never fully resolved; whether it could have been, had I addressed it and not crushed it, I do not know. Or was what happened spontaneously the unavoidable error, necessary as a form of corrective experience? Whatever, it certainly re-established my narcissistic equilibrium. I am in agreement with Dr. Kernberg: many cases terminate when their narcissism has been sufficiently bolstered.

- As a fascinating subset, I have seen a number of sons of famous fathers, who exhibit a grandiose self without infiltration of pathologic aggression and yet were unable to tame their excessive demands for success. I came to the conclusion that the utter impossibility of ever becoming victorious in competing with their rival fathers interfered with any potential resolution and reconciliation. The acceptance of a more realistic assessment was too great a defeat, leaving too great a gap between a father's and son's accomplishments, creating at times disastrous consequences.
- The cases of suicidality in a non-depressive character structure are quite mystifying when first seen. The activation of this dissociated self-destructive state, associated with denial and impulsivity, disappeared as rapidly as it appeared. The bland indifference occupying the unconcerned non-suicidal side of the split can be maddingly frustrating. Only the HMO's refusal to continue reimbursing her hospitalization, since there was no evidence of depression, was more frustrating. On a more positive note, these cases were more reachable and treatable, since they presented a more typical borderline structure that developed an intense, dependent transference, thus locking in the treatment.
- Never underestimate the enormity of revenge, betrayal, and triumph over the external representatives of persecutory internal objects with whom they are totally dependent and upon which the only escape from their victimization is death. One hospitalized suicidal woman's family refused

to continue her treatment, requiring her to be sent to a state institution. A week before the mandatory discharge, she asked permission to attend her favorite niece's wedding for just two hours on a Saturday morning. She pleaded, "I wouldn't do anything to destroy my favorite niece's wedding," appealing to my acknowledgment of her basic human decency. How could I refuse? Two weeks later, she was finally found, discovered by the stench of her decayed body, hidden under the oil tank in the basement of her family home. The revenge was on a grand scale, lasting for generations. This resoundingly echoed the grandiose control, revenge, and triumph over her family, over her fear of death, and over the unbearable pain of living with such rage, loneliness, envy, and self-loathing. The family actually offered me condolences.

CONCLUDING THOUGHTS

Cases of the sort mentioned above lead us to consider the fascinating concept of the 'dead mother' by Andre Green (1980). Of course, he meant the phenomenological death as experienced by a child whose mother is depressed or emotionally absent or not there. The patient is in a mirror-identification with the 'deadness' to be one with her, to feel dead himself, and is drawn to the inner world of no object. He is empty in his body-self, and feels dead or inhuman in his psychic-self. The inner representation of his mother is a picture frame without its picture, likened to the stolen Rembrandt whose empty frame remains on the wall in the Isabella Stewart Gardner Museum in Boston. These patients fear looking into the mirror and seeing nothing. Now, Kernberg and Green may be describing the same phenomenon, but I don't think they arrived there from the same conceptual starting point or utilize the same treatment strategies. Green (1975), from my understanding, bases his theory on a loss of representation taken from Freud's (1911–1913) theory of primary expression, a decathexis of not only libido from the object, but its internal representation as well. Nothing is left except the experience of a 'hole,' as in Schreber's delusion of 'the end of the world.' This is opposite to secondary expression, which is a countercathexis to the object which is still extant, but buried from conscious and pre-conscious awareness. Now of course the self-representation is included in the withdrawal in decathexis and countercathexis. According to Freud, rage reactions against the internal objects are restitutive phenomena to fill the void. They are secondary, not primary. Of course, this was before the dual instinct theory and aggression was only seen as reactive. For Green (1997, 2002), since the longing for primary absolute narcissism in union with the good mother in heavenly bliss was unattainable, it was replaced by its opposite negative narcissism, a solution of despair, of being drawn to nothingness. Is this a defect from deficiency? Green (1993a) seems to prefer to rely on a Winnicottian transitional space (Winnicott, 1953) to provide vitality, aliveness, and interest for the analysand.

My experience takes me in both directions. In agreement with what I assume is Kernberg's conflict theory, the experience of emptiness in the body-self can be defensive, behind which rage and violence are concealed, as well as introjects or hidden inner objects secretly and protectively buried (Singer, 1977a, 1977b). These patients are saying, in body language, "I want to appear weak and empty but I'm really not empty; I'm full of hate, rage, and/or buried treasure." Fascinatingly, the etymology of 'emptiness' is Germanic, meaning 'fury' (Singer, 1988). Furthermore, the experience of deadness or non-humanness in the mental self is defensively saying, "If I am a person who can't even experience the quality of my own existence, then I am too weak and insignificant to be responsible for such heinous sexual and aggressive crimes as you might accuse me of."

On the opposite side, the analysis of a pathologic narcissist with multiple sadomasochistic and exhibitionistic perversions revealed, once the many layers were worked through, that he was left with a profound sense of emptiness, loneliness, and not feeling alive. Were these perversions restitutive phenomena to fill the void? Of course, behind the emptiness could be more rage and behind the rage more emptiness, etc. My point here is that it takes many years of treatment, double digits for sure, to finally get to the bottom of the trough and you are still not sure.

Finally, Dr. Kernberg's treatment of the antisocial narcissist is the most ambitious of undertakings. I can add nothing of value since I've treated only a very few and unsuccessfully. I do, however, offer the Baseball Rule of three. For borderlines, I tell them three strikes and they're out if there are aggressive enactments outside the established limit setting. For the sociopath, they are presented a rule of three strikes and we're out. Strike one, there is no payment. Strike two, they say the check is in the mail. Strike three, you guessed it, the check bounced—they're gone and you're out.

Chapter Eight

Three Literary Characters in Search of Revenge

Eve Holwell

The founder of psychoanalysis, Sigmund Freud, concluded his 1933 lecture on femininity by saying to his audience that "if you want to know more, enquire from your own experiences, or turn to the poets" (p. 135). At other occasions (Freud, 1916, 1920a, 1920b), he cited great writers and poets and acknowledged that the insight he gained about a certain matter had been readily available to them. Freud's respect for the informative potential of literature is my inspiration to undertake this brief essay on a particular aspect of human experience, namely, the phenomena of revenge and vindictiveness.[1] In it, I will attempt to highlight the complexity of retaliation with the help of three prominent sources from classical literature, namely Euripides's (431 BCE) *Medea*, Emily Brontë's (1847) *Wuthering Heights*, and Herman Melville's (1851) *Moby Dick*. My choice of these particular works is a bit arbitrary and I am aware that many other literary texts could be chosen to shed light on the phenomena involved. Prominent among them are William Shakespeare's (1602) *Hamlet*, Alexandre Dumas's (1844) *The Count of Monte Cristo*, Honoré de Balzac's (1846) *La Cousine Bette,* and in a more light-hearted vein, F. Scott Fitzgerald's (1920) "Bernice Bobs Her Hair." On the popular and contemporary scene, Stieg Larsson's (2004) *The Girl with the Dragon Tattoo* also revolves around the scenario of narcissistic injury and revenge. Clearly, one has to pick and choose even at the risk of being somewhat idiosyncratic and arbitrary.

THREE LITERARY TEXTS

Euripides's *Medea*

Euripides's *Medea*, written in 431 BCE, is a play about a horrific and violent act of revenge. Medea, left for another woman by her husband, Jason, murders both Jason's new wife and her own children fathered by Jason. The acts are not carried out in a fit of passion. They are premeditated and born from Medea's pain and anger at Jason's betrayal. The murders achieve a couple of purposes—they punish Jason and reclaim power for Medea. They punish Jason through destroying his role as a husband and father, thus forcing him to experience a parallel loss to the one Medea experienced as a wife and mother when he left her for another woman. Retaliation provides Medea with a sense of justice over the wrongs done to her. Vengeance also gives her an outlet for her pain and anger as well as power over a situation that has hurt her.

From the opening of the play, Medea's pain at Jason's betrayal is linked to her feelings of anger and her desire for revenge. Medea's nurse first describes the intensity of Medea's sorrow, saying she "lies there eating nothing, surrendering her body to her sorrows, pining away in tears unceasingly since she saw that her husband had wronged her" (p. 4). Her nurse goes on to point out that "this her grief has a terrible momentum" (p. 6) and that "it will be by no trivial action/that my mistress will lay her anger to rest" (p. 6). This combination of hurt and anger fuels Medea's desire for revenge. Once Medea appears on stage, she immediately vows that "may I one day see him and his bride/pounded to nothing, house and all, /since they have dared to wrong me unprovoked" (p. 5). Here Medea expresses, along with her fantasy for revenge, a sense of outrage that she did nothing to incur such an injury. She believes that Jason shouldn't have remarried considering the vows he took to be her husband and the fact that she has been a good wife. When she confronts Jason, she points out his transgressions. She says, "I am at a loss to understand whether you think that the gods you swore by no longer rule or that men now live by new standards of what is right" (p. 14). Along with her loss of him as a husband, she has lost faith in a just world since Jason has simply gone back on his vows.

Since Jason has transgressed without ramification, Medea takes it upon herself to bring justice to the situation through revenge. She carries out the murders as acts of vengeance, explaining to Jason, "You were never going to shame our bed and lead a pleasant life and laugh at me—nor was the princess or Creon, the man who made this marriage for you—he was not going to throw me out of this land and get away with it. So now call me a lioness even, if you want, and Scylla who took her abode on the Etruscan rock. I have done what I had to—I have stung your heart" (p. 37).

Medea believes that Jason could leave her without ramifications in part because of the relatively weak position of women in society. This fact heightens Medea's outrage at Jason as well as her desire to seek vengeance. She laments that married women have "to take a master for our body" (p. 5) and be confined to the house while men can do things in the outside world. Medea is clear that she does not want to be viewed as only inhabiting the traditional roles for women. She says, "Let no one think of me as weak and submissive, a cipher—but as a woman of a very different kind, dangerous to my enemies and good to my friends. Such people's lives win the greatest renown" (p. 23). She also often remarks that she has a desire "not to bring laughter to yourself" (p. 12). Her fear of being slighted and overlooked comes from her sense of inferiority as to her place in society. She avoids this fate by committing murders and engineering an escape to Athens.

Medea's anger at Jason's betrayal and desire for revenge is intensified by the fact that she betrayed her father and country for Jason. Jason first came to Colchis, where Medea was a daughter of the king, seeking to win the golden fleece. Falling in love with Jason, Medea helps him steal the fleece. She also kills her brother in order to make their escape easier. That Medea has betrayed her father and homeland for Jason only makes his betrayal harder to bear. When Medea confronts Jason, she reminds him of the sacrifices she has made. She says to him, "Where can I turn now? To my father's house? But I betrayed it, and my fatherland too, when I followed you here. Or to the wretched daughter of Pelias? How warmly they would welcome me in their house—I killed their father!" (p. 14). Medea doesn't regret doing these actions. Rather, she regrets doing them for a man who hasn't proved worth it. She says bitterly to Jason, "What a wonderful husband, what a trustworthy one, I, wretched woman, have in you" (p. 14). She wonders, too: "For well I know that the man who was my everything has proved the vilest of all—my husband" (p. 14). She feels indeed that it is worse to be deceived by those for whom one has made the highest sacrifices.

While Medea has relatively little trouble killing Glauce, Jason's new wife, she wavers before killing her own children. She is not insane; she knows killing her children is wrong and yet she justifies the action both as an act of revenge and as an outlet for her own anger. Citing her own anger, she says, "I am overwhelmed by the evils which surround me. And I know what evil deeds I am about to do, but my fury against Jason is stronger than my counsels of softness, and it is fury that leads to the greatest evils for mankind" (p. 29). Here Medea explains her evil actions by citing the evil world in which she lives. It is a tenuous moral claim but the emotional truth of the statement must be considered. And yet another side to the emotional repercussions of killing her children is that Medea herself will be caused pain. She will lose her children. At one point, she says, "I could never do the deed. Goodbye to my former plans. I shall take my children from the land. Why should I, as I seek to pain their father through their sufferings, win twice as much agony for myself? I will not do it" (p. 29). In the end, however, she steadies herself to committing the task because it is the best way to avenge Jason's wrongs. She reminds herself that she will not "make myself ridiculous by letting my enemies go unpunished. I must face the deed. Shame on my cowardice in even letting my mind dally with these weak thoughts" (p. 29). Medea convinces herself that she must kill her children or else Jason's actions will not be properly avenged.

In the final scene of the play, Jason confronts Medea after she has murdered his wife and their children. Medea gets to see Jason experience the pain and anguish that she feels he had created for her. Though Jason accuses her of being cruel and heartless, Medea feels blameless. Jason has destroyed her in the only realm she had power as a woman—namely, as a wife and a mother. She then denies these roles existence through killing Glauce and their children together, thereby regaining a measure of power. She shows Jason that, in committing those murders, she has written the final chapter to their story together. She is no longer the victim but the victimizer. This is a powerful reason for revenge and she leaves unscathed in having carried it out.

Emily Bronte's *Wuthering Heights*

Brontë's (1847) *Wuthering Heights* is a brooding, passionate tale set in the moors of England. Orphaned and abandoned, Heathcliff is brought by Mr. Earnshaw back to Wuthering Heights. There, Heathcliff meets Mr. Earnshaw's daughter, Catherine, and the two fall in love. However, class and the actions of others separate them as they grow up. When Catherine intends to marry Edgar Linton, the owner of Thrushcross Grange, Heathcliff disappears. He returns years later, after acquiring a fortune, and seeks revenge on the people who separated him from Catherine—namely Edgar and Hindley, Catherine's brother. He retaliates through destroying their happiness and acquiring Wuthering Heights and Thrushcross Grange. When he gains ownership of both properties, he aims to destroy them as a way to demonstrate his power over the places that treated him as an outsider and denied him Catherine. However, this comes about years after Heathcliff's return as well as many years after Catherine herself has died. A sudden and strange turn of events finally causes Heathcliff's obsession with revenge to lessen and the book ends with a hopeful move toward redemption and forgiveness.

On a business trip to Liverpool, Mr. Earnshaw finds Heathcliff on the street, penniless and alone, from no one knows where, and, deciding he cannot leave the child as such, brings him home to Wuthering Heights. However, when Heathcliff is brought back to Wuthering Heights, he is not welcomed. Mrs. Earnshaw tells her husband not to let "that gypsy brat into the house" (p. 19) and Hindley immediately views him "as a usurper of his parents' affections and his privileges" (p. 27). The Lintons don't think highly of Heathcliff either. One time, when Catherine and Heathcliff are walking the moors, they come to Thrushcross Grange. Catherine hurts herself and the Lintons take her in. Mrs. Linton, Edgar's mother, however, is shocked that Catherine might be found "scouraging the country with a gipsy!" (p. 36) and won't let Heathcliff into the house, calling him "a wicked boy, at all events . . . and quite unfit for a decent house!" (p. 36). Hindley, Catherine's brother, compounds Heathcliff's early feelings of rejection by banning him from being a member of the house after Mr. Earnshaw dies. Indeed, still sore at his father for defending Heathcliff, Hindley decided to "deprive him [Heathcliff] of the instructions of the curate, and insisted that he should do hard labor out of doors instead, compelling him to do so, as hard as any other lad on the farm" (p. 33). This act separates Heathcliff from Catherine by putting a clear class distinction between them. Denying Heathcliff education also lowers his sense of himself and he soon feels embarrassed in front of Catherine's growing knowledge and sense of the world.

Hindley adds to Heathcliff's growing insecurity through repeatedly shaming him in front of Catherine. Catherine stays a while recovering at the Lintons and when she finally returns, Hindley tells Heathcliff to "come and wish Miss Catherine welcome, like the other servants" (p. 40). Naturally Catherine is excited to see Heathcliff and yet she is also moved by his obvious differences from the refined Lintons. She makes a comment to this effect, harmlessly in her own mind, but it alienates the growing sense of shame within Heathcliff. One Christmas, when the Lintons are coming to Wuthering Heights, Heathcliff cleans himself up to impress Catherine in front of Edgar. Hindley makes fun of Heathcliff's attempt, which Heathcliff quickly retaliates at by lashing out at Edgar. It is after this event that Heathcliff first mentions his desire to seek revenge on Hindley. Heathcliff tells Nelly, the housekeeper at Wuthering Heights, that "I'm trying to settle how I shall pay Hindley back" (p. 44). When Nelly says God should be the one to take care of it, Heathcliff answers, "No, God won't have the satisfaction that I shall. . . . I only wish I knew the best way! Let me alone, and I'll plan it out; while I'm thinking of that, I don't feel pain" (p. 44). Heathcliff evokes the traditional idea of 'an eye for an eye' when he says he wonders how he will justly pay Hindley back. He also reveals another purpose for committing revenge: to lesson his own pain.

The magnitude of Heathcliff's hate for Hindley and his unquenchable desire for revenge in part stem from the fact that Hindley's banishment builds on previous abandonments in Heathcliff's life. As an orphan, Heathcliff has experienced desertion and rejection already, so when Hindley exiles him to be a servant it opens a previous wound. Furthermore, the very act exacerbates Heathcliff's feelings of being inadequate and different from the inhabitants at Wuthering Heights and Thrushcross Grange. There is a poignant scene where Nelly tries to persuade Heathcliff not to pull away from Catherine once she has returned from her recuperation at the Lintons. Heathcliff is hesitant; he tells her, "But Nelly, if I knocked him [Edgar] down twenty times, that wouldn't make him less handsome, or me more so. I wish I had light hair and a fair skin, and was dressed, and behaved as well, and had a chance of being as rich as he will be!" (p. 41). The feelings expressed here show that Heathcliff feels inferior to Linton because his appearance is different and because he is not rich. Indeed, Heathcliff has completely stopped believing that Catherine has feelings for him even though she is still in love with him. When Heathcliff overhears Catherine telling Nelly that she would be lowering herself if she married him, he simply leaves town. He doesn't stay to hear the rest of the conversation where Catherine confesses her eternal love for Heathcliff. Instead, he anticipates her rejection and, in order to avoid it, leaves town.

During Heathcliff's absence, he acquires a fortune and then returns to claim Wuthering Heights from Hindley. He finds that Hindley, whose wife died during childbirth, has become an alcoholic who gambles recklessly and neglects his son, Hareton. Heathcliff is generally "delighted to witness Hindley degrading himself past redemption" (p. 47) and exploits the situation. He lends Hindley money to gamble to such an extent that Heathcliff eventually owns Wuthering Heights. Ownership is Heathcliff's ultimate design and gives him power over a place that had initially displaced him. He wasn't believed to be a son and treated as an outsider, and so he attempts to heal that wound through one day owning the very place that didn't deem him good enough.

Heathcliff seeks further revenge on Hindley through debasing Hareton in the same manner that Hindley did to him. While Hindley is still alive, Heathcliff stops Hareton's education. Hareton tells Nelly that his education has been stopped—that "the curate should have his—teeth dashed down his—throat if he stepped over the threshold—Heathcliff promised that!" (p. 81). Hareton is too young to understand what Heathcliff has done, or hold any resentment against Heathcliff for doing it. Upon Hindley's death, Heathcliff keeps Hareton with the express purpose of raising him as a servant. After Catherine's marriage to Edgar, Nelly accompanies Catherine to Thrushcross Grange. Seeing that Hareton is Catherine's nephew, Nelly tries to take Hareton from Wuthering Heights to come and live at Thrushcross Grange. However, Heathcliff won't let her. On the day of Hindley's funeral, Heathcliff says to young Hareton, "Now, my bonny lad, you are mine! And we'll see if one tree won't grow as crooked as another, with the same wind to twist it" (p. 138). The first crooked tree is Heathcliff; he hopes to make Hareton into the second. The choice of metaphor is important; it signals that Heathcliff knows himself perverted and destroyed, and that he seeks, for revenge, to pervert and destroy the next generation.

Heathcliff's largest disappointment is naturally the rejection by Catherine herself. The sting of this builds on his initial desertion by his parents. Heathcliff won't hurt Catherine because he loves her, and yet he makes it clear to her when he returns that he is angry. He tells her, "I want you to be aware that I know you have treated me infernally—infernally! Do you hear? And if you flatter yourself that I don't perceive it, you are a fool—and if you think I can be consoled by sweet words you are an idiot—and if you fancy I'll suffer unrevenged, I'll convince you of the contrary, in a very little while!" (p. 82). While Heathcliff feels Catherine has treated him unjustly, in truth Heathcliff never tried to marry Catherine. He never even fully pursued her but rather abandoned her before she could make a choice. Nonetheless, Catherine did marry Edgar, and the pain this causes Heathcliff makes him lash out on the Linton family.

Heathcliff finds a way to retaliate against Edgar through marrying Edgar's sister, Isabella Linton. After Heathcliff returns, he visits Catherine at Thrushcross Grange. During his visits, Isabella Linton falls in love with him even though Catherine and Edgar warn her that Heathcliff loves Catherine. Heathcliff quickly takes advantage of the situation and feigning love, he marries Isabella. Once they are married, however, his true nature is revealed. As Isabella tells Nelly, Heathcliff "wishes to provoke Edgar to desperation—he says he has married me on purpose to obtain power over him; and he shan't obtain it—I'll die first!" (p. 112). Heathcliff treats Isabella horribly. When Isabella becomes pregnant with Heathcliff's child, she flees to have the baby far from Heathcliff's abuse. She stops at Thrushcross Grange to see Nelly before her departure. There Nelly urges her to stay and yet Isabella knows she cannot. Heathcliff would never allow her to be happy and peaceful; he would come and bring her back to Wuthering Heights, where he could make her miserable.

Heathcliff accomplishes his final goal act of retaliation and self-justification through acquiring Thrushcross Grange. He does this through a series of manipulative and outright wrong actions. He first forces Catherine and Edgar's daughter, named Catherine as well, to marry Linton, his son with Isabella. Catherine is long gone by this time; she died in childbirth. Isabella too has died and though Heathcliff hates their son, he takes Linton back in order to get Linton to marry the young Catherine. Linton is sickly and weak and Heathcliff lures Catherine under exaggerations of the boy's illness to Wuthering Heights. There, Heathcliff locks Catherine in the house and forces her to marry Linton. Catherine does marry Linton—willingly, because she takes pity on her sickly cousin—and when her father, Edgar, dies shortly thereafter, Linton becomes the owner of Thrushcross Grange. Heathcliff himself soon after becomes the owner of Thrushcross Grange when Linton dies soon after. Heathcliff has forced Linton to leave the manor to him instead of young Catherine. Apart from gaining ownership of Thrushcross Grange, there is an odd parallel in Heathcliff forcing young Catherine to marry his son. He is almost remedying the fact of his own rejection by forcing a marriage between his son and Catherine's daughter. And yet he is also affirming his lack of worth because he knows Catherine doesn't love Linton, who naturally serves as sort of an extension of Heathcliff himself.

In the end, Heathcliff finds himself unable to commit the final act of revenge for which he has worked for so long: leveling the two manors. He admits this much to Nelly, telling her, "It is a poor conclusion, is it not . . . an absurd termination to my violent exertions?" (p. 237). He relents because he has been reminded of his first love with Catherine in a way he couldn't have anticipated and initially tries to stop. Young Hareton, raised as ignorant as Heathcliff, and Catherine Linton, raised as a wealthy landowner's daughter at Thrushcross Grange, begin to fall in love. They both find themselves under the same roof at Wuthering Heights after Catherine has been forced to marry Linton and then Linton dies, having left everything to his father, and Catherine penniless and alone. Catherine slowly begins to befriend Hareton. Initially Heathcliff is enraged by this friendship; the sight of them together, falling in love, causes him agony and goes against his plans to ensure unhappiness to this next generation of his enemies. And yet ultimately, the young love awakens him to his own memories of love and softens him. Referring to young Catherine and Hareton, Heathcliff tells Nelly, "Those two who have left the room are the only objects which retain a distinct material appearance to me; and, that appearance causes me pain, amounting to agony" (p. 237). He goes on to say, "If I try to describe the thousand forms of past associations, and ideas he awakens, or embodies . . . five minutes ago, Hareton seemed a personification of my youth, not a human being—I felt to him in such a variety of ways, that it would have been impossible to have accosted him rationally" (p. 238).

Soon enough Heathcliff leaves Hareton and Catherine alone and he allows himself to live fully in his memories of Catherine. He stops eating and sleeping and yearns towards death, where he believes he will be again with Catherine. He dies shortly thereafter, and when he does, Catherine Linton and Hareton become engaged to be married. It is a poignant end to a tortuous love story. Indeed, there is nearly redemption and there is certainly forgiveness—carried out by Catherine and Hareton—for the original sins and the cruel revenges of their parents.

Herman Melville's *Moby Dick*

Melville's *Moby Dick*, written in 1851, is a decidedly grim tale about obsession and revenge. Captain Ahab, who lost his leg to Moby Dick, is obsessed with hunting down and killing the White Whale. Ishmael, along with the rest of the crew, learns of Captain Ahab's intent to hunt Moby Dick only after the *Pequod* sets sail. Early in the voyage, Ahab calls the crew together to tell them of his plans. When Ahab asks the crew to pursue the whale, it is as if he is rallying soldiers for battle. And, like soldiers responding to war cries, they wholeheartedly agree. It is surely insane to pursue one whale in a very wide ocean and yet there is something intense and compelling about Ahab's revenge. Unlike the kinds of revenge that take place in *Medea* or *Wuthering Heights*, the acts of retaliation in *Moby Dick* are against something non-human that has come to represent man's relative weakness in the face of nature. Ahab seeks to destroy the White Whale and this weakness. Yet, the story ends with Moby Dick destroying the *Pequod* and drowning every member of the crew save for Ishmael. Thus, unlike the other works explored, *Moby Dick* is also a story failure, with implications about the purpose and efficacy of revenge itself.

The *Pequod* takes to sea without anyone aboard knowing its true mission besides Ahab. The two other captions of the *Pequod*, Captains Bildad and Peleg, assume that Ahab has completely recovered from the loss of his leg. They outfit the *Pequod* while Ahab has a new leg made. It isn't until a couple of days offshore, clear from land, that Ahab emerges from his cabin. When he does, his whole being trembles with intensity. Ishmael notes an "infinity of firmest fortitude, a determinate, unsurrenderable willfulness, in the fixed and fearless, forward dedication of his [Ahab's] glance" (p. 109). There is awe in Ishmael's description. Ishmael is equally moved by the sense of tragedy and grief within Ahab. He describes Ahab standing "with a crucifixion in his face; in all the nameless regal overbearing dignity of some mighty woe" (p. 109). Ishmael no doubt feels there is something of a tragic hero in Ahab and before such greatness, he is both unable and unwilling to protest. Even the one dissenter—Starbuck, the first mate—cannot resist the pull of Ahab's need. Starbuck knows that Ahab's obsession with hunting down Moby Dick isn't sane and yet he finds himself unable to protest the old captain's desires.

Ahab's ability to persuade the crew to hunt Moby Dick illustrates his purpose and power in his pursuit of the White Whale. Both serve as antidotes to the humiliation Ahab experiences from the loss of his leg. By all accounts, before he lost his leg, Ahab was a very skilled and seasoned sea captain. Indeed, his reputation was such that even after he lost a leg, he gained a ship to take out quite easily. Nonetheless, there were capabilities that he lost. Ahab required a special hole cut in the deck in which to put his prosthetic leg, which was made of whale bone, so as to steady himself against the rolling sea. He also had a carpenter and a blacksmith on the *Pequod* in case he had to make repairs to his whale-bone leg, which could get banged up and displaced from activity. These alterations to his independence must have been significant to a man whose identity was tied up in captaining a whaling ship. Indeed, captains of whaling ships were not a gentle sort; casualties were common and it was a difficult two years spent away from port.

The tremendous wound Ahab sustains when he has loses his leg leads to his obsessive search for revenge. As Ishmael describes, Ahab is "gnawed within and scorched without, with the unfixed, unrelenting fangs of some incurable idea" (p. 158). Ahab's desire for revenge is as permanent as the reality of his lost leg. Indeed, he seems to better bear the loss of part of his physical self by preserving the integrity and power of his identity, which slowly begins to revolve around avenging his loss. In one scene, Ahab defends chasing down Moby Dick by saying that "ye seen an old man cut down to a stump; leaning on a shivered lance; propped up on a lonely foot. Tis Ahab—his body's part; but Ahab's soul's a centipede, that moves upon a hundred legs" (p. 418). The metaphor here is powerful. Ahab at once admits he is cut down and belittled by his loss and yet simultaneously asserts that his soul, far from being disfigured, outstrips his body in legs and potency. He demonstrates this potency through avenging the loss of his leg, thereby gaining a measure of control over a situation where he was out of control and victimized.

The intensity of Ahab's desire for revenge also points to the fact that this wound also comes to represent past injuries Ahab has sustained without the satisfaction of revenge. Indeed, Moby Dick seems to have become a reservoir for all the various hurts and disappointments of Ahab's life. Ishmael offers this explanation when he states that Ahab "at last came to identify with him [Moby Dick], not only his bodily woes, but all his intellectual and spiritual exasperations. The White Whale swam before him as the monomaniac incarnation of all those malicious agencies which some deep men feel eating in them, till they are left living with half a heart and half a lung" (p. 156). The word 'exasperations' here indicates that these difficulties aren't necessarily evil itself but rather the sort of problems and frustrations that one accumulates while living. Likewise the term 'malicious agencies' isn't a definite and known ill; it is rather a collection of assorted problems that slowly eat away at a man, reducing his sense of agency and power in the world.

Ahab's own words further illuminate the nature of his despair. At one point, he laments the cruelty of the wind, which has no body and therefore nothing upon which man can defend himself. He says, "Would now the wind but had a body; but all the things that most exasperate and outrage mortal man, all these things are bodiless, but only bodiless as objects, not as agents. There's a most special, a most cunning, oh, a most malicious difference!" (p. 420). Something that is 'bodiless as an object but not as an agent' is a fine description of what would give rise to the 'intellectual and spiritual exasperations' of which Ishmael says Ahab has experienced. It is fitting that Ahab, disgusted by such agents of evil, would make as his scapegoat an animal that does wrong, has a substantial body, and yet is not an agent of evil.

In addition to building on past discontents, Ahab's obsessive hunt for revenge also serves as an outlet for the madness he experiences after he has lost his leg. Ishmael learns about the days following Ahab's dismemberment upon returning to land as the sole survivor of the *Pequod*. Ishmael finds out that Ahab entered a sort of delirium after losing his leg. The ship he captains is turned toward home and for a while Ahab remains indisposed with grief. But recover Ahab does, and at the time everyone assumes he has regained his sanity. Ishmael, however, knows that Ahab's madness had "subsided not, but deepingly contracted" (p. 157). Ishmael believes that "far from having lost his strength, Ahab, to that one end, did now possess a thousand fold more potency than ever he had sanely brought to bear upon any one reasonable object" (p. 157). Ishmael understands how Ahab's insanity has fixated on his desire for vengeance, thus bringing an uncommon intensity and power to his quest.

Captains Bildad and Peleg, the two other owners of the *Pequod*, undoubtedly believe Ahab to be sane enough to captain a ship. However, once out in the ocean, Ahab's behavior reveals his obsessive desire for revenge and the inner turmoil that has created such a desire in him. Ahab's obsession with the whale is often described by various fire-associated terms—such as 'scorched within' and his 'fiery hunt.' Ishmael describes how the whole boat would hear Ahab cry out in the night and then Ahab would "burst from his state room, as though escaping from a bed that was on fire" (p. 169). Ahab is also often referred to as a monomaniac. Monomania is a psychiatric term, now dated, but used during the period when Melville wrote, to describe an otherwise sane person who is preoccupied with one idea—in the case of Ahab, the one idea is that of killing Moby Dick. Interestingly, it often seems that Ahab's obsession allows for the degree of sanity he maintains, as if seeking revenge gave his insanity some focus and place to act. Indeed, his capabilities as captain of a substantial vessel are not compromised. One gets the idea that the people on shore who thought Ahab sane were not dumb, but rather that Ahab is largely sane with rather substantial pockets of insanity.

Another interesting feature of Ahab's obsession with killing the White Whale is that he believes it is fated to happen. Fate is often linked to revenge in order to give it a sense of the inevitable and of being backed by a divinely inspired sense of justice. Ahab evokes fate in order to link his efforts with some sort of larger purpose. Towards the end of the book, when the *Pequod* is closing in on Moby Dick, Starbuck pleads once again with Ahab to relent in his chase. Ahab refuses. He tells Starbuck that he will not relent—he says, "Ahab is forever Ahab, man. This whole act's immutable decreed. 'Twas rehearsed by thee and me a billion years before this ocean rolled. Fool! I am the Fates' lieutenant; I act under orders" (p. 418).

For all of Ahab's unwavering intensity, there is a notable moment when Ahab wonders what exactly he is fighting against. His doubt comes during a calm day at sea, when the earth's beauty moves and soothes him. The effect of the day on Ahab is described as "the step-mother world, so long cruel—forbidding—now threw affectionate arms round his stubborn neck, and did seem to joyously sob over him, as if over one, that however willful and erring, she could yet find it in her heart to save and to bless" (p. 405). This passage, coming towards the end of the novel, captures Ahab's belief that the world is a cruel and dark place. This belief builds on the unfortunate circumstances surrounding his childhood: his mother, already a widow, died when he was only one year old. In light of such a beginning, it is no wonder then that he views the world as a cruel place and a 'stepmother' since he lost the embracing love of his mother when he was still an infant. Occasionally thereafter, as during the above quoted passage, he comes into contact with the world in such a way that he feels it a gentle place and such experience softens his anger and reveals his sorrow and pain. In that scene, he tells Starbuck that he is "deadly faint, bowed, and humped, as though I were Adam, staggering beneath the piled centuries since Paradise. God! God! God!—crack my heart—stave my brain!—mockery! mockery! bitter, biting mockery of grey hairs, have I lived enough joy to wear ye; and seem and feel thus intolerably old?" (p. 406). Ahab allows himself more vulnerability in that speech than he has in nearly the whole book. Starbuck then understands Ahab, in all his sadness, and responds by saying, "Oh, my Captain! My Captain! noble soul! grand old heart, afterall!" (p. 406). Starbuck also urges Ahab to relent. Of course Ahab can't. His misery has long ago hardened into anger and a desire for retaliation and, ultimately, revenge eludes him. He cannot have it. He drives the *Pequod* on to destruction and the death of all the crew save for Ishmael.

COMMON PSYCHODYNAMIC ELEMENTS

Relying upon the principles of metapsychology (Freud, 1915; Rapaport, 1960), the consideration of the three protagonists discussed above ought to delineate the genetic, topographic, economic, dynamic, and adaptive aspects of their hateful behavior. A genetic perspective can also be taken vis-à-vis Heathcliff and Captain Ahab. Both were orphaned and the depth of their reaction to later traumas undoubtedly has roots in this childhood one. Ontogenetic and developmental information on Medea is missing, though one can speculate that the intensity of her rage at her adult life trauma seems a bit overdetermined; tributaries other than those consciously stated registered certainly have played a role here. As far as the dynamic and adaptive perspectives are concerned, breaking the narratives down into their central components is helpful: (i) the occurrence of severe trauma, (ii) the stirring up of great fury, and (iii) the powerful wish to turn the tables and get even with the perpetrator. Let us now take a clear look at each of these elements.

In Medea's case, the trauma inflicted is at the hands of Jason, her husband. When Jason abandons Medea for the daughter of Creon, king of Corinth, he has ruined her stable life with him as well as embarrassed her. Interestingly, Medea talks little about missing Jason. She says nothing about loving him. Her pain instead seems to come from her feelings of humiliation. A comment from Pine (1995) as to the nature of Medea's injury is particularly illuminating:

> But Medea's internal experience is different from either of these. It is, instead, an experience of being slighted, insulted, mocked, reduced. Here, after all of the killings, in brief [before I quote more extensively] is the final exchange between Medea and Jason, in which they talk past one another, Jason only hearing his view of Medea's actions as a response to his leaving her to sleep with another, Medea emphasizing the insult to her sense of self. . . . Medea's internal experience is a compound of a sense of injury—a sense that builds to imagined public humiliation—and a sense of righteousness. (108–109)

These injuries are made worse by the fact that Medea murders and lies so that Jason can take the golden fleece from Colchis. Medea has then essentially become a traitor to her homeland for Jason and so when he leaves her for another, she feels foolish. The injury stings worse for what she has previously done for him.

Heathcliff's injury in *Wuthering Heights* is similar to Medea's since it also surrounds a romantic relationship. And yet, unlike in *Medea*, the injury is not clearly at the hands of his love. Their separation has many causes, apart from Catherine, that include both societal and class expectations, Hindley's actions, and Heathcliff's own shame and fear of rejection. Catherine does her best in a patriarchal society where she herself has little hope for an independent future apart from marrying Edgar Linton. Ultimately their separation is indeed part misunderstanding, and part situational. As a result, Heathcliff feels his injury occurs not just from one person—as Medea does from Jason—but rather from multiple sources, including Hindley and the Lintons. Also unlike Medea, Heathcliff repeatedly pines for Catherine. He continues to love her absolutely and yet his love for her is completely wrapped up as well in his experience of debasement at the hands of Hindley. Hareton becomes an alter-ego for Heathcliff once Heathcliff exiles him to a servant position after Hindley's death. Heathcliff comments on Hareton's—and thus his own—pain when he tells Nelly, "I know what he suffers now, for instance, exactly—it is merely a beginning of what he shall suffer, though. And he'll never be able to emerge from his bathos of coarseness, and ignorance"

(p. 161). And yet Heathcliff is proved wrong; as chance would have it, Hareton is saved from such a fate by Catherine Linton's love.

In contrast to the trauma experienced by Medea and Heathcliff, Ahab's injury in *Moby Dick* is both concrete and symbolic. It is concrete because the injury is the physical loss of his leg. The injury is also symbolic because it comes to represent a loss of independence that is particularly troubling to Ahab because Ahab was orphaned as a baby. Only one sentence of the whole book is devoted to the situation; Captain Peleg mentions in passing that Ahab's mother, already a widow, died when he was just one year old. And yet one could surmise that Ahab had to learn independence from a young age and that this ability became particularly important to him such that any minor decrease of independence becomes a huge blow. Manninen (1996) offers insightful analysis into what the loss of his leg represents to Ahab. He writes:

> To Ahab, losing a member of his body seems to have grown into an insurmountable trauma, because it inexhaustibly and continually brings him under the destiny he most abhors. Now he could be forced to resort to other people and be at the mercy of their good will. Even occasional need of help would constitute an unbearable insult to him, and remind him of the painful incompleteness of not only his body, but of his whole self. (p. 8)

In each work, the characters process their narcissistic trauma through rage. Indeed, anger is the defining emotional state of the three characters. It seems to be the more acceptable emotion rather than, say, sadness that each undoubtedly experiences. *Medea* opens with Medea's nurse saying that "hatred has corroded everything" (p. 1) and notes that Medea "will not give up her rage" (p. 3). Indeed, we soon see that Medea will *not* give up her rage: from the moment she comes onto the stage, Medea is not so much a sorrowful, abandoned wife as a bitter, hateful seeker of revenge. She spends no time wondering if she has done something to drive Jason away or thinking herself unworthy of Jason's love in comparison to his new wife. Instead, she heads right towards anger, saying that Jason, who "was my everything has proved the vilest of all" (p. 7). When Jason enters, Medea calls him "vilest of traitors—yes, I can at least call you that, the most cutting insult against a man who is no man" (p. 13). She refers to him as "the worst of all husbands" (p. 19).

The response of rage to traumatic narcissistic injury is common, and has been outlined by others. Kohut (1972), in his paper on narcissistic rage, writes that the "narcissistically vulnerable individual responds to actual (or anticipated) narcissistic injury either with shamed faced withdrawal (flight) or narcissistic rage (fight)" (p. 10). Kohut also notes that "the desire to turn hurt into anger is fueled by a desire to turn a passive experience into an active one" (p. 11). Medea fulfills this desire in the sense that she becomes the perpetrator when she murders Jason's new wife and their own children. As to why she might be narcissistically vulnerable, the most likely explanation seems to be that she killed her brother and was essentially a traitor to her country for Jason. Having traded her old family for Jason's love, Medea is all the more hurt when Jason forsakes her.

The rage of Medea is memorable and yet Heathcliff and Ahab hold competitive places in our literary canons as characters who are consumed by rage. Heathcliff's anger in *Wuthering Heights* completely withdraws him from other people. He is angry at nearly everyone save for Catherine, and even for her, his love is mixed with anger for having been unfulfilled. His anger causes him to lash out and abuse others. He abuses Edgar's sister, Isabella, who falls in love and eventually marries him. He then goes on to abuse his son, Linton, whom he hates, and forces the boy to woo Catherine Linton (Catherine and Edgar's daughter). Linton does not want to trick Catherine. Rather he is terrified of his father; Nelly describes the "mortal terror he [Linton] felt of Mr. Heathcliff's anger" (p. 200). Indeed, Heathcliff's anger is often right below the surface; one time, when provoked by Catherine Linton, Nelly describes how Heathcliff's "black eyes flashed, he seemed ready to tear Catherine to pieces" (p. 235). This rage has its first source in being parted from Catherine and came to be seen in full effect when, after his return, Nelly tries to part him from her again. Nelly describes his reaction as, "He gnashed at me, and foamed like a mad dog, and gathered her to him with greedy jealousy" (p. 119).

Of the three, Ahab's rage in *Moby Dick* is the most isolated and pervasive. It is not directed at another person and has nothing to do with love or loss of a relationship. It is rather completely fixed on a whale and takes place on the sea, set apart from society and the everyday concerns and relations of the human world. In this way, Ahab's rage completely rules the world of the story and his whole character. There is nothing else—it is the purpose and driving force of the *Pequod.* What seems to have been a whaling journey turns out to be something very different. His anger defines him; he is described as dark and as having "fiery eyes of scorn" (p. 390). Ahab believes himself to be so consumed by anger that he calls himself "demonic" (p. 143) and indeed others call him the devil. The comparison is apt; Ahab is the leader of the *Pequod* and has bent it on killing Moby Dick. The others fall into line and in this sense, Ahab's anger consumes and directs the actions of the crew in a way that the anger of Medea and Heathcliff does not.

The desire for retaliation is for all three characters the culmination of their injury and ensuing anger. Medea seeks revenge against Jason for leaving her. He is the prime target and yet she carries out her retaliation through killing his current wife and their children. The aim of these murders is to cause Jason pain and rob him of what she lost when he left her. Nonetheless, the person upon whom she seeks retaliation is not the only person harmed. Arguably the most lasting and permanent harm is done to those she has murdered. And yet, Medea undoubtedly hurts herself as well when she kills her own children. However, these losses feel worth it because she gets to avenge what Jason has done to her. Furthermore, Medea feels that there is justice in committing this act of retaliation. Horney's (1948) 'openly aggressive vindictiveness' captures the nature of Medea's drive for revenge well. Horney writes:

> It looks uninhibited in action. The person may aggressively strike out at others. He is openly exploiting. He is usually proud of this capacity, although, as mentioned, he does not experience the vindictive character of these actions. He may feel that his is simply more honest and straightforward than others, that he merely is doling out justice, that his dignity refuses to be insulted. (p. 2)

Heathcliff bears a wound similar to Medea's in that both are of a romantic nature. However, Heathcliff and Catherine's separation is by no means as causal as one leaving the other: circumstances such as class, Hindley's jealousy, Heathcliff's pride, and even Catherine's relative powerlessness in a patriarchal society are all contributing factors. As such, Heathcliff does not directly seek to cause Catherine pain, as Medea does to Jason. He seeks instead to debase Hindley and Edgar, as well as to gain eventual ownership of Wuthering Heights and Thrushcross Grange. Heathcliff seeks retaliation over years and in various acts; this is different than Medea's revenge, which is carried out through the murders, and is then complete. However, Heathcliff was abused and belittled by Hindley for years. His desire for revenge grows not only from his anger at being separated from Catherine but also from his shame at being made to feel inferior. As Horney (1948) points out such humiliation often creates a character structure replete with rage and revenge fantasies:

> The need for vindictive triumph stems from many sources. There is mostly an early history of having suffered thoughtless or openly cruel humiliations. There are later experiences felt as humiliations on account of neurotic pride. All of these, consciously or unconsciously, make a person long for an ultimate triumph over his offenders. Together with his hopelessness in regard to a constructive development of his own life, triumph may become the only goal worth striving for. (p. 6)

In the end, Heathcliff decides not to destroy both manors. Such a change of heart is suggestive of someone who has forgiven and yet Heathcliff has not. Rather, the growing love between Hareton and Catherine Linton, which parallels his love with Catherine, brings a sort of reunion to him and Catherine. As the two young ones fall in love, Heathcliff himself drifts farther from life and into memories of Catherine.

In contrast to Heathcliff, Ahab never relents and yet his act of revenge is a failure. While he does finally find Moby Dick, the final battle is unsuccessful. The *Pequod* goes after the White Whale three times; on the third try, the whale destroys the boat and kills all the men save Ishmael. The first two encounters are dangerous; Ahab knows that hunting Moby Dick might kill the whole crew. Starbuck even begs Ahab to relent. But Ahab can't. He is obsessed with seeking vengeance on Moby Dick. Indeed, he can't hear anyone who tells him not to chase Moby Dick and he won't tolerate any distractions. A passing whaling boat asks for the *Pequod*'s help in finding lost members at sea. Though the other captain makes a moving plea, Ahab ignores it and just moves on to finding Moby Dick. An appropriate comment about the unceasing desire for vengeance from Kohut (1972) touches on this very dynamic:

> The need for revenge, for righting a wrong, for undoing a hurt by whatever means, and a deeply anchored, unrelenting compulsion in the pursuit of all these aims which gives no rest to those who have suffered a narcissistic injury—these are features which are characteristic for the phenomena of narcissistic rage in all its forms and which set it apart from other kinds of aggression. (p. 10)

CONCLUSION

In this contribution, I have delineated the theme of revenge and its relational backdrop with the help of three major literary works. I have included both male and female protagonists and sought to trace the sources of their narcissistic mortification and rage, which, I propose, were the *fons et origo* of their unquenching thirst for revenge. In elucidating the nuances of these literary texts, my goal has been to deepen the understanding of the phenomena of revenge and the emotional states that accompany it.

From the portraits drawn by Euripides, Brontë, and Melville, the drive for revenge seems to be an understandable, if destructive, aspect of human nature. To mitigate its destructive effects and to move forward, one needs to understand the traumas that precede revenge-seeking. When a traumatized and angry person feels heard and understood, the possibility of his letting go of the rage appears on the horizon. Without such witnessing and validation, one stays stuck in the past. This brings to mind the title of Desmond Tutu's (1999) book, *No Future Without Forgiveness.* Tutu emphasizes that there has to be forgiveness in order for people to move forward, an observation that has been upheld in the psychoanalytic literature (Akhtar, 2002; Siassi, 2013).

Without forgiveness, one cannot have a meaningful future. Obsessed with rage and vindictiveness, one keeps repeating the past in one's present.

NOTE

1. As would be readily apparent, the title of my essay is modeled after Pirandello's (1921) famous play *Six Characters in Search of an Author*.

Chapter Nine

The Ubiquitous Nature of Revenge

Biopsychocultural Perspectives

Rama Rao Gogineni and April E. Fallon

The universal response of ire and a desire to even the score against those who we perceive have hurt or betrayed us is one of the most primal and intense human reactions. For the individual, it can become a lifetime obsession. Edmond Dantes, the central character in *The Count of Monte Cristo* (Dumas, 1844), after a wrongful imprisonment, spends the next twenty years seeking revenge against the three people responsible for it. For families, it can fuel generations of cyclical feuding. The Hatfield–McCoy feud is just such an example. The two Appalachian families began feuding over the theft of a hog, which escalated into more than a dozen killings of family members and lasted more than thirty years. For nations, it can result in centuries of atrocities, as in the case of the bloody dispute between Albanians (Muslims) and Serbs (Eastern Orthodox) over control of Kosovo. Albanians claim it as the original inhabitants and Serbs as the origin of their church. From the perspective of advancement of society, preservation of human life, and quality of living, such examples of revenge with the wisdom of distance and time would be condemned. Yet, revenge as a motive and social behavior is woven into the fabric of everyday interaction and accepted by ordinary people. Revenge spans a broad spectrum of behaviors ranging from mildly retaliatory acts in the workplace and tit-for-tat in social encounters to the extreme destructiveness of genocide. The consistency of themes of retaliation throughout recorded history of civilization as well as their popularity in contemporary social media venues suggests the ubiquity of the desire and the importance in understanding its function to the individual and society.

Throughout the other chapters in this book, revenge is explored as an understandable, yet dysfunctional psychological compromise. In this chapter, we examine revenge through the lens of its function in ordinary life and suggest that in its nuanced form the act or threat of revenge with its biological basis has an evolutionary function which unfolds within the social context and serves to keep the other (individual or group) from further transgression. It can restore social equilibrium for an injured party who has no other recourse. However, its original function can be sullied by misattributions as to the satisfaction it provides and can go awry in judgments of an 'acceptable' payback.

This chapter explores the biological and evolutionary, social and cultural underpinnings of revenge. We begin by presenting two examples of revenge and use them to highlight the definition of revenge and distinguish it from related terms such as retribution. Next, we review the omnipresent nature of revenge examples existing in mythology and religious texts, occurring throughout history. We then examine the evolutionary function of revenge and explore underlying social and cultural mechanisms that may contribute to the range of revenge enacted. Our final section discusses instances of revenge having gone awry and examines empirical evidence and explanations for why this may have occurred.

CONTRASTING HISTORICAL EXAMPLES

Example One: The Mongol Invasion of Khwarezmians

In the early thirteenth century, Genghis Khan wished to develop a trading alliance with the Khwazermid dynasty ruled by Shah Ala ad-Din Muhammad. When he sent a five-hundred-man caravan from Mongolia to the city of Otrar, the governor attacked the caravan, charging that it contained spies, and later refused to repay for the destruction of the caravan. Genghis Khan then sent three ambassadors, two Mongols and a Muslim, to meet the Shah instead of the governor. The Shah ordered the men shaved and the Muslim decapitated and sent his head back with the two remaining diplomats, an obvious insult to Genghis Khan. Genghis Khan sent 200,000 soldiers to invade and defeat Khwarezmian and then ordered the massacre of many civilians, enslaved the rest, and murdered the governor by pouring liquid silver into his ears and eyes, as revenge for his deeds. Genghis Khan then sent two generals with 20,000 men to hunt down the Shah. He moved the capital and then charged two of his generals with completely destroying all aspects of the Khwarezmid Empire, including buildings, people, and farmland. Pyramids of severed heads were constructed as a symbol of victory (Medbib.com/GenghisKhan, accessed 6/30/13).

Example Two: The Story of Chanakya

In the subcontinent of India 345 BC, Chanakya is credited with defeating the powerful Nanda Empire, run by a tyrant, Dhanananda, and establishing the new Maurya Empire. Chanakya was the son of Chanak, a famous teacher of public policy and an influential Brahmin outspoken in his opposition of the bad governance. For this, Chanak was beheaded and his head publicly displayed, as a warning to anyone who would oppose the king.

Chanakya fled to Takshashila, a university city, where he studied economics, public policy, and chemistry, and became a teacher. Years later, Chanakya returned to Magadha and confronted Dhanananda; subsequently, he was humiliated and imprisoned. He was rescued by Chandragupta (grandfather of Ashoka the Great), a young man also opposed to the king. Chanakya vowed to avenge his father and his own humiliation. Chanakya had groomed Chandragupta with his developed sutras in the art of ruling a kingdom. The two engaged in some brilliant maneuvers of deception and managed to unite the many bickering kings of the subcontinent to march against Dhanananda. They are credited with destroying the Nanda dynasty and setting up a strong republic with good governing principles which was the first in recorded history to rule most of the subcontinent. His two well-known surviving texts—*Arthashaastra* and *Neetishastra*—outline duties of a ruler, and the dos and don'ts of running a kingdom (Acharya and Jain, accessed 6/30/13).

The Diversity of Revenge

These two examples from history that contrast and highlight the range of revengeful stories differ on several dimensions. In both cases, humiliation is experienced and payback is sought. In the former case, the wrong is a public disregard of a request and destruction of members of the requesting group, but it was not directly experienced by Genghis Khan. In the latter case, there was personal humiliation and destruction of the immediate family. In the former case, brutal vengeance was carried out not only on the perpetrators, but innocent victims who simply had in common a cultural identification; there is eventual eradication of all traces of the dynasty.

In these two examples, there is a range in the degree of vengeance or vindictiveness with which the injured party pursues. In the former case, Genghis Khan pursues with brutality that exceeds most of his other conquests; the goal is destruction of the injurer and inclusion of bystanders who may not have even agreed with or been a part of the original offense. Identification in the group is enough to yield punishment for others' misdeeds. The end goal is eradication and destruction. With Chanakya, revenge occurs, but is transformative as well as rebuilding for the social good, without destabilizing a nation or making it weak for foreign invasion. In the latter case, ideological revenge is sought for the personal harm and humiliation with the goal of societal betterment. Although quite capable of a more brutal and vindictive attack on the harm doer, it achieves payback that revenge was designed to serve without total destruction.

Deterrence is often considered a major function of revenge. Genghis Khan's grand scale of vengeance serves as a warning to other groups who might not be respectful of his 'invitations.' Chanakya's strategies are clever and perhaps more subtle. His maneuvers required some deception and therefore may not have permitted a public announcement of his intentions and acts. Without a public announcement of humiliation and payback, the impact of the revenge act as a deterrent may be limited.

These two examples contrast two philosophies that often underlie humans' pursuit of revenge. In the former, payback is eradication and destruction whereas in the latter, payback is the institution of a new ideology, the hope of reformation, which transcends time. At the extremes, as in these two examples, vengefulness and revenge can be distinguished from retribution and retaliation. However, often, this distinction is much less clear. With only the outcome in view and without intimate knowledge of the victim(s), it is difficult to appreciate the intensity of the affect. In addition, as we will argue later, the 'fairness' of the payback is dependent upon the individual's perspective in the transaction.

DEFINING REVENGE

Revenge, retaliation, retribution, and vengeance are often used somewhat interchangeably. The dictionary indicates that all of these terms involve a payback for a wrongdoing to oneself or those felt to be like oneself. They differ in the nature of the payback. Both retaliation and retribution involve a 'just or deserved or equal' action. Vengeance (and often revenge), however, involve a retaliation that is judged by others to be vindictive, spiteful, or excessive. Useful also are Zdaniuk and Bobocel's (2012) other distinctions for revenge and retribution: in retribution, moral limits are drawn on permissible punishment, whereas in revenge there are no limits; revenge has greater emotional and behavioral intensity than retribution; and revenge acts are often intended to inflict pain, suffering, and diminution whereas retribution is aimed at assertion of moral truth and providing the victim with equality. Gerber and Jackson (2013) distinguish between two dimensions often merged in the discussion of revenge: the desire to punish an offender to 'get even' by making the offender suffer (*retribution as revenge*) and the desire to restore justice through proportional payback from the transgressor (*retribution as just deserts*). When we refer to others' work, we respectfully use their terminology. When we are delineating our views, we reserve retribution and retaliation for deserved payback for harm incurred. We use vengeance to indicate punitive and excessive payback.

Revenge Is Everywhere

Revenge appears to have existed throughout time. It "contributes to warp and woof of the world's history, to the plots of drama and literature, to the role of government, law and religion. . . . It seems to persist as immutably as the second law of thermodynamics by its insistence that for every wrong there must be an equal and opposite righting" (Seton, 2001, p. 78). We provide a few diverse examples to illuminate its universality.

Historical Example: The Ancient Greeks

Through Greek mythology, we know that revenge and retribution played a significant part in Ancient Greece. The Olympian gods and goddesses Zeus, Hera, and Poseidon rose to power as a result of a series of battles (Titanomachy). Their father, Titan Cronus, had disfigured his father, Uranus. Because Uranus had been castrated to avenge the loss of his siblings, Uranus was unfit to rule and was succeeded by Cronus. From the blood of Uranus came the three Furies, sisters Alecto ('the angry'), Megaera ('the grudging'), and Tisiphone ('the avenger'). These cruel earth goddesses symbolized the divine vengeance and persecuted crimes of disrespect, injustice, arrogance, and intra-familial murder. Their thirst for punishment was unbounded, for they would punish a transgressor even after death, until he demonstrated remorse. Cronus, attempting to avoid the fate of his own father and his destiny, would eat each of his children as they were born. When the last child was about to be born, his wife, upon the advice of her parents, presented a rock to Cronus instead of the child. The child, Zeus, was whisked away. As an adult, Zeus, through a series of tricks was able to have Cronus regurgitate the other siblings and the battles began, eventually resulting in Zeus ruling from Olympus. Nemesis was also an important goddess,[1] the spirit of Divine retribution. Described as a remorseless god, she punished those afflicted with hubris.

The Judaic-Christian Tradition

The old testament of the Bible is often considered to represent the code of ethics to which both Christians and Jews have followed in the last two thousand years. It seems that nearly half the Bible is filled with stories of revenge—revenge that God exacts and revenge that individuals and groups take on each other with various outcomes. It is clear that those writing and reading the text have deep concerns about this aspect of human nature. Any group or individual looking to take revenge or not take revenge can find a verse in the Bible to support their desire.

The common parlance phrase of "an eye for an eye" (Exodus 21:24) is used as support for the notion of reciprocal justice and proportionate revenge. The story of Samson (Judges 13–16), a complex story with cyclical and multiple acts of revenge, provides an example. The context of the story is that God had been punishing the Israelites by allowing them to be ruled by the Philistines. Samson, born of Israelite parents, had been identified at birth to be a servant of God. Samson woos a Philistine bride. On his wedding day, Samson poses a riddle that the Philistines cannot answer. They are enraged and threaten to burn his wife if she does not obtain the answer. He discovers this and kills thirty Philistines and burns their crops. They rape and kill his wife and father-in-law. Samson kills more in revenge. The Philistines capture him, and he kills a thousand of them. The Philistines cut his hair (the source of his strength), blind him, and confine him to women's work. He regains his strength and destroys the Philistine temple killing all in it including himself, freeing the Israelites (Wikipedia, accessed 6/6/13).

Stories such as these in the Bible generally do not have happy endings for those specifically involved. Perhaps this is to acknowledge the destructive nature of revenge. There are many other scriptures, even within the Old Testament, that do not support revenge by man. For example, in Leviticus, the concept of forgiveness is prescribed: "Do not seek revenge or bear a grudge against anyone among your people, love your neighbor as yourself" (Leviticus 19:18). There are also references to the notion that only God may seek revenge: "Avenge not yourselves, but *rather* give place unto wrath: for it is written, Vengeance *is* mine; I will repay, saith the Lord" (Romans 12:19). Thus, in this model, ordinary people should not seek revenge, but leave it to a higher authority who presumably may act dispassionately.[2]

Contemporary World Cultures

Today around the world, revenge acts are in abundance. Anthropologists have documented such behavior in traditional societies such as Papua New Guinea (Diamond, 2008) and the various tribes in the Amazon rain forests. We review atrocities such as events from Yemen, 'honor killings,' and school shootings. But there are more ordinary acts of revenge that occur at work, in school, and in intimate relationships. We examine a few.

Yemen

In 2008, the *Yemen Post* reported that almost 5000 people had been killed in the past decade due to revenge killings (Al-Zaidi, 2008). The most common appear to be what is referred to as tribal killings. In this case, a feud begins because of what might appear to us to be a relatively unimportant object—

the killing of donkey or sheep or a dispute over a tiny plot of land. These become increasingly complex over time with more severe payback. These revenge killings are on the rise since the outbreak of unrest in 2011. Most likely this is due to a government unable to enforce laws, a corrupt judiciary system, and the spread of firearms (Shamlan, 2013). A second kind of revenge killing are the political vengeance killings. For example, many want to kill General Ali Mohsen Al-Ahmar, who led the government's war against the Shiite Houthi Movement (supported by Iran) in the previous regime. Houthi fighters continue to clash with forces loyal to the general. This kind of revenge can be much more dangerous as it goes beyond the family and local disputes, potentially escalating to a more civil war.

Honor Killings

In Somalia in 2008, Aisha Ibrahim Duhulow, thirteen, was dragged to a hole while a thousand people watched, buried up to her neck, and stoned by fifty men for adultery. After ten minutes, she was dug up, but still alive and so was reburied to be stoned to death. Her 'crime' was that she was raped by three men (Fiske, 2010). In 2000, the United Nations estimated approximately 5000 honor killings[3] a year, although Chesler of the *Middle East Quarterly* (2010) believes this to be a significant underestimate. Many women's groups feel it exceeds 20,000 per year (Fiske, 2010). Although men can be victims, it is predominantly a fate that is suffered by women. In her study, Chesler (2010) found that honor killings have significantly increased from 1989 to 2009. Over half of the victims were daughters and sisters of the perpetrator. However, honor killings are a family collaboration, with two thirds of the victims killed by their families of origin; most murders had multiple perpetrators. Offenses varied by region. In North America, over 90 percent are murdered for being "too Western"[4] whereas in the Muslim world, a little over half were for sexual offenses. In Chesler's study there were two different victim populations. One group was composed of young girls (average age seventeen) and the other was made up of older women (average age thirty-six), usually mothers. Honor killings are rarely categorized as such and judicial systems even in the West have been reluctant to directly give these issues full court press due to cultural sensitivities.[5]

Revenge in the School Setting

In the period between 1974 and 2000, there were thirty-seven incidents of school shootings identified by a branch of the Secret Service. We are aware of the high-profile shootings such as Columbine, Colorado, Oakland, California, and most recently, Sandy Hook, Connecticut, but there have been many others as well. The number-one articulated motive for these shootings was revenge. Alfred University conducted a large-scale national Internet study of seventh- to twelfth-grade students with over 2000 participants to assess students' perceptions of their safety in school. Responses were weighted to reflect national representation. Eighty-seven percent of the students indicate that they believe that shootings are motivated by a person's desire to "get back at those who have hurt them" (Gaughan et al, 2001). Almost the same number indicated that "other kids picking on them, making fun of them, or bullying them" was the cause for another student to use lethal violence. About a third of them indicated that they thought there were other students in the school who might shoot someone. About 20 percent of respondents reported that they personally overheard a peer talking about shooting someone at school. Is it the adolescent prefrontal brain not fully developed and the available means that permits a wish to be so easily transformed into an act? Do social media give notoriety to events such as these so that such acts appear to be the norm rather than the exception?

The teacher-student power differential also seems to foster a more subtle form of revenge. While teachers ultimately have the power to promote or stifle a student's success, students have developed various mechanisms for seeking revenge when they feel that they have been unfairly treated or not given what they expected. Official student evaluations of faculty allow students to rate teachers. One of the biggest concerns about them is the positive relationship between them and their anticipated grades. A survey of college students indicates that 8 percent admit to using the evaluations as tools of revenge (Boysen, 2008). Many students do not trust the formal evaluation process as they feel that some faculty may seek revenge by assigning lower grades to them. Internet sites such as ratemyprofessors.com and ratemyteacher.com allow for more anonymity to trash their teachers. Yahoo supports a site, answers.yahoo.com which allows for posts on 'How to get revenge on your teacher.' Teachers are not unaware of this urge and need for protection; there are web pages devoted specifically to best practices for teachers to protect themselves from students' revenge and parents' lawsuits as well (Nelson, 2009). In this, we begin to see the elaborate dance of perceived threats and effort to deter harm that subtly unfolds.

Romance and Revenge

Google billionaire executive Omid Kordestani's ex-wife spent millions of 'his' dollars on her next wedding with surgeon Reza Malek to avenge his affair with a younger co-worker. The lavishness was recorded by paparazzi who happened by looking for Jennifer Aniston. The revenge of this telecom executive turned philanthropist was clearly payback where it might most hurt. In all relationships, acts such as these are destructive communications that are likely to strain what relationship might exist. A survey of revenge acts in significant relationships revealed that most events that provoke revenge responses have to do with rule violations, particularly exclusivity and mate responsiveness (Boon et al, 2009). Much less common were transgressions that damaged the participant's self-esteem or social standing. When asked about their decisions to retaliate, most expressed that they wanted to deter their partners' future acts and they wanted partners to empathize with their suffering as well. Revenge acts helped victims deal with their own feelings. Revenge also helped them to feel that they had restored justice. In the choice of revenge responses, most chose bending or ignoring tacit rules that govern relationships (Boon et al, 2009).

Of course, there is a great deal of individual variation in revenge responses. Ignoring a phone call is measurably different than setting fire to an ex-husband's penis as he watches TV and drinks vodka. In romantic revenge, if the relationship is to be maintained, it may not always feel possible to allow the transgressor to know of the deed. In a women's group, a woman who had been physically abused by her spouse but who felt unable to leave him spoke of her revenge of the previous week. She had served dog excrement in a beef stew. She reported the great satisfaction that she felt in watching him eat the stew. One by one, other women in the group reported similar acts—two others who used small amounts of rat poison in food preparation, just enough to make their spouse very sick, but not enough to kill them. In the discussion, it became clear that for some, the act was a compromise between the wish for a much more gruesome punishment and their own moral values. They justified their responses as not even proportionate to the harm that they had received. For all, the discussion of it appeared to have a cathartic effect; it felt empowering and was momentarily restorative to their self-esteem.[6] Of course, not every abused woman would exact such acts of revenge.

Sheppard and Boon (2012) investigated personality differences in honesty, humility, and vengefulness in decisions to retaliate against romantic partners in a non-clinical population. Honesty and humility, not surprisingly, were inversely related to vengeance. They also found that those low in honesty and humility were more likely to see desirable benefits in revenge and to minimize the costs (Sheppard and Boon, 2012). While clinicians might expect this to be the case in examples of individuals with significant narcissism, this finding extends to the non-clinical population as well.

Theories on the Evolution and Function of Revenge

After her boyfriend, teenage heartthrob Justin Bieber, broke up with her, Selena Gomez, also a teenage rock star, sought revenge by dating his best friend, Alfredo Flores. The media portrayed it as an attempt to make Justin jealous and as an act of revenge, not an uncommon phenomenon in adolescent breakups. Why do ordinary people seek revenge? There are many theories that address aspects of why an individual might seek revenge in certain situations and why groups may do so. Likely, biology, psyche, and culture are tethered to produce beliefs and actions of revenge. Indeed, some notions of revenge appear diametrically opposed.[7] In light of a missing comprehensive theory, we present a mixture of individual, interpersonal/social/cultural, and biological theories that account for various forms and aspects of revenge. We make no claims as to the comprehensiveness of the presentation and simply present some popular ones that appeal to us.

Evolutionary Function of Revenge

The ubiquity of revenge in almost every culture and throughout time suggests revenge has or at least once had an overarching evolutionary function. An evolutionary model suggests that genetic components of revenge provide some advantage in survival and fitness and thus would be selected for. Fehr and Gächter (2002) first proposed the evolutionary hypothesis of revenge as a key motive in understanding cooperation among genetically unrelated people, a necessity for survival of a social group larger than kin. Although the term 'revenge' is never used, a closely related term, 'altruistic punishment,' is defined as an act of punishment that an individual delivers to another who has transgressed a social and expected norm, even when the punishment is costly and results in no material reward to the avenger. They experimentally demonstrate that cooperation flourishes if altruistic punishment is possible and deteriorates if it is not. Even the behavior of those predisposed to cooperation deteriorates quickly in the presence of others acting only in self-interest. They concluded that negative emotion was the proximate mechanism involved. At an intuitive level, an evolutionary function of revenge and its importance in the welfare of a society makes good sense. Chaos emerges when there is no strong reciprocation of rewarding cooperators and punishing norm violators (Buckholtz and Marois, 2012). Revenge is often viewed as a deterrent. Acts of revenge by an individual will signal to the larger group that certain behaviors will elicit vengeance (McCullough et al, 2010). In their formulation, the purpose of revenge is to prevent future transgression rather than responding to a single immediate harmful offense. Yet questions emerge as to the underlying mechanisms of how exactly revenge or altruistic punishment improves individual reproductive fitness and group survival.

Chagnon (1988) in his study of the Yanomami—South American Indians of the Amazon—suggested that the propensity to engage in revengeful acts might improve individual reproductive fitness. In his twenty-three-year examination of this group, he found that almost half had killed someone and about a third of the deaths were due to violence. Those males who had killed an enemy (referred to as *unokais*) had more wives and more children than those who had not. Having more wives directly improves chances of passing your avenging genes onto the next generation. However, even if reproductive fitness is not substantially improved, individuals who have a proclivity toward revenge will be dominant, have more prestige, and can obtrude their will and beliefs on the larger social group.

However, later Beckerman et al (2009), studying the Waorani, the most violent and revenging group in South America, found evidence to the contrary. The most zealous and aggressive warriors had fewer wives and fewer children. They suggest that the norms of revenge are different, having a more inclusive group of targets that span the generations. Thus, a straightforward biological explanation of a 'revenge gene' maximizing genetic fitness is likely to be too simplistic to account for the range of revengeful responses in an individual or society. An evolutionary model of revenge becomes more palatable when it can be demonstrated that other species exhibit those traits or behaviors. Chimpanzees near the village of Tongo in the Congo have been reported to have killed at least ten people, which has been attributed to the human population encroaching on their lands (Abraham and O'Callaghan, 2012). It is more than a biological response to overcrowding. Groups of chimps wait for weaker targets of women and children to surround and attack. Many children have scars and have lost ears and fingers due to chimpanzee attacks (Wandimoyi, 2012). A laboratory demonstration with the same species suggests that their acts are more than reflex aggression. Jensen found that when given the opportunity, chimps retaliated against humans who took their food and ate it by collapsing the food table, which ruined the remaining meal. Yet, when adults gave taken food to another chimp, they did not retaliate (Jensen et al, 2007). Jensen interpreted the motivation for this revengeful behavior to be a deterrent for future acts of theft.

The evolutionary function of revenge becomes even more appealing when a biological substrate can be connected to it. In the last decade, positron emission tomography (PET) scans and functional magnetic resonance imageing (MRI) technology have permitted brain substrate and process mapping. There is indeed accumulating evidence for a neuroscience of revenge. Studies that use this technology usually involve a variation on the Prisoner's Dilemma Games in which participants believe that they are involved in a cooperative game with one or more people. Participants are manipulated into thinking that another has not contributed equally, which would result in the participant not receiving a fair settlement. Participants are given various options with different rewards or costs to them. While they are deciding on the option, a PET scan or fMRI is utilized to understand which parts of the brain are activated (show increased use of oxygen). These findings, as well as the accumulated knowledge on brain functioning, leads investigators to infer what cognitive and emotional tasks are being processed. Of course, more than one substrate is involved in each decision and multiple cognitive and emotional events often are processed in the same region.[8]

The anterior cingulate cortex has been implicated in social and comparative signaling (Rilling and Sanfey, 2011). Its activation sends an alarm that social norms have been violated, such as when one agrees to cooperate and then breaks that agreement by taking an unfair share. The dorsolateral and ventromedial prefrontal cortices are activated in fMRI studies when there are decisions of whether to penalize norm violations, particularly when avenging is costly (Buckholtz et al 2008; Buckholtz and Marois, 2012; de Quervain et al, 2004). These areas are generally responsible for many executive functions that involve integration, planning, and regulation. The former area is involved in overriding self-impulses, as when making a decision to cooperate rather than take more than your share (Rilling and Sanfey, 2011). Sanfey et al (2003) found that this area was activated after opponents presented unfair offers. The ventromedial area is associated with regulating emotional responses, including the suppression of emotional reactions such as anger. The magnitude of punishment appears to be more directly linked to areas where affective processing occurs, such as the amygdala, and medial prefrontal and posterior cingulate cortices (Buckholtz et al 2008).

Both the caudate nucleus and structures in the ventral striatum are understood to be the reward centers of the brain (Rilling and Sanfey, 2011). When participants punish others who have treated them unfairly, these two centers become activated (de Quervain et al, 2004; Singer et al, 2006). It appears that these areas motivate revenge; there is an anticipation of satisfaction when transgressors are punished and justice is re-established. This finding appears to be true when a third party rather than the participant has been unfairly treated (Buckholtz et al, 2008). However, the caudate nucleus is more activated when the punisher has been directly affected or when the punishment is strong, although gender moderates this relationship (Strobel et al, 2011). For men, the greater their desire for revenge, the greater the activation in both the caudate nucleus and ventral striatum is correlated (Singer et al, 2006). Consistent with this was the finding that those men willing to incur greater costs in order to avenge the transgressor have greater activation as well (de Quervain et al, 2004). For men, the desire for revenge works in conjunction with reduced empathy when they perceive unfairness. These same brain centers also become activated when individuals rewarded others who cooperated (Rilling et al, 2002). It seems that people experience greater striatum activity when they are anticipating a satisfying outcome (both social and non-social), and thus the same brain center that "brings us together can also break us apart" (Knutson, 2004, p. 47). Interestingly, this center is also activated by pleasant tastes. 'Revenge is sweet,' an expression linking the two experiences, is common in current culture to express the satisfaction that revenge brings. The first author that we know who linked the two was the Greek poet

Homer. In *The Iliad*, he speaks of revenge, "It is sweeter far than flowing honey" (XVIII, 109). Living around the seventh century BC, he predates our biological understanding of the connection between taste and revenge by approximately nine thousand years. It gives new meaning to the unconscious!

Although enthusiasm in the correlation between brain activation and revenge is warranted, until genes can be more directly implicated, the evidence for an evolutionary function of revenge remains incomplete. In the last two years, some preliminary support for the genetic variation being a mechanism underlying revenge has been found. Strobel and colleagues (2011) investigated whether genetic variation in dopaminergic function could account for variations in neural activation when individuals are considering revenge options. The neurotransmitter dopamine is a significant contributor in the brain system that is responsible for reward-motivated behavior.[9] It was previously found that variations in the genes associated with dopaminergic function influence the responsivity of the reward system (Dreher et al, 2008). Strobel et al (2011) specifically examined whether carriers of the COMT Met alleles would evidence stronger nucleus accumbens and dorsal lateral prefrontal cortex activation during the contemplation of punishing offenders versus subjects in control trials in which there was no offense. They found a relationship between COMT genotype and punishment-related neural activation in the nucleus accumbens, the brain's pleasure center, during punishment trials. Thus, it appears that carriers of the COMT Met alleles experienced greater pleasure when anticipating punishing offenders. All other things being equal, it is a simple and classic behavioral paradigm of response-reward. The genetic carrier of COMT Met alleles, like Skinnerian rats pressing bars for food, is rewarded when avenging the perceived transgression. We might infer that it is just such a person who becomes the zealous warrior, anticipating the satisfaction of revenge.

A purely genetic model is suspect. If revenge takers are selected for, over time, there is likely to be increased aggressiveness and expression of it, which may have the unwanted (or perhaps desired) effect of reducing the population. Such a model would not be viable unless the gene additionally is linked to something else that is even more valued for genetic fitness (such as strength or superior cognitive capacities). Lastly, it is also possible that its selection is interwoven with cultural elements that may have evolved to quell or contain expression of revenge (such as forgiveness, as suggested by McCullough). We now turn our attention to the cultural components of revenge.

Cultural Components of Revenge

Embedded in a biological and genetic framework, the norms that dictate the expression of revenge are not universal. When harm is experienced, the reflexive impulse is to pay back. Whether and how that happens is heavily influenced and determined by culture, family, and the groups to which one belongs. Biological components are ensconced into the cultural backdrop of the nature of the transgression—who is entitled to address it, the timing, emotional state, and the rituals that must accompany it. Cultures vary on each of these.

Groups or cultures that value revenge offer more social support to those pursuing revenge avengers (Price, 2009). In an examination of cultural differences in assigning blame to a harmful act, South Koreans and Americans assigned blame (i.e., 'wronged me') to an individual who was responsible either intentionally or unintentionally for a negative outcome. Americans assigned higher blame than Koreans when the act was intentional, but lower blame than Koreans when it was unintentional, suggesting that for Americans, intentionality is an important variable, whereas for Koreans it is less so. Cultural differences nicely aligned with collectivist versus individualistic attitudes. Those embracing collectivists' attitudes are less interested in intentionality when it comes to assigning blame. In a second study, an infringement of individual rights versus duty to others was varied. In those embracing more collectivists' attitudes, duty transgressions were judged more harshly. Individual rights violations were seen as more blameworthy by people embracing individualistic attitudes than collectivist attitudes (Shteynberg et al, 2009).

In decisions to pursue revenge, societies do the equivalent of a cost-benefit analysis, weighing the importance of punishment for order with the significance of maintaining relationships. (This is a notion that has been developed extensively by McCullough in his discussion of revenge and forgiveness.) At one extreme is revenge for every transgression, as illustrated by this passage in the novel *The Godfather*:

> They call it business. OK. But it's personal as hell. You know where I learned that from? The Don. My old man. The Godfather. If a bolt of lightning hit a friend of his the old man would take it personal. . . . And you know something? Accidents don't happen to people who take accidents as a personal insult. (Puzo, 1969, p. 146)

At the other extreme, injustice is met with some form of forgiveness. Gandhi's position on passive resistance and *Satyagraha*[10] is an example of a philosophy which embraces this position. Louis Fischer (1947), in his book *Gandhi and Stalin*, contrasts the approach of each of these men that contains a version of a quote that is frequently attributed to Gandhi. "The shreds of individuality cannot be sewed together with a bayonet; nor can democracy be restored according to the Biblical injunction of an 'eye for an eye' which, in the end, would make everybody blind" (O'Toole, 2010).

The Relationship of Revenge to Formal Laws

Anthropologists view revengeful acts as a way that a society maintains order and predictability where laws and enforcement are not present or applicable. We discuss three kinds of circumstances in which some variation of this occurs in our present-day world: when lawlessness is the norm, instances where groups operate outside the law, and when groups are actively feuding.

In places where laws are either not available or not agreed to by all factions, revenge may play a prominent role as no other avenues of punishment are available to those who harm others. An example where rules of revenge have been elaborated is in northern Albania. Norms dating back to the Bronze Age but more recently codified in the fifteenth century by the Albanian prince Lekë Dukagjini are used as justification for retaliatory acts. In a nation with corruption and an ineffective court system, the ancient code of Kanun articulates who can and must retaliate, who are legitimate targets, blood vengeance, etc. For example, Djilas (1958) writes of the retaliation that clan members must carry out to avoid the shame:

> The word "blood" . . . meant . . . a life that flowed together from generations of forebears who still lived in the tales handed down. Their blood coursed in all the members of the clan, and in us, too. Now someone had spilled that eternal blood, and it had to be avenged if we wished to escape the curse of all those in whom the blood once flowed, if we wished to keep from drowning in shame before the other clans. Such a yearning has no limits in space, no end in time. (p. 105)

Last year, *USA Today* reported on a killing of a seventeen-year-old girl and her grandfather in Albania (Cohen, 2012). The outcry was not about the killing itself, as her family had been feuding with another over land, but it was about the killing of a child, as this was a breach in ethical code where only adults outside their homes are appropriate targets.

For groups that operate outside the law, such as gangs and the Mafia, a code of conduct that includes revenge often appears significant. In the novel *The Godfather*, this is articulated nicely: "I don't trust society to protect us, I have no intention of placing my fate in the hands of men whose only qualification is that they managed to con a block of people to vote for them" (32). The workings of the American Mafia have fascinated authors (e.g., *The Untouchables* by Eliot Ness, *The Sicilian* by Mario Puzo) and film directors (e.g., Francis Ford Coppola's *The Godfather*, Brian De Palma's *Scarface*, and Sergio Leone's *Once upon a Time in America*) for decades. The code, the exclusivity, the violence and primitive vengeance have allowed all of us vicariously to have the sweet taste of revenge. In this group that operates outside the law, avenging outsiders and 'members of the family,' there is a code of ethics that restricts revenge (Raab, 2005; Repetto, 2004). Family members could be killed by those close to them for breaking rules. In the 'blood-for-blood' custom, if a member kills another member, no one could seek revenge until the boss grants permission. For example, Angelo Bruno (the 'gentle Don' of the Philadelphia crime family) was shot by his consigliere, Antonio Caponigro, without the Commission's permission. In turn, Caponigro was suffocated, beaten, multiply stabbed, shot, and found in a trash bag with $300 inserted into his rectum, symbolic that he had become too greedy. With the Mafia, revengeful acts were often accompanied by symbolic gestures. For example, the breaking of the well-known 'Omerta' code of silence, even if it was not intentional or known, was cause for retribution. Dominick Napolitano was a very loyal and devoted Mafia member. In 1981, he had his hands severed after he was murdered because he had allowed an undercover FBI agent who had infiltrated the Bonanno family to shake hands and be introduced as a 'friend of ours' (Wikipedia, accessed 6/5/13).

While there may be intra-group rules to address harm, ongoing friction between groups may have no legal recourse. These conflicts seem to be fueled by cyclical retaliatory acts and yet they may also serve to moderate the rageful vengeance between the groups. Such is the case between Israel and Palestine. In an elegant paper that utilizes the Mediterranean and Middle East, Albania, the Balkans, and South American tribes as illustrations, Elster (1990) reviews the norms of revenge and makes the case that where factions are feuding, the behaviors of revenge seem closely linked to honor. How honor is achieved and maintained is dependent upon societal norms toward both forgiveness and revenge. He asserts the attainment and ongoing maintenance of honor is the province of 'free' men who directly subdue equals or those superior. Women, children, and servants are usually exempt, as there is no honor in the conflictual interaction with lower-status individuals.

Black-Michaud (1975) argues that feuding is a conflict over material resources in which individuals attempt to manipulate the norms of revenge by presenting what is in fact a material dispute masked as a conflict of honor. Elster (1990) disagrees:

> Asserting one's honor, like enjoying other people's envy of one's assets, is an aspect of a deep rooted urge to show oneself to be superior to others. . . . It depends on actions not assets. The paradigm of the striving for honor is Hegel's master-slave dialectic. . . . The master derives it from his willingness to risk his life and thus ignore the purely material aspects of existence. . . . Honor is not acquired for the sake of consumption. Its aim is sheer self assertion and self esteem. (pp. 883–884)

Our earlier example of Genghis Khan supports Elster's notion that honor is more important than the materialistic aspects. Genghis Khan's revenge was to assert superiority by pure destruction of the entire society—men and women. No material gains were realized in the destruction of all the fertile farmland. Elster (1990) also notes many feuding societies require that acts of revenge be publically announced and recognized. A person acquires honor by humiliating the transgressor in the presence of others. As further evidence of this, he notes that in Albania, it is dishonorable to kill and not announce it. Likewise no retaliation against an assault results in disgrace. "In Corsida, the man who has not avenged his father . . . can no longer appear in public. Nobody speaks to him" (1990, p. 871). The importance of public announcement of the revenging act can be seen in our past decade of interaction with fundamentalist groups. The events of 9/11 led to the U.S. invasion of Iraq and the hunting down of Saddam Hussein. Radical fundamentalist groups took responsibility for the bombings in Bali. A few years later, U.S. Navy Seals, in a well-planned and well-executed operation, located and killed Osama bin Laden. Ten days later two suicide followers of Al Qaeda walked into a paramilitary center training men to confront Pakistan's Al Qaeda groups and killed eighty. Each deed was followed by a group's public claim of credit. No material wealth was acquired in any of these events. It was the re-establishment of honor that was sought. Imagine if we had not gotten credit for killing bin Laden.

Public announcement may also permit the avenger to learn whether the act of revenge is understood. Gollwitzer, a European psychologist, attempted to tease out satisfaction for the avenger. He found that only when the transgressor indicates an understanding of the revenge act does the avenger have satisfaction. Misunderstanding or no acknowledgment of the wrongdoing is as satisfying as no revenge at all (Gollwitzer et al, 2011).

REVENGE AND THE INDIVIDUAL

Deterrent to Bad Behavior

McCullough views individual acts of revenge as "a deeply human and sometimes very functional behavior" (Carey, 2004, accessed 10/17/13). It is a deterrent to unacceptable and harmful behaviors rather than merely punishment or a reflexively angry response. Individual acts of revenge announce to others—individuals as well as the group—that some responses will yield retaliatory events. It functions (i) to discourage transgressors from committing the same harmful behaviors, (ii) to delineate norms of acceptable behavior and avoid future confrontation, and (iii) to coerce cooperative behaviors (McCullough et al, 2010).

Revenge as a Homeostatic Mechanism of Identity

Using Erikson's notions of sociobiological development of the social self and Edleman's theory of neuronal group selection, Seton (2001) suggests that revenge is part of the individual's neurobiological homeostatic system to rebalance a disordered sense of self. In this model, transgressions toward the individual self can evoke a homeostatic reflex response to restore identity. One method of restoration is revenge. "Because identities run the full gamut of stability from rock-firm to jury-rigged, people vary greatly in their susceptibility to affronts and their readiness to respond vindictively" (p. 83). How easily this occurs depends not only upon ego-strength, but also how far and the degree to which the self extends into the environment (and cultural group). Here, affect is important, as it may regulate the sensitivity of a disordered or threatened self and identity. Whereas Seton sees affect as modulating the assault to identity and self-esteem and thus the propensity for a revengeful response, Carlsmith and colleagues (2008) place emphasis on acts of revenge as functioning to repair emotion or mood. While revenge in anthropological and social psychological circles is generally discussed in terms of a payback to another for a wrongdoing, revenge can be turned toward the self or parts of the self (see Kernberg's chapter in this book). Revenge also can be behaviorally enacted against the self even though the payback is toward another, as is often the case in adolescent suicide. Seton's view of the function of revenge as restoration of identity easily accommodates acts of self destruction as well as those against another.

The Relationship of Attitudes and Gender to Revenge

The clinical setting encourages the intrapsychic and relational understanding of revenge, in contrast to social psychology researchers who have sought to identify social attitudes existing in the broader social context (and primarily a non-clinical population) that correlate with the beliefs and expression of revenge. While the analytic couch has considerable advantage in exploring in depth and beyond the conscious attitude, the latter can assert more than impressionistically the broader existence and range of the phenomenon in ordinary people.

Gender has figured prominently in the expression of aggression. Cross-culturally, boys are more likely to express aggression physically whereas girls use verbal means (Lansford et al, 2012). Crime statistics reveal that a large portion of murders are committed by males in response to minor provocation (Daly and Wilson, 1988). Men are more likely than women to physically retaliate with trivial provocation. Lorena Bobbitt is the exception and not the rule, which is one of the reasons that it was so noteworthy. The biology of revenge suggests that there may be some gender differences in the revenge response. Singer et al (2006) found that when watching the punishment of a transgressor of a social norm, different parts of the brain are activated for men (striatum) than for women (anterior cingulate cortex). The former activity was associated with revenge motivations and the latter associated with empathy. A series of studies examined gender, anger, revenge, and physical aggression.[11] In all three studies, men's reports of revenge motivation were higher than women's, but there were no differences in angry feelings between the two groups. Revenge motivation, but not anger, predicted aggression (Wilkowski et al, 2012). Once the revenge motivation is taken into account, there is no difference in gender. Interestingly and consistent with Carlsmith's notion that revenge may repair mood, this study confirmed that revenge motivation and physical aggression in men was associated with positive emotion, but not with anger. This suggests that in men, the tendency to seek revenge is associated with positive emotional experiences rather than angry emotion. From a purely behavioral perspective, revenge has the capacity to be hedonically reinforcing.

There are three personality characteristic attitudes that social psychologists relate to revenge: social dominance, authoritarianism, and 'belief in a just world.'

- *Social dominance* is defined as "a preference for hierarchical relations between social groups as well as for in-group domination over out-groups" (Gerber and Jackson, 2013, p. 66). Individuals who endorse a social dominance orientation have a competitive worldview. They express a preference for inequality and believe in reinforcing status boundaries. They prefer their own group to dominate. These individuals support the use of harsh punishment. They view punishing offenders as a method to restore balance in society and power to the victim. They desire revenge as a measure to get even and have offenders suffer (Gerber and Jackson, 2013). It has also been linked to personal vengeance (McKee and Feather, 2008). Timothy McVeigh, previously a Gulf War veteran sought retribution against the tyranny of the 'left wing' federal government's handling of the Waco siege of April 1993, and Ruby Ridge incident. He felt that federal workers had become soldiers and that he needed to attack their 'command centers.' He detonated a bomb mounted on a rental truck in front of a federal building in Oklahoma City, Oklahoma, on April 19, 1995 (the second anniversary of the Waco raid). The Oklahoma City bombing killed 168, including children in the building's daycare, and injured over 600, and is known as the deadliest act of domestic terrorism within the United States prior to September 11, 2001. McVeigh's preference for social dominance is evident in press interviews when he indicated that the 19 children killed were "collateral damage" (Borger, 2001).

- *Authoritarianism*[12] is a personality and ideological view originally developed by Altemeyer (2006). Authoritarians are individuals who are submissive to authorities they believe are legitimate (authoritarian submission). They follow social convention and established norms, endorsing uniformity and group authority (conventionalism). They are punitive and endorse coercion toward others who do not adhere to tradition and established authority (authoritarian aggression). Individuals who endorse authoritarianism support suffering and getting even for an offender with the motive of restoring in-group conformity (Gerber and Jackson, 2013). But unlike someone who is high in social dominance, authoritarians endorse a more proportional punishment and believe in the possibility of restoring connection with the offender if they can identify the offender as a member of their group.
- People need to view their social world as predictable and orderly. Social psychologists have dubbed this '*belief in a just world*,' where good things happen to virtuous people and bad things befall to evil people (Lerner, 1980). The more strongly this view is held, the more distressed an individual becomes when this view is challenged and the more motivated he or she becomes to redress this challenge to the equilibrium. In a fortuitous opportunity, Kaiser et al (2004) measured students' beliefs in a just world before the September 11 attacks and then their desire for revenge and distress two months after. Those individuals who held strong beliefs about a just world were more likely to experience terrorism-related distress and more likely to desire revenge after the September 11 attacks. For many people, this event was a major challenge to physical safety in the world. More recent research has suggested that belief in a just world reduces distress when the stressors are more minor, and in this instance may reduce revenge and encourage forgiveness (Strelan and Sutton, 2011).

Revenge Gone Awry: Misattributions of Revenge

Equity theory (Walster et al, 1978) suggests that people are motivated to seek equality in their social interactions. If a transgression violates that equilibrium (physically, socially, or psychologically), the offended party is motivated to rebalance this inequity by pursuing justice. This theory seems to hold in many social transactions, and those who feel transgressed upon tend to act as equity theory would predict (Stillwell et al, 2008). If revenge functions purely to restore the inequity for initial transgression, how come there are so many instances in which endless feuding happens? The definition of proportionate restorative justice can be different depending upon the perspective. For example, when King Prasutagus of the Celtic Iceni tribe died, he left the kingdom to his wife, two daughters, and the Roman kingdom. The Romans, not known for fair play, ignored the will, took over the country by calling in loans, and raped and beat Boudicca and her daughters. While Rome was occupied in North Wales, Boudicca obliterated and burned three Roman cities, killing 80,000 people (della Quercia, 2010).

Social psychologists have created short-term relationships and collaborations in the laboratory to study and manipulate these variables. Although reductionistic in approach, many of their findings illuminate what we can observe in the social world. One possibility is in the misperception of 'fairness.' That is, there is a divergence in the perception of what is reasonable to restore equity to both transgressor and victim. In normal college students, recipients of transgressions describe these as more severe and unresolved than do their perpetrators (Baumeister et al, 1990). This has been termed 'the magnitude gap.' In an attempt to relate these findings more to the real world, researchers asked students about instances of revenge in their lives. They found that when avenging a transgression, they were more likely to rate the revenge action as a way of restoring equity to the relationship and to indicate that the perpetrator deserved to suffer, whereas when recipients of the revenge they rated it as relatively severe (Stillwell et al, 2008). In addition, both avengers and the recipients were angry at the time the event took place and felt justified in their feelings. Both saw themselves as victims; avengers viewed themselves as victims of the initial transgression, seeking revenge in an attempt to restore equity, and recipients viewed themselves as victims of excessive revenge. It is this magnitude gap that at least partially explains the cyclical and ongoing feuding between the Hatfields and McCoys. Although both avengers and victims took some responsibility for blame, avengers less so. When avengers viewed the revenge as a fair restoration of equity, they felt satisfied, but when they acknowledged that it was excessive, they felt less comfortable.

For all those instances in which revenge is sought for some transgression, there are many times when it is not sought. What determines whether one seeks reparation? In a study designed to examine revenge in the workplace, Aquino et al (2006) found that revenge is more often sought when there is no effective delineated procedure for resolving interpersonal conflicts and when the victim is of lower status than the perpetrator. Victims with higher status were more likely to reconcile or forgive the perpetrator. Even when individuals decide not to seek revenge, they still feel that the transgressor deserves to suffer revenge but feel that revenge would not be practical (would make it worse) or is immoral. Even when events have passed, those who do not take revenge reported still feeling more angry than those who have taken revenge (Stillwell et al, 2008). About half the instances reported that regardless of whether revenge was sought or not it resulted in a significant deterioration of the relationship, as a result in part of the particular interpersonal offense.

The Promise and Disappointment of Revenge

Nietzsche wrote "to witness suffering does one good, to inflict it even more so . . . an old powerful, human all-too-human proposition . . . in punishment there is so much that is festive" (Nietzsche, 1887/1996, p. 50, cited in Carrabine et al, 2013, p 306). His writing captures the beliefs of many people that revenge has a cathartic effect and will bring satisfaction and closure to those who have been harmed. However, many social psychologists have discovered that in the laboratory, an individual's ability to punish those who offend does not decrease anger or reduce the desire to aggress subsequently. Those who believed in catharsis punished more severely than those who did not believe in its effect. Yet, contrary to expectation, those who punished most severely felt more angry instead of less (Bushman et al, 2001). That is, those who can punish feel worse than those who are not given the opportunity to do so (Carlsmith et al, 2008).

What is even more interesting is that people did not anticipate this effect. Carlsmith and colleagues had students participate in a 'free rider' paradigm laboratory game. Players could cooperate and earn money, but a non-cooperator could earn more while the others earned less. The optimal money earned as a group would be greatest if everyone cooperated, but an individual could maximize his or her personal gain by not participating. Then some participants were given the chance to 'punish' the free rider, at some personal cost. Almost all given the chance would punish the free rider. Those given the opportunity to punish and those not able to punish anticipated that they would feel better if they were able to punish the free rider. However, those who did punish felt worse afterwards than those not given the opportunity to punish. This negative feeling did not extend to those who witnessed another punishing a free rider. Thus, it is clear that people do not predict the emotional costs of punishing an offender; they underestimate the degree to which initiating the punishment will make them continue to ruminate about the offender, rather than forget it. This is especially true if they are the one who is permitted to administer the punishment. By implication, those who do not have the opportunity to take revenge psychologically move on and feel happier (Jaffe, 2011). Despite feeling better not avenging a transgressor, the paradox is that people still think they would feel better if they could take revenge (Price, 2009). It is suggested that the reason revenge 'may stoke anger's flames' may be that when we are not able to redress our loss, we may come to terms with it by trivializing the significance of the transgression. Perhaps Milton was more accurate than Nietzsche when he wrote, "Revenge, at first though sweet/ Bitter ere long back on itself recoils" (*Paradise Lost*, Book IX, line 171).

The Interface Between Revenge and Forgiveness

Even though there is some evidence that we may be genetically programmed to seek revenge when we are harmed, not every harmful action results in a revengeful act. How can we understand this? We have offered a variety of explanations in our discussion of culture, individual, and gender differences. McCullough has introduced another sociobiological explanation that can be applied at both the individual and group level (McCullough et al, 2010, 2013). This involves a cost-benefit analysis with each hurtful or insulting act that balances the necessity of revenge for the deterrence of harmful behaviors and the importance of the maintenance of a positive emotional connection with the other. Revenge carries with it certain costs for the avenger and the victim that may include the detrimental effects of distrust, distance, or severing of the relationship. For relationships significant to one's well-being—attachment and affectional bonds, future or current mates—the cost of revenge may be too high. The victim can condone, 'forget,' or deny the transgression, which is harmful to the victim's physical being and/or psychic reality. The victim also can excuse (implying extenuating circumstances) or trivialize the transgressor's offense, which still may involve a distortion of reality. Or the victim can forgive the aggressor. From an evolutionary perspective, forgiveness is a secondary adaptive set of thoughts, feelings and behaviors that serve to restore important relationships (McCullough et al, 2013). As McCullough and colleagues suggest, the revenge response is inhibited after assessing the risk of future harm by the transgressor and the anticipated importance of an ongoing connection with the avenger. Forgiveness involves inhibiting revenge behaviors and engaging in reparation. According to McCullough and colleagues, this involves recognizing the harm, signaling to the aggressor that the victim has been harmed by his or her actions, but despite that is willing to engage in ongoing mutually beneficial interactions if the aggressor will abstain from future damaging behavior. This is becoming a popular notion in psychology and economics. However, forgiveness is an intraspsychic construct which involves no longer feeling intense negative affect toward the aggressor, but rather over time a more positive reaction.

Barry Schwartz (1978), in his paper "Vengeance and Forgiveness: The Uses of Beneficence in Social Control," also sees revenge and forgiveness as centrally linked to social stability. Although forgiveness can take the form of complete refrain from harm to a transgressor, both forgiveness and revenge can be fused into one act whereby a behavior is punished but in a fashion that is measured and retrained. According to Schwartz, this allows the wrongdoer to continue as part of society and milder retribution evolves as a cultural principle. Quakers, with their non-violence platform, take this to an extreme and seem to value transgressors as an opportunity to practice their moral values. This integration highlights how "forgiveness and punishment are intimately linked; the one dramatizes and lends significance to the other. In this sense, punishment stands out as a reaction to a wrong which is not forgiven" (Schwartz, 1978, p. 666).

CONCLUSION

In this chapter, we have illustrated the universal nature of revenge—throughout history and in present-day life. While killing is the most dramatic of revenge responses, there are more subtle ones that take place within the family, between friends, neighbors, co-workers, bosses, etc. We view revenge as a deterrent of harmful behavior serving an evolutionary function. There is accumulating evidence for a biological and genetic basis. This biological response is shaped further by an evolving set of cultural norms. Individual differences are explored. Studies from social psychology suggest that the appropriateness of the revenge response varies depending upon perspective. These observations and studies may contribute to our understanding of the unending conflicts between individuals and cultures.

NOTES

1. Nemesis is described by some as the daughter of Zeus, but others believe that she was the child of Nyx alone.
2. We have said nothing about the New Testament chiefly because we were interested in a broader Judaic–Christian perspective. The New Testament, however, is almost exclusively concerned with containing the wish for revenge by forgiveness.
3. Human Rights Watch defines honor killings as acts of vengeance, most often death. These are committed by male family members against female family members, who are held responsible for bringing dishonor to the family. These can be for a variety of acts such as infidelity, being a victim of rape or sexual assault, requesting a divorce, or even dressing inappropriately (Wikipedia, accessed 6/9/13).
4. Not subservient enough, wanting an advanced education, having non-Muslim friends and boyfriends, wanting to choose a marriage partner.
5. There are some exceptions with Danish, German, and British courts convicting fathers of honor murder. The Canadian government is also informing new immigrants that "Canada's openness and generosity do not extend to barbaric cultural practices that tolerate spousal abuse, 'honor killings,' female genital mutilation or other gender-based violence. Those guilty of these crimes are severely punished under Canada's criminal laws" (Mills, cited in Chesler, 2010).
6. This is used as an example of revenge in an unhealthy romantic relationship. The lifting of their moods was only temporary as their situations had not changed, it did not accomplish the important deterrent function of revenge, and it did not restore their social esteem as they were not able to find a healthy solution for themselves.
7. For instance, the Pushtun Proverb suggests, "Revenge is a dish best served cold," suggesting that the passion and anger accompanying the original offense should have dissipated at the point that revenge is to be enacted. In contrast, Djilas (1958), in describing the Albanian customs of retribution, suggests that "revenge is an overpowering and consuming fire. It flares up and burns away every other thought and emotion."

8. The discussion here is certainly not exhaustive of all the research in this area; for instance, the anterior insula appears to be involved as well, as it functions to consider decisions to restore equity in an unfair situation.

9. Addictive drugs such as cocaine and amphetamines amplify the effects of dopamine.

10. This is loosely translated as 'insistence on truth,' which is a philosophy of non-violent resistance developed by Gandhi.

11. The studies included both questionnaires and a lab study where expression of aggression was measured by the administration of a loud noise blast to a competitor.

12. Sometimes also referred to as 'right-winged authoritarianism' or 'authoritarian personality.'

Chapter Ten

Narcissism, Rage, and Revenge

Concluding Commentary

Henri Parens

The phrases in the title of the symposium on which this book is based, "The Wounded Self: Narcissism, Rage, and Revenge," hang together cogently. But I cannot be sure that we all agree on how exactly narcissism, rage, and revenge are connected with each other. In this volume, detailed reports of the analytic treatment of two children and one adult shed some light on how these human beings became so rage-filled and driven to revenge. "The wounded self" seems to have had everything to do with it. Novick goes directly to the point: revenge is in the service of preserving the self. Freeman tells us that when evolving development hits a wall—I would say a 'parent-built' wall—"crises may lead to deflation, rage, and sometimes impulses toward revenge."

Kernberg focuses on narcissism and takes us to a clear exposition of the complexly different constellations of severe narcissistic pathology, giving us years of experience-acquired insights into the clinical implications of these conditions. Well-established among the premier scholar-clinicians of narcissistic pathology and borderline conditions, Kernberg tells us that patients with these conditions "have been severely traumatized by physical or sexual abuse or gross neglect in their infancy and early childhood." We will find, in turning our attention to the clinical analyses detailed by Novick and Freeman, that, indeed, the psychogenesis of rage and revenge manifest in their patients' fantasies, behaviors, and symptoms has its roots in their having been harshly traumatized, leading to their experiencing severe narcissistic injuries suffered at the hands of their primary caregivers, which forged their "wounded self."

In this chapter, I propose to test yet again with clinical analytic cases other than my own and those I have supervised the applicability of one of the nuclear concepts of the 'multi-trends theory of aggression' to the assemblage of these words: 'narcissism, rage, and revenge.' *The multi-trends theory of aggression* holds that one of its three trends, namely, *hostile aggression/destructiveness*, is generated by (*excessive*) *psychic pain*; formally stated: "Excessive Unpleasure Generates Hostile Destructiveness" (Parens, 1979, p. 111). This early childhood observational data-derived hypothesis, a hypothesis readily replicable, led to my proposing that this explanation of and accounting for destructiveness in humans is provable. From 1979 on, I have emphasized that *psychic pain* gives to aggression the *affective* quality characteristic of dysphoric affects ranging from annoyance to anger, and increasingly *excessive psychic pain* does so for hostility, hate, and rage.

I will not revisit all that went into my proposing the 'multi-trends theory of aggression' (Parens, 1979). Started in September 1970, the project that gave rise to this revision of the psychoanalytic theory of aggression consisted of approximately 1,350 hours of direct anthropological-type observation of a group of ten normal healthy enough mothers (who were not psychiatric patients[1]) and their eventual sixteen newborns. The same mothers and very recently born infants and the psychoanalytically oriented research team met together[2] every Tuesday and Friday morning from 9:00 to 11:00 am, for eleven months of the year, continually over a period of seven years. Results from a nineteen-year (from the actual project starting date) follow-up study were published in 1993, and two later follow-up studies, at thirty-two and at thirty-seven years, are documented in a DVD (Parens, 2008).

I felt on still firmer grounds when I found that the hypothesis 'excessive unpleasure (psychic pain) generates hostile aggression/destructiveness' could be explained by the following biological model that is basic to all living organisms:

> Unpleasure has a somatic root: irritability of the protoplasm. By virtue of the irritability of the protoplasm . . . , the noxious accumulation of tension in the cell (organism) is experienced psychically as unpleasure. This sensory reactivity of live matter . . . , [irritability of the protoplasm,] serves to protect against the destruction of the [organism] and acts primarily to rid the [organism] of [any] noxious [agent]. From the adaptive point of view, it may be said that this experience of pain-unpleasure, on hand since birth, is the first workshop of the hostile destructive trend in aggression which from the outset [is] deflected toward the outside (to rid the organism of noxiae) onto the environment. The somatopsychic force in this ridding activity is aggression. The activity is effected by primary autonomous [ego] functions [and is compelled by the self's] primary narcissism. (Parens, 1979, p. 110)

Let me say one more word regarding what I have called 'excessive unpleasure,' that is, excessive psychic pain. Pain is a biological self-preservative reaction of organic tissue; it signals that something is wrong and that we need to do something about it, lest some part of us, however vital or not, becomes destroyed. But we know that not all pain is equal or equivalent and that we need to distinguish between physical pain and psychic pain. Not all physical pain causes excessive unpleasure; our inborn sensitivities (low or high thresholds) and reactivities (rapid or moderate) and the nature of what causes us pain co-determine what we experience as physical pain, and even more so, whether that physical pain brings with it psychic pain, or excessive psychic pain. If someone inadvertently steps on your foot, it will cause pain; but if he conveys to you that it was an accident, you won't want to slug him! If, on the other hand, that person does it intentionally to nastily make some point with you, you are likely to immediately indeed want to slug him! In the former case, even though you feel physical pain, your narcissism is not injured and you may feel no psychic pain. In the latter, on the contrary, your narcissism is injured and the psychic pain you experience is most likely even greater than the physical pain. It is reasonable that it is so. In brief, the intensity of psychic pain experienced—which is what determines the generation of hostile aggression/destructiveness—is dependent on a number of parameters such as (i) who is causing the pain, (ii) what is causing the pain, (iii) how intense it is, and most critical (iv) what is its meaning to the self, and (v) is it intentional. Psychic pain, inflicted on us by those whom we love, count on for protection and nurture, is much greater than being abused at the hands of a bully or an enemy.

I have found support for the multi-trend theory concept that excessive psychic pain is what generates hostile destructiveness during many years of clinical analytic work with children and adults. During this symposium, we heard about three cases reported by two experienced child analytic clinicians who tell us that their patients from early on in life experienced much rage and were bent on revenge. Does the concept that excessive psychic pain generates hostile destructiveness in humans hold up for these cases?

THE CLINICAL CASES

Ali

In "Green Wounds," Kerry Kelly Novick sensitively details the analysis of ten-year-old Ali, who, she found, turned "himself into a weapon of destruction in order both to create and protect a sense of self, and revenge himself on his parents for their impossible [and therewith narcissism-injuring] demands." Novick proposes, from what she learned working analytically with Ali and also working weekly psychodynamically with each or both of his parents, that the parents' expectations and blindness to Ali's developmental needs and his individual experiencing of them threatened the integrity of his evolving sense of self and healthy primary narcissism. On the basis of much work with both the child and his parents, Novick found clinical evidence that, despite their very real concerns and love for their son, their parenting was "an assault on [his] core identity [which evoked] deep fears of annihilation, obliteration, non-being." Ali had, Novick says, "no choice but to find some way, any way, to survive, to retain agency and existential identity." And she asserts that "deep and intense rage in reaction to the assault on" Ali self-fueled in him efforts to find a solution.

Here Kerry Novick comes close to Rocklin's (1973) proposition that aggression is elicited by a perceived attack on the self; that is, the threat of narcissistic injury rouses aggression. She tells us that "one solution [for Ali was] the . . . construction of a sadomasochistic character organized around omnipotent beliefs in the right and power to exact revenge from those responsible for rendering [him] helpless. . . . [These individuals hold to] the litany and justification for sadism, envy, vindictiveness, selfishness, lack of empathy, and all the other nasty qualities of those obsessed with the need and desire for revenge." In achieving his revenge, Novick tells us that Ali seemed to take "the initiative in avenging [himself against his parents,] attempts at soul murder by developing . . . his neurotic symptoms and character pathology. For Ali, these were his desperate efforts to preserve his very self. [And these efforts had] the hallmark qualities of rage, resentment, vindictiveness, and meanness that signal . . . revenge motives."

In her work with his parents, Novick learned that Ali's parents had themselves been painfully traumatized. His mother had been raped as an adolescent, which resulted in her aversion to males that led to her wishing her son had been born a girl (more on this below) and with Mother's having serious difficulties with both her son and her husband. Ali's father felt deeply pained and enraged by his own parents' neglecting him; he felt marginalized by them as they favored his older brother, who eventually, in Novick's words, turned out to be a 'deadbeat.' Surely, Ali's significantly traumatizing first decade of life experienced at the hands of his own traumatized parents constituted a severe narcissistic injury which generated in him intense feelings of hostile destructiveness, indeed, of rage, that in turn elicited in him wishes for revenge.

Chris

In "As the Twig Is Bent, So Grows the Tree," Dan Freeman tells us that for the first six months of life, Chris had been idolized by his mother, who thought he was the 'perfect child.' At about that time, because Father's physician believed Father suffered stress-related cardiovascular symptoms, he recommended that Father take a therapeutic vacation. Mother and Father left Chris and his six-year-old sister for one week with resentful, unempathic grandparents. When the parents returned, not recognizing them, six-month-old Chris did not welcome them back. Failing to understand the dynamics operative in her son's failure to welcome their return, his mother felt rejected and narcissistically injured by it; in silent rage, she totally withdrew from him. Emotionally abandoned by his heretofore adoring mother, what promised to evolve into a blissful symbiosis with emerging good basic trust and their evolution into libidinal object constancy was abruptly disrupted and derailed. Fortunately for Chris, his father seemed to not have felt rejected by his son's puzzling reserve on reunion, maintained a loving relationship with his son, making himself emotionally available to Chris when present therewith, making it possible for Chris to develop, as Freeman proposes, images of a caregiving, 'partial-object-father,' images which refueled Chris imaginatively in transitional fantasy—in the blur of the often played spinning game. With his father's emotional investment in him, Chris achieved a degree of partial 'paternal-object' constancy. Freeman further notes that biting his blanket, spitting, and banging his head during the 'game' channeled Chris's rage and impulses toward revenge aimed at his rejecting 'dead mother,' who always was in the background.

Remarkably, Chris creatively devised strategies for coping with the severe trauma he experienced at the sudden rejection by his previously idolizing mother. The narcissistic injury he experienced was enormous. The good mother had become the hurtful-rejecting bad mother. Chris's rage reactive to, in fact I have proposed *generated by,* the narcissistic injury his mother inflicted on him, and the wishes and fantasies of revenge that devolved from it, challenged his young self and ego and led to the struggle within him, as Freeman tells us, to mediate the highly conflicting feelings of intense ambivalence toward her. Unable to mediate *his rage toward* and *his need for* the good mother to whom his attachment had gotten under way, Freeman holds that Chris used splitting of the good and bad mother for years to come, complementary to which he developed a split in his self-representation, a good and a bad self.

From the time the trauma was inflicted on him, Chris labored day in and day out, painfully, even violently, to mediate his rage toward his rejecting, "zombified dead mother" and his need for the good mother of infancy; this struggle was also experienced by Chris with regard to his own good-and-bad self. Chris's imagination, creativity, cleverness, impressive persistence all readily revealed his resilience as he grew from six months to ten years of age, when Freeman began to see him. In the course of his work with him, Freeman saw a rich display of Chris's creative efforts as he labored to cope with his internal conflicts due to ambivalence at all levels of development, all preeminently influenced, in fact shaped by, his long struggle to mediate his rage and wishes for revenge against the bad mother, a therapeutic process made possible by the object constancy derived from his father, which was then substantially furthered via the transference during his analysis. Freeman's report also highlights the striking commitment Chris made to working on integrating his split self, enacting the central persisting conflict between his good and bad self, cleverly assigning the role of bad self alternately at times to his dummy, William, and at other times to himself. The struggles between his split self, Chris and William, evolved, and in time, with remarkable sublimation-bound analytic work and, again, his able use of the transference to his analyst, Chris progressively integrated his split-off selves. His self-analytic process of writing his novelette, with its many working-through versions, again revealed his capacity for sublimation and therewith his resilience. I cannot but wonder how much pain and agony he might have been spared had his parents brought Chris to see Freeman, and Ali's parents had brought him to Novick much earlier than at ten years of age.

Ruth

Twenty-some-year-old Ruth sought treatment because she had feelings of rage and impulses to get revenge which she experienced as dystonic, a fact that bode positively for her treatment outcome. As with Ali and Chris, Ruth has a narrative of hefty traumatization, coming from her own inborn diatheses as well as at the hands of her mother, especially so when, at age two, her father was drafted into then-compulsory military service.

Ruth had the misfortune of starting life with infantile atopic eczema, an inborn allergy-based condition[3] that leads to that well-known torture, intense itching, that reactively compels scratching, which, when too vigorous and ruptures the skin, may in turn cause further nagging pain; all in all, it makes an infant feel miserable. To get an infant with eczema to stop scratching is beyond the infant's ability to contain this itching-induced reflexive impulse. But the naïve strategy of tying the infant's hands down, as Ruth's parents did in order to prevent her scratching, compounds the infant's helplessness in the face of unbearable itching. The cumulative effect of unbearable itching and enforced helplessness to reduce it intensifies the excessive pain that comes with the eczema itself.[4] Of itself, the degree of *physical pain* inflicted by the infant's own body most likely brings with it some *psychic pain*; but the enforced helplessness effected by the 'outside' (not by the infant's own body) I assume brings with it even more intense *psychic pain*.

We now know that the infant's perception of the caregivers' libidinal and affect-motor handling of the misery-burdened infant is well registered over time by the infant and recorded in its midbrain (amygdala and hippocampus). Confirming Kernberg's proposition that 'self-object-affect' events are experiential psychic building blocks (1966), observing infants, Stern hypothesized that repetitive everyday events, as well as especially painful events, are recorded in the infant's psyche and become patterned expectation and reactivity; he spoke of these as "Representations of Interactions that have been Generalized (RIGs)" (Stern, 1985, p. 97). Even before frontal cortex connections to the midbrain activate the integration of affective experience and its ideation (Kagan and Herschkowitz, 2005), the affective self-object event is perceived and reacted to emotionally and behaviorally by the infant.

The average psychologically sensitive observer of infants will be able to readily infer the qualitative character of the infant's reactive experience to the caregiving efforts. In this, then, one can infer the infant's perception that the object is sympathetically trying to make the infant feel better, or the object is not. I am speaking of no more than that nigh-magical TLC,[5] a key component of what Mahler coined 'libidinal emotional availability.' Even when the emotionally available caregiver cannot make the pain or the itching go away, TLC makes the infant 'feel better.' This is well-illustrated in, say, a four-year-old who has an earache and painfully complains to Mother that it hurts. The emotionally available mother will affectively and motorically make efforts to make the child feel better—and many a child stops crying and, indeed, gives the impression of feeling better. The pain is still there; but the child-object affective experience seems to help the young child bear the pain better. To the question, At what point in infantile brain functioning can such a mother-child interaction have its miraculous effect? infant observers will uniformly say from birth on.

We are led to understand that not only was Ruth *not* tended to empathically by her emotionally not-available mother but that, in addition, the enforced helplessness (her hands being tied down) to getting even momentary relief by scratching multiplied Ruth's experience of being tortured. Cumulatively, the *psychic pain* Ruth experienced was large. It may be that Ruth's parents were not able to tolerate the demands for help their infant made and, at wits end to soothe the baby, and/or narcissistically self-consumed as Ruth's mother seemed to be, Mother experienced her baby as an obnoxious irritant; she failed to grasp that Ruth was in distress and pleading for comforting, and the anger the distressed baby's behavior roused in her led Mother to withdraw, if not actually attack her baby. This reaction on the part of her mother was later affirmed by Ruth (see below).

Compounding these torturous beginnings, Ruth reported that when she was two years old, she had a series of surgical procedures to attempt to reduce her congenital right eye strabismus. At a time when separation from libidinal objects—however ambivalent the attachments—and familial surroundings are again heightened, that is, during the rapprochement subphase of separation-individuation (Mahler et al, 1975), Ruth, experiencing intense separation anxiety and, as Freeman says, feeling abandoned, was again subjected post-surgery to having her arms restrained to prevent her from touching her bandaged eyes. As she no doubt did in infancy, Ruth struggled against the restraints. Freeman tells us that Ruth "had . . . a 'half-crazed feeling' of panic as she awoke, remembered wanting to bite the men who were bandaging her eyes, and wanting to take revenge on her mother for having left her." Furthermore, in rage, "she would move her eyes about violently inside the bandages." Fighting those who had tried to rebalance her eye muscles, masochistically, perhaps in regressed 'organismic' distress (Spitz, 1965), she directed the rage against herself and destroyed the efforts to help her. Her rage was almost universally discharged; her affect flat, she wanted only to "go home to her pet dog!" She wanted everyone around her to "get away from me! [declaring,] I hate you all!" Libidinal objects so hated, Freeman tells us that "she did not attain libidinal self- and object- constancy."

Living during that era with maternal grandparents because her father was then serving in the military, Ruth's separation anxiety intensified by her highly ambivalent attachments, she resisted intensely the separation that comes with going to bed. She felt desperately the need to be with people and her grandfather was the one who responded to her pleas and would 'rescue' her by taking her out of her crib and trying to comfort her. At one point, Freeman tells us, her unmoved "conscientious 'tiger mom'" gave Ruth a "Sears mail-order catalogue to rip up in the crib, saying, 'Spare me your RAGE!'" Do we not construe from this 'caregiving' and this remark the height of maternal sadism? Given such sadism on the part of one's mother or father, but mothers perhaps even more so, the psychic pain experienced by the child is enormous. Many a child would rather get beaten than be so emotionally maltreated by Mother! It compels my observing again the problem that while physical abuse is duly recognized to have the potential of being harmful, not enough attention is given to the fact that *emotional abuse* at the hands of one's parents or by teachers can in fact be equally if not more harmful (Parens et al, 1995). I need not elaborate further on Ruth's traumatizing early development.

How Do Narcissism, Rage, and Revenge Hang Together?

The characters in all three cases suffered much psychic pain at the hands of their caregivers. Surely, born a normal infant, Ali's traumatizing first decade of life, given that it was at the hands of his own very troubled parents, was experienced by him as a severe narcissistic injury. The clinical evidence documents that this generated in him intense feelings of rage that elicited intense pressure for revenge. Novick believes that his solution to this state of experiencing was to develop a sadomasochistic character formation which contributed to his serious neurotic symptoms and seriously jeopardized relationships.

Chris, the 'perfect child,' was shockingly traumatized at six months of age in his sudden fall from being idolized by his mother, who, narcissistically injured by his not welcoming her home, abruptly turned away from him emotionally, abandoning him at the height of his symbiotic phase. We learn that he exerted much of his adaptive energies in coping with the rage he experienced and the intrapsychic and relationship conflicts it created, and that even into his analysis early in his teen years, he struggled to manage his rage toward both his bad mother and his bad self. While he dealt with this load of rage better than did Ali or Ruth, using remarkably creative strategies to do so, we are left with little question that his trauma was experienced as a severe narcissistic injury which unleashed his rage and intense pressure to act on it.

Surely, in the case of Ruth, her somatic diatheses led her to experience much physical distress and would have been taxing on any infant and her caregivers to moderate. Rather than being comforted, her misery was further intensified when her hands were tied down. Then at two years of age, her mother's sadism peaked when following unsuccessful eye surgery after which her hands were, again, tied down, Ruth experienced this assault on herself as directed by her sadistic, emotionally depriving mother. Her much accumulated rage and strivings for revenge governed her life well into her analytic experience.

I am emphasizing the genesis of the generation of hostile destructiveness in these cases as explained by the multi-trends theory of aggression. The explanation put forward by this model of aggression is, of course, not the preferred explanation among all of us. Kernberg, who agrees that these patients, like those who in adulthood suffer from borderline and malignant narcissism disorders, "have been severely traumatized . . . in their infancy or early childhood," turns rather to the explanation given us by Freud's second drive theory, which holds the duality of libido and aggression as devolving from *the life instincts and the death instincts* (Freud, 1920a, 1930), the 'death instincts' being the basis for Freud's theory of aggression. As I wrote in a 1979 review of Freud's evolving instinctual drive theories,

> While Freud had only tentatively [indeed, with trepidation and declared uncertainty] put forward the [hypothesis that the] death instinct [is the source of human destructiveness] in 1920, by 1930, despite the resistance met with "even in analytic circles," he noted that the death instinct had "*gained such a hold on me that I can no longer think in any other way.*" (1930, p. 119) (Parens, 1979, p. 55; italics added here)

Freud repeated this just italicized phrase in 1937 in a letter he then wrote to Marie Bonaparte. I have elsewhere raised some questions about these two models of aggression, which I revisit very briefly here.

Several Questions About These Two Theories of Aggression

Does the death instinct model of aggression hold up more than ninety years after its initial publication (Parens, 2011a)? Given that I do not challenge trivially anything Freud wrote, I have also asked if the multi-trends theory of aggression holds up since I put it forward forty years ago (Parens, 1973). Two further questions follow from these:

(i) Can we document directly by replicable observation evidence of aggression being driven by a death instinct? Similarly, can we document directly by replicable observation evidence for the multi-trends model of aggression? If we cannot and only inference informs us, is the evidence sufficiently convincing so as to make its refutation very difficult? And

(ii) Since both are 'working models,' what is the heuristic value of each?

In answering the first question, can we document evidence, directly or strongly inferably, that our patients' destructiveness is fueled by a death instinct, that is, by an organic self-destructive tendency that is turned outwardly? When in the transference, we are the object of our patient's hostility, so is it our tendency to ascribe it to a death instinct derived aggression? Are we not likely to look for an underlying past 'self-object-affect' *experience,* an experiential 'schema' (Slap and Slap-Shelton, 1991) externalized into the transference that gave rise to this hostility? My clinical experience and, for long now, my inclination is to look for one or more past experiential sources responsible for and determining of the patient's currently experienced hostility toward me, the object of his or her transference.

What would generate such past experiences? If we assume an inner pressure that derives from a death instinct, how would we explain that? When I ask, "Does the assumption advanced by some psychoanalysts hold up that infants come into the world driven to attack the object?" I assert that I have not seen evidence in support of that assumption. *Caution:* infants who give evidence of an outright pain-inducing diathesis (like asthma, or as was the case for infant Ruth who suffered from atopic eczema) or pain from a somatic immaturity (such as an esophageal atresia, or even just plain colic) or due to some in utero toxicity (as found in mothers who drank much alcohol or used addictive drugs during pregnancy) or yet some other organic disorder that causes pain, such infants may seem to spontaneously become angry, cry, and even scream. But I submit that these infants experience substantial physical distress and/or pain which then unavoidably brings with it much psychic pain. Given such a discernible, readily replicable biological source for their distress, of their experiencing excessive unpleasure, I hold that it would be a psychobiological non sequitur and an error to assume that it might/must arise from a death instinct derivative.

Efforts have been made to document robust evidence in support of the hypothesis that a death instinct operates in us, but none to date has held up.

Some have invoked phenomena such as neonatal 'cell death' and the rare dramatic medical disorder progeria as proof of a self-destructive tendency in living organisms. Accepted explanations for each of these phenomena do not support the hypothesis of a self-destructive instinctual or organic drive to return to an inorganic state. 'Cell death' has been explained[6] to be a normal neonatal phenomenon believed to serve to reduce overcrowding of neurons to optimize space for the formation of specific neural pathways. One source of evidence for this explanation is that a stained cervical ganglion of a just newborn rabbit[7] is all black! Such a ganglion stained several days after birth is no longer all black; it is a patch of black networks of strands in a whitish field. The evidence for progeria is far less clear. It is an insufficiently understood acceleration of aging; attempts to document the play of a death instinct in this disorder have proven as challenging and unattainable as it is to ascertain it in the psychoanalytic situation.

To the question of documentation, I say that we can amply observe and replicate the fact that when an infant experiences unpleasure, there is a good chance that if the unpleasure mounts, at first anger and gradually hostility of greater intensity will become evident. As I briefly detailed in the introduction, excessive psychic pain generates this hostility; and I proposed a biological model for it that can be demonstrated. Many analysts and researchers in adjacent fields relevant to psychoanalytic questions have reported explanations consonant with the multi-trends theory explanation for the generation of hostility in humans (Parens, 1979 [2008, Intro., chaps. 2 and 3]).

I am confident that the component of the multi-trends theory of aggression that details the nature of hostility in humans has merit and can be documented and replicated. I do not have the same confidence in the explanation that a death instinct within us, countered by our life instincts, compels us to externalize our aggression (hostility) onto others. We cannot prove that we have a death instinct and we cannot disprove it. I, therefore, can no more accept the death instinct theory of aggression than I can discard it.

This leaves me to ask: What is the heuristic value of each theory (Parens, 2011a)?

1. It is warranted that we reconsider Freud's (1932) answer to Einstein's question "Why war?" Freud held that war is inescapable given man's inborn death-instinct-based need to self-destroy, which self-preservatively is diverted toward the outside. I find it problematic that when Freud spoke of human aggression, he did not consider the most widespread trend in aggression, namely *prey aggression,* what I have spoken of as 'non-affective destructiveness' (Parens, 1979 [2008]). Doing so, I intend therewith to point out that this type of destructiveness is not driven by hostility but by the biological self-preservative need to supply our body with alimentation. The lioness that chases an antelope is not angry with it; rather the lioness likes the antelope; it's exactly what she and those dependent on her need for dinner! But ignoring

> 'prey aggression' is not the most problematic factor with the death-instinct-based theory of aggression.

More important is that it has given the stamp of inevitability to the question of war. Let me quickly emphasize, as I wrote elsewhere, that "Freud is not totally pessimistic. His reasoning leads him to ask [Einstein], 'Why do you and I and so many other people rebel so violently against war? . . . After all, it seems to be quite a natural thing, to have a good biological basis and in practice to be scarcely avoidable' (Freud, 1932, p. 213). Now then, it is justified! But [I asked,] is it? Freud then puts forward the critical and meritorious argument which I noted earlier that H. Kilian and I, independently, have subsequently made, that 'For incalculable ages mankind has been passing through *a process of evolution of cultures . . . (i.e., 'civilization'). . . .*[8] Now war is in the crassest opposition to the psychical attitude imposed on us by the process of civilization, and for that reason we are bound to rebel against it [also on p. 213]. . . . This is not merely an intellectual and emotional repudiation; we pacifists have a *constitutional* intolerance of war. . . . [And] one thing we *can* say: whatever fosters the growth of civilization works at the same time against war' (pp. 214–215)" (Parens 2013a, chap. 1; 2013b). Freud saw our progressively evolving into yet more civilized human beings. But was his uncertain theorizing about the unavoidability of war right? I have come to believe that it was not. Nonetheless, his hypothetical explanation for it has gained some favor in society.

At a roundtable on aggression and genocide,[9] held at the New York Psychoanalytic Institute's Philoctetes Center, the opinion was voiced by a prominent personage who was present that humans are inherently driven to destroy; all we need do to document this, he opined—as have others before—is to look around at all the destructiveness around us. How, asked this thoughtful person challenging my having put forward the multi-trends theory of aggression, can excessive unpleasure experiences and the generation of hostile destructiveness to which you say it leads explain why we have wars? Well, I asked, how much does life bring with it experiences of excessive unpleasure, be they experienced individually or in social groups due to abuse (e.g., bullying or malignant prejudice), neglect (be it in child care or in minority sectors of society), narcissistic injury (including especially that brought about by shaming at home, in school, in society), joblessness, intentional destruction by another of one's possessions (be it individually or as is only too frequently done in genocide), etc.? How much of this is there? I put forward one example: according to a fairly recent study, "An estimated 40 million children globally under the age of fifteen suffer from violence, abuse, and neglect, said UNICEF, [according to a UN-sponsored study led by Paulo S. Pinheiro, in what is deemed to be] the first detailed look at how children experience violence all over the world, and what must be done to prevent and end the scourge" (Pinheiro, 2005). I hold that large prevention strategies will be much more readily considered feasible if we know that the cause of much of human hostility is the product of experiences that can be prevented or at least mitigated than if we assume that all over the world children's death instinct must be tamed!

2. In considering the heuristic value of the multi-trends theory of aggression, assuming that wars are triggered by experiences of excessive psychic pain rather than by a death instinct, we bring a very different set of propositions to the question "Why war?" Challenged by my self-imposed application of this question to the multi-trends theory of aggression, I am currently laboring to address how, in fact, in the history of civilization, cultures, societies, and nations, for multifaceted reasons—historical, ethnic, religious, political, economic, and philosophic—we have come to visit upon each other the sequentially causative dynamics of narcissism, rage, and revenge (Parens 2013a, chaps. 3–8). Without going into detail here, I have found the application of the hypothesis that excessive unpleasure generates hostile destructiveness is as applicable to large groups as it is to individuals. Freud's observations on the "narcissism of minor differences" (1930, p. 114) plays its due part, not, I believe, under the sway of the obligatory nature of finding an external object onto whom to discharge one's psychobiologically generated need to destroy (death instinct); rather, it is by virtue of reciprocal injuries visited upon each other in consequence of historic-cultural narratives of narcissistic injury and revenge. That is, simplifying matters and recognizing that there is pattern variability, past 'X-group's hyper-narcissism has led it in one way or another to narcissistically injure Y-group, which often, in time, has in turn led to a reconstruction/re-inflation of Y-group's (hyper)-narcissism which then took on the challenge of causing X-group a revenge-based narcissistic injury,' a cycle that has often over time repeated itself among X and Y neighboring groups (see section below, Reflections on the Two Invited Chapters). For example, the wars in Europe and beyond of the past several centuries amply document such a psychodynamic cyclicity (Parens, 2013a, chap. 4).

But coming back to this chapter's concern, the newborn's dysphoric experiences and behaviors, a critical determination follows from understanding that hostility-laden behaviors are driven by a death instinct versus that they are the by-product of excessive unpleasure experiences. What follows in the attitude of the caregiver toward the baby from the assumption that this baby is endowed with a heavy dose of death-instinct-based aggression is vastly different than when the caregiver recognizes that it is rather much psychic pain and distress that is being revealed by the baby's crying, flailing, or even screaming (for help)! I believe that assuming it is death-instinct-generated aggression may be, and in fact has been found to be, harmful for the baby's future mental health and life. For example, the overburdened mother, who, not inclined to react sympathetically and comfort her infant who is crying and flailing, may tell you, "It's the evil in him" and angrily tell him, "Stop crying or else!"—whereby she intensifies his psychic pain and generates in him more hostility toward her while she also raises her own level of hostility toward her own child. Whereas, in fact, I have seen mothers react in growth-promoting ways when their baby is crying and flailing, and the mother assumes that he is hurting—such as by sympathetically trying to guess and search for, even ask the infant, "what's wrong?"—all the while comforting and setting herself the task of fixing whatever it is. And often, such mothers do succeed in 'fixing it.' This consideration alone, and there are others, makes the heuristic value of the death-instinct-based theory of aggression highly doubtful! I should say in passing here that the assumption of a normal paranoid-schizoid position based on the assumption of the death instinct theory of aggression which leads the young child by externalizing his inborn destructiveness to want to destroy the mother is an equally highly problematic and unprovable assumption.

Further Thoughts Elicited by Clinical Findings Reported in This Volume

In our field, we do not all agree on what takes place psychologically in the infantile psyche during the first twenty-four months of life. Ego psychologists and Kleinians, for instance, conceptualize early psychological development very differently; and for complex conscious and unconscious reasons we each choose which concepts make most sense to us, that is, which 'we believe in.' This variance in conceptualization is unavoidable given that psychoanalytic findings and explanations are foremost based on subjective interpretations of what we infer in the clinical situation; objectivity, certainty, and proof are only too often unattainable. This, in fact, is what led Hartmann (1950b), Kris (1950), and Anna Freud (1958), independently, to urge that when it comes to psychoanalytic conceptualizations of post-natal psychological development, at a time when infants cannot confirm or reject our subjective grasp of their experiencing, we should attempt *by means of direct observation of very young children* to test our hypotheses about what we can best discern and infer may be taking place in their heads. I can assert from years of observing infants and young children that while we can make inferences about what they may be experiencing by virtue of their affective and motoric behaviors, we cannot get infants to corroborate *verbally* what we infer is going on in their minds when they fuss and cry or when they seem satisfied with life!

About Splitting

Considering Chris's plight, Freeman tells us that he used splitting as a principal defense in coping with his intense ambivalence toward his love-objects.

One wonders—did he do so from the time his mother withdrew from him, causing him intense narcissistic injury? As I considered elsewhere (Parens, 2011b, p. 31), Klein, Mahler, and Kernberg all seemed to propose that splitting is a primary, inborn state of adaptive functioning in early life. We now understand better that it is reasonable to assume that good experiences and bad experiences are mediated and catalogued in separate neural/brain networks. For example, in discussing[10] 'affective' in contrast to 'predatory aggression,' neurologist Reis

> advanced the view that various biochemical compounds "believed to function in the central and peripheral nervous system as neurotransmitters may serve to modulate the expression of aggressive behaviors. These agents . . . norepinephrine, dopamine, serotonin and acetylcholine . . . are synthesized, stored, and released *by specific and discrete neural systems* . . . [and they may then mediate] *two neurologically* distinct classes of aggression: *affective and predatory aggression*." (Reis, 1973, p. 1) (Parens 1979, pp. 113–114, italics added)

Can we similarly assume that the separate cataloguing of bioaffective experiences which might be considered by some to be a form of 'primary splitting' might, rather, occur because different neural pathways mediate each type of feeling? That is, we know, for example, that from birth on, there are different receptors in the skin for pain and touch. Would we be off the mark if we assume that these receptors belong to different dedicated nerve fibers that carry each category of experience to a specific dedicated locus in the brain? Might not the experience of psychic pain and of pleasure also seem 'split' but that this is, in fact, due to these experiences being mediated by different neural pathways and systems? Thinking of young Chris's traumatizing pain, should we consider his reaction to it, his struggle to cope with the polarity of feelings it generated to be 'primary splitting'? Would we think of it as a primary defense or some other kind of primary phenomenon?

The same question can be posited with regard to the concept of 'primary repression.' This question may be easier to address. Pain, as a biological signal that attention must be given to a part of the self that is being threatened or is in fact being injured, reflexively activates reactions necessary to stop the injurious process from progressing. This reactivity is biological; it is best illustrated in the 'fight or flight' reaction in the face of threat to life (Cannon, 1928). But we know that while connections between the midbrain and frontal cortex are believed to occur from about twenty-four months, sufficient cortex functioning exists at birth to make conditioned learning possible, which is demonstrable at birth (Kagan and Herschkowitz, 2005). In fact, Kagan and Herschkowitz discuss the fact that fetal conditioning has been repeatedly demonstrated. Might we not then assume that if the pain persists despite reflexive efforts to stop it, might 'primary autonomous ego apparatuses,' which Hartmann (1939) proposed are inborn, be activated to protect the predominantly midbrain-functioning newborn—that is, the newborn child with very limited input from a sufficiently cognition-operative frontal cortex (Kagan and Herschkowitz, 2005)? Let's bear in mind that many species of the animal kingdom—so-to-speak species 'below' Mammalia—operate with minimal cerebral cortex; yet with little or no frontal cortex to think with, these species have survived for who knows how long. Might pain at times post-birth be so intense that it might induce an automatic reactive disconnect between the pain and primitive perceptual conscious system, thereby effecting a form of 'primary repression'? Can we similarly invoke such activity for 'primary splitting'? While I say 'yes' to 'primary repression,' I cannot be so sure about 'primary splitting,' because I think splitting is a more complex function than a reactive biological reflex-self-protective-'not feeling,' despite the dangers this reaction might allow. I am inclined to assign splitting as a psychic defense that requires action by a functioning psychological agency beyond primary autonomous ego functions.

I hold, following Freud (1923) and Hartmann (1939, 1950a), that the ego, that agency of the self's psyche responsible for adaptation, has the task of integrating experiences perceived as bad or good. Splitting, erected by the ego due to the anxiety produced by rage feelings and destructive wishes toward love-objects which it cannot mediate, is a defense, a secondary, acquired psychic function (Parens, 2011b, p. 31). This is in contrast to the assumption of 'primary splitting' put forward by Kleinian theory which follows from the conviction that we are born with a self-destructive (death) instinct. If we do not accept the hypothetical assumption of a death instinct, then the hypothesis that there is a biological-level 'primary splitting' becomes more difficult to accept as well.

About the Emerging Self

But this question can be taken up in the context of the proposition that in early life, given that painful ('bad') and non-painful sensory experiences (including 'good') are channeled by different neural systems, there may be an un-integrated state of early life affective and adaptive experiencing, which in fact was proposed by Glover (1947). He held that these different categories of experiencing lead to a structuring of 'ego nuclei.'[11] Interestingly, Glover's model has not been given much attention; it seems to have faded, as has the concept of part-objects. But perhaps we have not paid enough attention to Glover's idea; indeed, some have ignored it.

Stern (1985), for instance, argued for a primordially integrated 'self' from birth on. While Mahler was not explicit on the question of a primordial self (see below), her view and Stern's on the very beginnings of extra-uterine life were not in accord. But their disagreement lay more explicitly around Mahler's concept of a 'symbiotic phase.' Mahler proposed that from about eight weeks to ten or so months, self and object are emotionally experienced by the infant as one, experienced as if within a 'symbiotic membrane,' an intrapsychic representation I conceptualized as "a fused construct of vaguely delineated actual self and actual object, experienced as 'self' libidinally, thus: 'I–not-I'" (Parens, 1971, p. 104).[12] It is with this that Stern and also attachment theorists each for their own reasons rejected the concept of 'symbiosis.' When soon after emerging from the 'symbiotic phase,' the 'practicing subphase' child easily separates from the mother in order to more or less energetically explore his immediate universe, due to progressively developing reality testing at about eighteen months this free-to-explore toddler rather suddenly re-experiences a heightening of separation anxiety whereby it initiates the phase of 'rapprochement,' a renewed compelled hanging on to the mother. Not finding evidence in support of Mahler's conceptualization of separation-individuation, Lyons-Ruth (1991) wondered whether this 'rapprochement' is rather an 'approchement' due to better reality-testing-based heightening of separation anxiety that resurges.

One more word on my experience of what Mahler and colleagues thought and discussed many times regarding Mahler's views on the emerging 'self.' While in her formal presentation of separation-individuation theory, Mahler had proposed that in his earliest post-natal development, the infant is in a "normal autistic phase" (Mahler et al, 1975), at urgings by Anne-Marie Weil, Marjorie Harley, and H. Parens, in later years Mahler abandoned the term although she did not write a revision of the first phase of separation-individuation theory to account for it. The urgings by Mahler's colleagues were based on the concern that Mahler had adopted a term that derived from her earlier work on autistic and symbiotic childhood psychosis (Mahler, 1952; Mahler and Gosliner, 1955) and carried what we felt was the erroneous notion that the normal infant is in a state of introversion and withdrawal vis-à-vis the object environment.[13] On the basis of Spitz's (1965) observations (reported in the final integration of his studies on 'the structuring of the libidinal object') as well as what I found in my studies, I suggested to Mahler in personal communications that holding to Freud's concept that the infant is in a 'primary narcissistic state' would be closer to what is readily observable, because we saw much evidence of the infant being intently interactionally engaged with the caregiver from the first days of life. Many times, while being fed, we saw days-old infants stare persistently at their mother's "forehead-eyes-nose . . . configuration. . . . The sign Gestalt [which] centers around the eyes . . . which triggers the infant's smiling response"[14] (Spitz, 1965, p. 94). For example, I filmed a ten-day-old child staring uninterruptedly for a good ten minutes at his mother's 'forehead-eyes-nose' while she was feeding him.

It is a murky era, this developmental time period from birth to about twenty-four months, when neuropsychology tells us connections begin to develop between the frontal cortex and midbrain areas that record affective experience. Affective experience then becomes ideated and given declarative meaning. The two-year-old can tell you what she is experiencing. And what they can say is at times eye-opening! But at the same time, there is much evidence that in addition to conditioning learning, observable primitive cognitive processes are at play before age two years. For instance, Spitz (1965) described the process from about six or so weeks, when the social smiling response emerges and the structuring of the libidinal object gets under way eventuating at about six to eight months in the specification of the libidinal object, which, we assume, yields an 'internal representation' which the child can predictably recognize. With regard to aggression, I have said that the dysphoric affect, anger, begins to be evident from about six months, when in reaction to psychic pain experienced at the hands of her mother, the young child shows clear evidence of being angry or hostile toward the mother (Parens, 1991). By eleven to twelve months, the child's understanding that her anger or hostility can create very real problems with her mother compels the child to erect psychic defenses, such as the earliest and most readily observable in behavior *displacement* and *inhibition,* which are soon followed by observable behaviors manifesting *denial, object splitting*, and *externalization,* with readily inferable *projection* ("He doesn't like me"); more complex reality-distorting defenses begin to be observable in behavior from about five years of age on (Parens, 1979, chaps. 7 and 8; Parens, 2007b, pp. 93–95).

And, in further evidence that preverbal cognition emerges from (perhaps even less than) six to twelve months, I was stunned by a totally different observation. After an ashtray spill—yes, some mothers smoked in that day—one of our project mothers spontaneously said to her twelve-month-old son, "Get me a broom." Moments later, having gone to the closet where we kept the toy cart and casual cleaning equipment, he came to her with a broom! He could hardly speak a word, but he seemed to have understood not only her use of the word 'broom' but also what she intended to do with it!

I think we should not be unconditionally wed to our models of early development; while we do have preferences, we still need more data and further refining of our concepts to claim certainty for any of them. I, for one, am among those amazed by the enormous psychological importance of what happens between birth and two years along the spectrum of emotional (affect-cognitive) experiences and what gets laid down by them. In psychoanalysis, we have long recognized the first six years of life as formative of basic psychological development. But the tendency among too many of us is to ascribe greater importance to the latter part of that period. Infant and toddler observation and clinical work with mother-infant dyads reveals that it is a mistake to continue to do so; the earlier years have to be given their due balance of importance as well.

In attempting to conceptualize young children's experience, following Hartmann (1939, 1950a), I assume that ego functioning capable of integrating self-object experiences of pain (bad self-object) with experiences of gratification (good self-object) as Freeman tells us occurred in Chris—each experience in turn being a 'self-object-affect' building block (Kernberg, 1966) of psychic structuring—such integration, I believe, does not yet occur during the first six or so months of life. Hartmann's model of psychic structural development proposes that the ego's ability to erect psychic defenses such as splitting would perhaps emerge around the time that Chris suffered the traumatizing libidinal abandonment by his mother.

Attempting to ascertain the effects on Chris of the trauma he endured and how he coped with it, here again, hypotheses are at variance. My own observational research leads me to propose the following. With regard to the status of a neonatal 'self,' I am inclined to integrate a confluence of Freud's primary narcissistic state with Stern's idea of a primordial self that evolves during the period of the structuring of the libidinal object (Spitz, 1965) into an emotionally perceived symbiotic state of oneness with that object from which, then, the young child evolves through a separation-individuation process into the development of recognized separate entities of self and object bound by a libidinal relationship (Mahler) that, as Freud proposed, by "the *fixation* of libido to particular objects . . . often persists throughout life" (Freud, 1939, p. 151). With regard to early ego functioning, I lean on the model proposed by Hartmann (1950a). And this takes me again to Dr. Freeman's Chris.

The Play of Experience on Inborn Endowment

Freeman proposes that Chris was healing the split of good and bad self and object. I am wondering if, given that splitting is a decisive defense mechanism which Kernberg (1975) has guided us to understand is central to the formation of borderline functioning, Chris was heading developmentally in this direction. Attentive to Freeman's detailed descriptions, it would seem that from the outset, Chris was pre-disposed by his quite sturdy inborn givens to "introspecting, wondering, *trying to get a perspective on experiences of opposing . . . forces within.* A hurt-and-angry, biting-persevering, wounded-but-trying, 'never-give-up' child [who] retained a transitional potentially-optimistic fantasy of . . . idealized 'good' libidinally-constant *integrated representations* of a 'good-and-bad self' and a 'good-and-bad object. . . . Chris was able to wonder about" a lot of things (italics added). To what extent did the splitting attain stability, if he was an "angry . . . [but] . . . persevering . . . trying . . . 'never-give-up' child . . . [who] retained . . . [an] optimistic fantasy . . . [and] integrated representations of . . . 'good and bad' . . . self and object?" Highly ambivalent: yes; splitting: at what level of character entrenchment? Freeman proposes at "the intermediate level of character organization" (Kernberg, 1970, p.).

Thinking of Chris's capacity for it, we cannot assume that he was 'introspecting' before the latter months of year one. But, while connections between frontal cortex and midbrain are not yet wired to go, as with other early cognition-affective processing capabilities, might not infants younger than two years be capable of 'wondering,' an early kind of conceptualizing process that precedes formal 'introspecting'? Watching infants, they do at times seem to be wondering, trying to make sense of the world around them. One infant I filmed at fifteen weeks convinced me that she was trying to figure out what a set of rings on a string was all about (Parens et al, 1974); I assure you, she was wondering! For a stretch of about twenty minutes, she seemed fascinated by this gimmick, plastic colored rings on a string, that she was pushing, pulling, mouthing, and staring at; were she five years old, I would say she was studying that gimmick. I have no doubt that Chris was 'wondering'; he did a lot of it; he probably wondered who were these strangers who came into his home—one week after they had been away and he did not recognize them! I doubt that Chris wondered about his feelings; he just had them and they had a profound effect on him. I think infants around six months are capable of some form of preliminary mulling over.

Following Freeman's clinical-behavioral documentation of Chris's splitting—for instance, when he would over years interchange roles with his steadfast dummy companion, William—Chris shows his persisting efforts to cope with his pressing rage, a persistence of notable dimension. He struggled to contain, attempt to work through, and metabolize his intense ambivalence toward both his mother and his own raging self. I admire that, however conflicted he felt, his young ego seemed determined to tolerate experiencing his rage (toward his mother) to resolve his defensive self and object splitting. We see him at work: repeatedly setting up 'good vs. bad conflict-resolving interactions' between himself and William. I find his efforts admiring and see the merits of Freeman's work, our work as clinicians, to help him toward securing better mental health.

About Object Constancy

I also wonder this: at six months Chris suffered the traumatic shock of his formerly idolizing mother now abruptly rejecting him. This essential libidinal-object-in-the-making's (Spitz, 1965) early mirroring and idolization, gratifying his flourishing primary narcissism—that healthy biologically based source of self-value—was abruptly stopped! The potential good libidinally gratifying object suddenly became the bad libidinally depriving-object. Fortunately for Chris, though often not at home, his father nonetheless maintained his good-enough evolving attachment to his son. Father steadfastly held to his emotional investment in his son, which, as Freeman proposes led to Chris's developing a degree of object constancy, a partial 'paternal-object' constancy—as evidenced in the fact that Father's absence on Chris's first birthday was so vividly etched in Chris's memory from that very early age. I want to comment on two points following from this note in Freeman's case report: (i) that one week after his parents had been away, Chris did not recognize them on their return, and (ii) that Chris developed a degree of object constancy, "a partial 'paternal-object' constancy."

> 1. Why did Chris not recognize them? And, in complement with his mother's traumatizing reaction, what might be the consequences of this experience on his up-to-then promisingly good development toward object constancy? Again, having seen this type of just not recognizing the primary caregiver in one child in our project—during a home visit after Mother had been in the hospital for five days—both observers and the infant's mother were surprised. I came to understand the dynamics that led to this bizarre, perhaps even startling reaction. Like the infant we had observed twice weekly since her birth, in Chris's case, the mother's face, her total self and infant-caring functions which that face represented, which up to then was progressively stabilizing into an internal representation of the libidinal-object-in-process-of-becoming-structured (Spitz, 1965), the sudden disappearance of that predictable, reliable face created a sense of absolute loss. Given the large libidinal investment in that object, its appearing in the child's visual field became critical for Chris's psychic stability. But the face was gone. As Piaget (1954) taught us, the memory of this prized familiar object cannot yet be evoked by the infant at six months of age; that becomes possible at about sixteen months of age. The presence of the object can only be 'remembered' when her face appears in the child's visual field. Spitz (1965) catalogued the evolution of the structuring of that 'face' which, with the emergence of *separation* and *stranger anxieties,* indicated the specification that the libidinal object is now represented in the infant's psyche. Note too that Erikson (1959) added to our understanding of those critical emotional-state factors in development during this early era in proposing that the emotional state of *basic trust* or *basic mistrust*—critical for the development of object constancy—seems to attain a sense of formation at about six months.

Chris's failure to recognize his parents, I have proposed, was due to the fact that their failure to appear as usual caused him excessive psychic pain against which he protected himself by transiently suppressing their representation from memory, essentially transiently suppressing or disabling his recognitive memory. Add to this the following: Spitz's work on the loss of the recently structured libidinal object—he studied only mothers—and its failure to be returned to the child over a period of three or so months, he showed us, led to the development in the infant of 'anaclitic depression' (Spitz, 1946). While Chris's parents did return to him, his mother did not return as the same mother; she was now the rejecting, extremely hurtful, bad mother. We might then also allow for an element of anaclitic depression in Chris's early-life traumatization.

2. We cannot be surprised, then, that Chris's evolving potentially promising object constancy was derailed. Foremost, however, that derailment was caused not by the separation but by the sudden withdrawal of libido by his now angry and rejecting mother. His basic trust took a nosedive! But the father maintained his libidinal investment in his son. Being well-enough endowed psychobiologically, Chris could make the best of what he did get. He developed a sufficient degree of object constancy forged from his relationship with his father. Due to time limitation, I will just add here without examples that I have also seen such substantial elements of object constancy being forged in sibling relationships. This is very easy to observe in twins, but I have seen it with non-twin sibs as well. We all have come across many an older sibling who acted as a parent-surrogate for younger ones. I want to conclude with one further exploration afforded us by these clinical cases.

Effects of Trauma in Early Childhood

Consider the challenge to the very young child, from infancy to two years of age, of the experience of intense and/or protracted traumatizing psychic pain that overwhelms the emerging ego, leading to a dysfunction of the infant's inborn adaptive capabilities. What might be its effects on the young child's psychic structure formation? Let's look at some of the variables that might determine the outcome: (i) What are the parameters and impact of the trauma? (ii) What is the adaptive potential of the child's inborn dispositions? (iii) What is the character/quality of the child's object-environment, and what opportunities for optimizing adaptation does this environment provide? And, bearing in mind the 'narcissistic injury, rage, and revenge sequencing,' what outcome character formation might we anticipate? Let me condense my answer to these questions.

With regard to the parameters and impact of the trauma, of course, traumas are not equal nor are the factors that cause them. Among the central parameters that shape the character and intensity of trauma, (a) the age of the child (or adult) at the time the trauma occurs, (b) by whom and by what is the trauma perpetrated, (c) what is the intensity of the trauma, be it sudden or protracted, (d) is it intentional or accidental, (e) what is its meaning to the self.

For Ali, the unempathic child-inappropriate demands started to be made from the earliest months of age on; it is difficult to ascertain just when he began to experience his parents' demands as onerous, as disallowing his sense-of-self experiencing. The clinical material suggests that, given their own character formations, Ali's parents' demands were protracted, part of their everyday interactions with him. His reactions to them suggest that he experienced their demands as intentional—why could they not let him be himself! To put it simply, he felt rage toward them, but he needed them; attempting to compromise and retain mother's love, he yielded a central aspect of his sense of self by complying with her wish that he not be a boy.

Of Chris, we know that his mother suddenly caused him to suffer the horrendous psychically painful fall from grace with her at six months of age. Fortunately, mitigated by his father's libidinal sustainment, he was not utterly desolate. What could he make of it? Bewildered, not understanding what was happening to him, might he not have held her accountable, that is, that she did this intentionally? She had dropped him from heaven!

Ruth was tortured by her own body from the first weeks, or at least the first months of life, when atopic eczema can strike. But the objects in her world intensified her torture by tying her potentially helpful scratching hands down. She knew that this was intentional; she could not then grasp that it was a sadly naïve and hurtful effort to protect her skin. Months later, we learn, her mother's cold lack of empathy and harshness is reported. This of course was not new behavior on her mother's part; she no doubt had been that way from the time of Ruth's birth. How could Ruth not have felt that her mother's coldness and maltreatment were intentional?; that's the way her mother was. From early on, Ruth most likely felt that she hated her mother and that she herself was hateful—you cannot hate your mother without feeling that you are hateful yourself (Erikson, 1959).

What is the adaptive potential of the child's inborn dispositions? In our field perhaps better than in others, despite the major comparable similarities among humans—as Freud (1930) noted in his 'narcissism of minor differences'—we are daily made aware of the multiple parameters along which we vary in our inborn dispositions. Therefore, my comparing Ali, Chris, and Ruth in terms of their inborn dispositions can only be tentative. Nonetheless, their importance to our topic recommends this glance at them.

From Novick's report, we might guess that from the outset, Ali seemed to resist his parents' demands that he comply with their inappropriate expectations, yet, he yielded much of his genetically determined sense of self to overly comply with his mother's wish that he had been a girl. There is rigidity in adaptive capability when a young child *resists or yields excessively* to parental expectations. And we see the continuation of his psycho-adaptive inflexibility even by age ten, when Novick takes him into analytic treatment. I believe that his inborn dispositions did not give him the ability to compromise self-protectively and that this fostered his unyielding rage and need for revenge which turned him into a 'weapon of destruction.' And we saw how his transference to his analyst challenged her strong clinical talents and years of experience. Only her commitment and perseverance got to him and he could finally start to use her help.

Chris seems to me to have been quite positively pre-disposed to adapt. I read in Freeman's report that Chris did not overtly exhibit rage against his mother. Rather, able to make the most of what was available to him, his father's libidinal investment in him, he forged of it some degree of object constancy. We saw his ability to carry this object constancy in his trusting his analyst sufficiently to very meaningfully reduce and move toward resolving the harsh ambivalence that led to his costly need for splitting. With his therapist's help, again using what was available to him, Chris persisted in attempting to master and metabolize his rage, and advanced to increasingly favorable adaptation—and the successful treatment goes on.

I am inclined to credit Ruth with quite good psychological inborn endowment despite and in the face of her inborn biological burdens—eczema and a strabismus that would require surgery. Reacting to her mother's sadistic narcissism, which generated in Ruth intense rage and led her to prefer her dog to the humans in her world (including her caring grandfather), she adapted by developing a sadomasochistic character formation which, however problematic it was, seemed less pathological than turning to developing a borderline character. Unfortunately, Ruth did not have the good fortune to be brought to treatment in childhood, as did Ali and Chris. Her engagement in analytic treatment in her early twenties suggests a constructive, determined effort to improve her life and reduce the problems her traumatic childhood wrought. She was feisty, determined, and sought to constructively change herself. I would ascribe this positive undertaking as driven by her good inherent psychological endowment.

With regard to the character/quality of the child's object-environment and *the opportunities for optimizing adaptation their environment provided,* what I have just written addresses both questions. Given what we have learned about these patients' traumatic early life histories, traumas in large measure determined by their primary objectal environment, what character formation might we expect them to develop?

What Outcome Character Formation Might We Anticipate?

These cases speak quite clearly to the sequencing that severe-enough *narcissistic injury* will generate *rage*, which in turn presses for calculated discharge against the injury perpetrator, that is, *revenge*. How would we expect young children to react and attempt to cope with the traumas they experienced as well as with the rage generated in them? How would such trauma impact their developing sense of self? What cluster of self-protective psychological defenses could we expect them to develop in the face of their rage? What relatedness to objects will develop and become patterned in them? And more questions can be asked. Summing it all, given their inborn capability to adapt, their character formations would be jeopardized to a greater or lesser degree. Outcome sadomasochistic characterology, narcissistic disorder, borderline functioning, or a combination of these is virtually predictable. Trauma does not simply yield neurosis. Given the parameters of the traumas they sustained and the narcissistic injuries inflicted on them by their substantially hurtful object relationships, we can expect that they would have developed substantial character pathology. Ali, Chris, and Ruth gave us dramatically painful documentation to arrive at such conclusions, conclusions explainable by the theory that 'excessive psychic pain generates hostility' and that being wounded at the hands of their own caregivers can achieve in them what it did. For Ali and Chris, their chance to have analytic treatment in childhood could significantly reduce the chance, by reducing the need for the defenses they were compelled to develop to cope with what befell them, of their eventually becoming firmly entrenched narcissistic personality disordered or borderline.

In concluding this chapter, I welcome making the leap from considerations arising from clinical cases to considering what follows.

Reflections on the Two Invited Chapters[15]

Eve Holwell in her chapter offers a novel perspective on the phenomenology and dynamics of narcissistic injury and revenge by deconstructing three major literary texts, namely, Euripides's (431 BCE) *Medea*, Brontë's (1847) *Wuthering Heights*, and Melville's (1851) *Moby Dick*. In a step-by-step fashion, Holwell lays out the sequence of narcissistic injury, psychic pain, rage, and the desire to take revenge. She compares and contrasts the protagonists in these three works of fiction and links her dynamic proposals with those highlighted by Horney (1948), Kohut (1972), and Pine (1995). The seamless fit between what the novelist and the analyst offer in regards to the understanding of human emotions is indeed impressive here.

Following Holwell's chapter, Rao Gogineni and April Fallon present a richly informative review of biocultural aspects of revenge. In doing so, they add to the growing consensus among psychoanalytic and psychodynamic thinkers who believe that what we have learned from our depth-psychological clinical work with individuals can, with due caution, be applied to the psychology of large groups. The authors give us a number of examples that document historically well-known talion-principle-based cyclic reciprocal acts of revenge, including those of Olympian Greek gods irascible with each other; the reciprocal ravages between Genghis Khan and Shah Ala as-Din Muhammad; and the trials and tribulations of Samson, the Israelite, and the Philistines. In all these cases, crimes intended to cause a large narcissistic (individual and collective) injury evoked subsequent retribution in kind, a cycle that repeated itself many times among them. In large measure, this cycle of narcissistic injury and revenge accounts for the perpetuation of both, as it has over centuries in serial wars among neighboring tribes and nations (Parens, 2013a). The authors report that Gaughan et al (2001), who studied

2,000 seventh to twlefth graders, found that "87 percent of the students . . . believe that shootings are motivated by a person's desire to 'get back at those who have hurt them.'" Gogineni and Fallon also found in the two examples they selected from history, that of Genghis Khan and that of Chanakya, that "in both cases, humiliation is experienced and payback is sought."[16] Any sufficiently painful narcissistic injury will generate hostile destructiveness toward the perpetrator.

There is also much merit to the authors' discussion linking revenge with the restitution of injured honor. This facet of revenge is difficult to untangle, not in 'honor killings' within families or among groups that live by their own code of law as do street gangs and Mafia-type-groups, but in the context of terrorism. Terrorism, an increasingly employed mode of waging war, brings with it acts of revenge to raise terrorists' own and their group's battered self-esteem and honor. This is the 'Janus Dilemma': that what the perpetrator considers an act of valor and honor, the victim experiences as terrorism and criminality (Parens, 2007a).

Although we have all seen only too often cases where individuals and groups have demonstrated Nietzsche's[17] view that 'to witness suffering does one good, to inflict it even more so,' I share Gogineni and Fallon's opinion that "perhaps Milton was more accurate than Nietzsche when he wrote, 'Revenge, at first though sweet / Bitter ere long back on itself recoils."[18]

Gogineni and Fallon tell us that "there is some evidence that we may be genetically programmed to seek revenge when we are harmed." There can be no doubt that we are genetically so programmed. Our behaviorally evident inborn dispositions—for instance, whether we have a low/high threshold of irritability, a low/high threshold for pain, a tendency toward slow/quick reactivity—are determined by our built-in biochemical make-up and physiological reactivities and functioning. These genetically determined characteristics have everything to do with the threshold of our experience of unpleasure (psychic pain), the qualitative and quantitative generation in us of hostile aggression, and the character of our hostile aggressive reactivity. So, too, the status of our genetically determined adaptive capabilities, starting with our primary autonomous ego apparatuses/functions (Hartmann, 1939), contributes importantly to both—how we react to the experience of psychic pain and how we discharge the hostile destructiveness it generates. Then once born, our *genotype* will be given shape by our experiences, yielding our eventual *phenotype*. For instance, Eric Kandel (1979; Kandel et al, 1991) has found that experience determines synaptic formation and the structure of neural pathways in our inborn genetically programmed brain which, when all is said and done, mediates our behaviors. I thus assume that our *genotype-derived phenotype* will determine how each of us reacts to the generation in us of hostile destructiveness as well as the character of our tendency to discharge it in revenge.

But as Gogineni and Fallon tell us, and we all know well, "not every harmful action results in a revengeful act." Referencing McCullough et al (2013), they propose that the response to every harmful act perpetrated on us "involves a cost-benefit analysis . . . that balances the necessity of revenge . . . and the importance of [maintaining] a positive emotional connection with the other. . . . [That is,] For relationships significant to one's well-being . . . the cost of revenge may be too high. . . . [There is much evidence for this] sociobiological explanation that can be applied at both the individual and group level" (p. 34).

As I have detailed elsewhere (Parens, 2013a), McCullough et al's (2013) thesis played itself out significantly in the different aftermath that followed World War I and World War II. In a word here, while other factors came into play as well, central to these very differing aftermaths is the fact that whereas after World War I, 'the War to end all Wars,' the revenge sought by the French against Germany[19]—which the British and the Americans tried to mitigate—was so harsh that it contributed critically just two decades later to the eruption of World War II. That World War II to date has not been followed by another worldwide catastrophe—although the twentieth century has had its share of more-contained wars—is in good measure due to (i) the way the Allies dealt with defeated Germany and Japan, in Europe, especially for instance, with the Marshall Plan, and (ii) the deterrence that has come with the threat of an atomic catastrophe. Again, while other factors no doubt have contributed as well, that the Allies did not exact a bloodletting revenge on either Germany or Japan probably has played a significantly constructive part in the aftermath of World War II.

I find especially important Gogineni and Fallon's paraphrasing McCullough et al (2013) that "from an *evolutionary perspective,* forgiveness is a secondary adaptive set of thoughts, feelings and behaviors that serve to restore important relationships" (italics added). As I wrote elsewhere, "Freud put forward the meritorious argument which German social scientist and psychoanalyst Hans Kilian (1995) and I (Parens, 2011b), independently have subsequently made, that 'For incalculable ages mankind has been passing through *a process of evolution of cultures . . . (of civilization)* [my italics]. . . . Now war is in the crassest opposition to the psychical attitude imposed on us by the process of civilization, and for that reason we are bound to rebel against it. . . . This is not merely an intellectual and emotional repudiation; we pacifists have a *constitutional* intolerance of war. . . . [And] one thing we *can* say: whatever fosters the growth of civilization works at the same time against war'" (Parens, 2013b, pp. 214–215).

Gogineni and Fallon's referencing McCullough et al that "from an evolutionary perspective, forgiveness is a secondary adaptive [formation]" speaks just to this notion, that civilization is undergoing a process of evolution. Consider as well that as Gogineni and Fallon tell us, "Forgiveness involves inhibiting revenge behaviors and engaging in reparation. . . . [And that] this is becoming a popular notion in psychology and economics." They also refer to Barry Schwartz (1978), who held that when "behavior is punished . . . in a fashion that is measured and restrained . . . this allows the wrongdoer to continue as part of society *and milder retribution evolves as a cultural principle*" (p. 35, italics added). In my bias as a child developmentalist, I have often said that as happens with every child, civilization is developing over time, a collective experience-dependent maturation that accrues with the passage of time.

May we not consider the probability that along a Lamarckian path, humans evolve by entering changes in their experience-dependent *phenotype* that in some adaptive way enters/modifies their *genotype,* all in the service of optimizing their Darwinian fitness for survival? Humans have in fact gone as far as to modify the genetic makeup of plants to yield better fruit and produce (and even animals for medical and research purposes) which document the modifiability of a given genotype. Is it far-fetched to consider that by psychological and educational means human behavior can be optimized so as to create more positively adaptive co-existence with improvement of life for all? Interestingly, Gogineni and Fallon turn to the Old Testament among other sources to document the prevalence centuries ago of that ancient justice-morality talion principle "a tooth for a tooth, an eye for an eye," remarking that "nearly half the Bible is filled with stories of revenge." Then in a footnote, they tell us that "the New Testament . . . is [much] concerned with containing the wish for revenge by forgiveness."[20] However accurate their statement, there is little doubt that among many Christians, Jews, Muslims, and those of other faiths, we are familiar with Jesus Christ's benevolent "Forgive them for they know not what they do!" Is it not one of many illustrations of changes brought by the passage of time, in this case from the earliest writings of the Old Testament (the Torah) some 1700 years[21] before the writings of the New Testament, itself now 2000 years old? This thesis was voiced recently on National Public Radio (NPR). Aired on June 5, 2013, during a report commemorating the assassination of civil rights activist Medgar Evers in Jackson, Mississippi, on June 12, 1963, Julian Bond, social activist and leader in the American civil rights movement, said, "The change [since then] is just enormous!" Then again on NPR, on June 20, 2013, continuing said fifty-years commemoration, Dr. Jesse Lewis from Birmingham, Alabama, speaking of his experiences of desegregation in this hotbed of racism, said: "We've come a long ways."[22] And this is only fifty years ago. We are all witness in America to what Bond and Lewis said.

Just one closing word on the rich Gogineni-Fallon chapter: I do not think that "revenge [in its primary function is] a deterrent of harmful behavior [that serves] an evolutionary function." I am more inclined to think that while revenge or the counteraction to an attack at times acts as a deterrent—as do

Hiroshima and Nagasaki—more basically, revenge is driven by a self-preservative built-in psychobiological reactivity that ensures the survival of the organism (see the biological model at the beginning of this chapter [Parens, 1979, p. 110]). It is a mandate imprinted in all living things by Mother Nature that every organism in order to "preserve the species, must survive"—Biology 101.

NOTES

1. The mothers were selected from nearly fifty mothers from the Medical College of Pennsylvania (MCP) neighborhood who volunteered in response to a call to the community for volunteers to participate in a project taking place in the Children's Unit, where we would study their young children's development. I ascribe the response of so many mothers to our call for volunteers to the fact that the Children's Unit of MCP had a very good rapport with the lower socioeconomic housing project community just across the street from the Medical College. The selection of mothers for the project was based simply on the fact that they were in mid- to late pregnancy at the time of the selection meeting. Much advantage came from the fact that none was a primipara (first-time mother).

2. In the Day Room of the Children's Unit at the Eastern Pennsylvania Psychiatric Institute/Medical College of Pennsylvania.

3. According to dermatologist Bernard Kirshbaum (personal communication).

4. To the reader who has never experienced eczema, I can attest that it is a miserable problem. Never having had eczema, I was sympathetic to what it might make an infant or adult feel. But when in the course of writing my Holocaust memoirs, *Nachtraeglishkeit* (manifestation of a trauma years after its occurrence), I developed a blaring nummular eczema of which I still have some very low-key evidence, I was well informed on the misery of the condition. To not scratch takes all the discipline one can muster—a task impossible for young children to achieve.

5. Given that one rarely hears this old magical term these days, for the uninformed, TLC = tender loving care. It was long considered the prime healing potion nurses carried on their medicine carts.

6. The author apologizes for no longer being able to access the references from which he gathered his information regarding both 'cell death' and progeria. Needless to say, if the reader can find documentation to the contrary of the author's claim, the author would be indebted to the reader for sharing this information with him.

7. Following on my apology of n6, I am not certain that the laboratory animal was a rabbit or another animal.

8. I italicize this phrase.

9. "On Aggression: The Politics and Psychobiology of Genocide" held at the Philoctetes Center, New York Psychoanalytic Institute on February 28, 2009, Co-Directors Ed Nercessian and Francis Levy. Roundtable participants included Joyce Apsel; Benedict Kiernan, moderator and renowned author of *Blood and Soil* (2007); Taylor Krauss; Patricia McCormick; and Henri Parens.

10. Held in New York, December 1973, at one of a yearly Interdisciplinary Colloquium on Aggression which ran for several years at the winter meetings of the American Psychoanalytic Association.

11. My impression, though, to keep the terms as clear as we can, is that Glover used the term 'ego' to mean 'self' as did Freud until 1923 (The ego and the id), when 'ego' as Hartmann (1950a) proposed is the agency of the structural model that serves adaptation.

12. This proposition of an early life 'self' representation constituted transiently of 'I–not-I' during the symbiotic phase may in time remain [some 'earliest cathexes are indelible' Freud proposed (1939, p. 151)] as a component representation within the mosaic that ultimately constitutes anyone's overarching evolving 'self.' This conceptualization, while differently ar-

rived at, may have a bearing on Kohut's (1971) critical 'self-object' concept that remains part of our overarching 'self' throughout life. Kohut further proposed that while we all retain and even look for self-objects to sustain our self-esteem and with whom to identify, self-objects become a key factors in the patho-dynamics and the treatment of narcissistic personality disorders (Kohut, 1977, pp. 187–8fn).

13. This concern, that some of our premier earlier child analysts borrowed concepts applicable to psychotic conditions from their work with childhood psychosis but then derived assumptions from these to conceptualize normal childhood development. That is problematic. For example, the Kleinian proposition that the normal infant passes through a paranoid-schizoid position is not discernible in the behaviors of most infants. To assume that such a dynamic operates at an unconscious level and is not discernible in behavior is a very untenable assumption. Again, the caution I stated earlier in this text with regard to infants born with some pain-inducing diathesis might mislead the observer to assume the presence of a *spontaneous* manifestation of hostile destructiveness, which some have interpreted as evidence of the play of a death-instinct based manifestation of aggression. In fact, Klein was a vigorous advocate of this theory of aggression and proposed that the infant comes into the world driven to destroy the mother's breast (the representative part-object).

14. Spitz had already proposed ten years before that this fact is of great importance in that this 'sign Gestalt' triggers the innate releasing mechanism (IRM) that launches the infant's attachment process to the caregiver that will lead to the caregiver's becoming structured as 'libidinal object' (Spitz, 1965, pp. 94–95).

15. While the three main chapters (i.e., those by Novick, Freeman, and Kernberg) and their respective discussions were delivered as talks during the 44th Annual Margaret S. Mahler Symposium held in Philadelphia on April 20, 2013, two other chapters in this book were added later on. These are chapter 8, by Eve Holwell, and chapter 9, by Rao Gogineni and April Fallon.

16. Gogineni and Fallon describe the flow of the individual ruler's dynamics to embroil the people he governs. I am not the first to propose that the humiliations Hitler suffered in the course of his youth and adolescence long plagued him and probably contributed to his strongly personalizing the humiliation the German people suffered at the hands of the Allies following the armistice that terminated World War I. This likely contributed to his pushing the theme that Germany had been humiliated by the Treaty of Versailles for which the Germans in World War II harshly punished France (especially) and its allies.

17. Nietzsche, 1887/1996, p. 50, in Carrabine et al, 2013, p. 306.

18. *Paradise Lost*, Book IX, line 171.

19. The 1919 Treaty of Versailles, which exacted territorial losses and enormously high reparation costs—which Germany finally repaid in total ninety years later by the year 2010!—that, compounded with the economic crash of 1929, fueled much of the potential energy with which the Nazi-German hierarchy ignited World War II.

20. Note that Gogineni and Fallon do tell us, however, that even in the Torah (the first five books of the Old Testament dated to possibly 1700 BCE), some scriptures do not support revenge; rather they recommend forgiveness (e.g., Leviticus 19:18 and Deuteronomy 21:35). Nonetheless, revenge is much advocated in the Old Testament, a point Ben Kiernan makes as well (2007).

21. en.wikipedia.org/wiki/Dating_the_Bible.

22. Audie Cornish interviewed Dr. Jesse Lewis "in Birmingham, Alabama, where the city is in the midst of commemorating the fiftieth anniversary of the tumultuous and influential civil rights protests that occurred here. One place that might not come to mind when you think about this period is the golf course. Cornish asks: Were you afraid at all? Lewis: No. There were a white group behind us, and one of the person in the group was standing in the line of my backswing. If I brought the club back out, I would hit him. So I explained to him very nicely that I possibly can if he keeps standing there, I will knock his teeth out because I have a long backswing. And so he eventually moved back, and we played, and the only thing we've got was a few heckles. Cornish: When you look at the city golf courses today and who's playing. How far do you feel like Birmingham has come? Lewis: We've come a long ways. Birmingham is a landmark of discrimination. We have come a long ways. The key is what we do in 2014," www.npr.org/templates/story/story.php?storyId=128116806.

References

Abelin, E. L. (1971). The role of the father in the separation-individuation process. In: *Separation-Individuation*, eds. J.B. McDevitt and C.F. Settlage, pp. 229–252. New York, NY: International Universities Press.

Abraham, C., and O'Callaghan, T. (2012, October 11). Chimps attack people after habitat loss—life—11 October 2012—New Scientist. *New Scientist Life*. Retrieved May 30, 2013, from www.newscientist.com/article/dn22369-chimps-attack-people-after-habitat-loss.html

Abraham, K. (1920). Manifestations of the female castration complex. In: *Selected Papers on Psychoanalysis*, pp. 338–369. London, UK: Hogarth Press.

Abram, J. (2007). *The Language of Winnicott: A Dictionary of Winnicott's Use of Words* (2nd ed.). London, UK: Karnac.

Acharya, A., and Jain, M. (n.d). History: What are some of the best stories about taking reveng in history or mythology or folklore or real life?—Quora. Retrieved June 11, 2013. www.wuora.com/History/What-are-some-of-the-best-stories-about-taking-revenge-in-history-or-real-life.

Akhtar, S. (1999). *Immigration and Identity: Turmoil, Treatment, and Transformation*. Northvale, NJ: Jason Aronson.

———. (2000). Mental pain and the cultural ointment of poetry. *International Journal of Psychoanalysis* 81: 229–243.

———. (2002). Forgiveness: origins, dynamics, psychopathology, and technical relevance. *Psychoanalytic Quarterly* 71: 175–212.

———. (2003). Dehumanization: origins, manifestations, and remedies. In: *Violence or Dialogue? Psychoanalytic Insights on Terror and Terrorism*, eds. S. Varvin and V.D. Volkan, pp. 131–145. London, UK: International Psychoanalytic Association.

———. (2007). From unmentalized xenophobia to messianic sadism: some reflections on the phenomenology of prejudice. In: *The Future of Prejudice: Psychoanalysis and the Prevention of Prejudice*, eds. H. Parens, A. Mahfouz, S.W. Twemlow, and D.E. Scharff, pp. 7–19. Lanham, MD: Jason Aronson.

———. (2009). *Comprehensive Dictionary of Psychoanalysis*. London, UK: Karnac Books.

———. (2011). *Turning Points in Dynamic Psychotherapy*. London, UK: Karnac Books.

———. (2012). *Good Stuff: Generosity, Resilience, Humility, Gratitude, Forgiveness, and Sacrifice*. Lanham, MD: Jason Aronson.

———. (2013a). The compulsion to betray and the need to be betrayed. In: *Betrayal: Developmental, Literary, and Clinical Realms*, ed. S. Akhtar, pp. 117–134. London, UK: Karnac Books.

———. (2013b). *Psychoanalytic Listening: Methods, Limits, and Innovations*. London, UK: Karnac Books.

Akhtar, S., and Choksi, K. (2005). Bollywood and the Indian unconscious. In: *Freud Along the Ganges: Psychoanalytic Reflections on the People and Culture of India*, ed. S. Akhtar, pp. 139–173. New York, NY: The Other Press.

Alexander, F., and French, T. (1946). *Psychoanalytic Therapy*. New York, NY: Ronald Press.

Allen, T.E. (2009). A psychoanalytic look at Herman Melville from his use of source materials for "Moby Dick." *Psychoanalytic Review* 96: 743–767.

Al-Shawtabi, A.R. (2009, February 9). 4698 people died in revenge killings over 10 years (reports). *Yemen Post*. Retrieved from www.yemenpost.net/27/Reports/20081.htm

Al-Zaidi, H. (2008). NDI launches its campaign aiming to fight revenge killing. *Yemen Post*, May 19, 2008.

Altemeyer, B. (2006). The Authoritarians. Retrieved May 30, 2013, from home.cc.umanitoba.ca/~altemey/.

Amati-Mehler, J., and Argentieri, S. (1989). Hope and hopelessness: a technical problem? *International Journal of Psychoanalysis* 70: 295–304.

American Mafia. Retrieved June 6, 2013, from *Wikipedia*, the free encyclopedia, at en.wikipedia.org/wiki/American_Mafia#Symbolism_in_murders

Angelo Bruno. Retrieved June 7, 2013, from Wikipedia, the free encyclopedia, at en.wikipedia.org/wiki/Angelo_Bruno.

Aquino, K., Tripp, T.M., and Bies, R.J. (2006). Getting even or moving on? Power, procedural justice, and types of offense as predictors of revenge, forgiveness, reconciliation, and avoidance in organizations. *Journal of Applied Psychology* 91: 653–668.

Arlow, J.H. (1980). The revenge motive in the primal scene. *Journal of the American Psychoanalytic Association* 28: 519–541.

Bacon, F. (1909–1914). *Essays, Civil and Moral.* Vol. III, Part 1. The Harvard Classics. New York, NY: P.F. Collier and Son.

Balint, M. (1968). *The Basic Fault: Therapeutic Aspects of Regression.* London, UK: Tavistock.

Balzac, H. de (1846). *La Cousine Bette*. London, UK: Penguin Books, 1963.

Barash, D.P. and Lipton, J.E. (2011). *Payback: Why We Retaliate, Redirect Aggression, and Take Revenge*. New York, NY: Oxford University Press.

Bartleby.com (2001). www.bartleby.com/3/1/. [March 17, 13].

Bateson, G. (1972). Culture contact and schismogenesis. In: *Steps to an Ecology of Mind: Collected Essays in Anthropology, Psychiatry, Evolution, and Epistemology*, pp. 61–72. Chicago, IL: University of Chicago Press.

Baumeister, R.F., Stillwell, A.M., and Wotman, S. (1990). Victim and perpetrator accounts of interpersonal conflict: autobiographical narratives about anger. *Journal of Personality and Social Psychology* 90: 994–1005.

Beattie, H.J. (2005). Revenge. *Journal of the American Psychoanalytic Association* 53: 513–524.

Beckerman, S., Erickson, P.I., Yost, J., Regalado, J., Jaramillo, L., Sparks, C., and Long, K. (2009). Life histories, blood revenge, and reproductive success among the Waorani of Ecuador. *Proceedings of the National Academy of Sciences* 106: 8134–8139.

Beebe, B., Lachmann, F., Markese, S., and Bahrick, L. (2012). On the origins of disorganized attachment and internal working models: Paper 1. A dyadic systems approach. *Psychoanalytic Dialogues* 22: 253–272.

Berke, J. (2012). *Why I Hate You and You Hate Me: The Interplay of Envy, Greed, Jealousy, and Narcissism in Everyday Life*. London, UK: Karnac Books.

Bion, W.R. (1957). On arrogance. In: *Second Thoughts: Selected Papers on Psychoanalysis*, pp. 86–92. New York, NY: Basic Books.

Bleuler, E. (1908). *Textbook of Psychiatry*. transl. A.A. Brill. New York, NY: MacMillan.

Bloom, P. (2010). The moral life of babies. *New York Times*, May 5, 2010.

Blum, H.P. (1981). Some current and recurrent problems of psychoanalytic technique. *Journal of the American Psychoanalytic Association* 29: 47–68.

Blumenfeld, L. (2003). *Revenge: A Story of Hope*. New York, NY: Washington Square Press.

Bollas, C. (1999). *The Mystery of Things*. London, UK: Routledge.

Boon, S.D., Deveau, V.L., and Alibhai, A.M. (2009). Payback: the parameters of revenge in romantic relationships. *Journal of Social and Personal Relationships* 26: 747–768.

Borger, J. (2001). McVeigh brushes aside deaths. *The Guardian*. Retrieved from www.guardian.co.uk/world/2011/mar/30/julianborger.

Boris, H.N. (1986). The "other breast"—greed, envy, spite and revenge. *Contemporary Psychoanalysis* 22: 45–59.

Boysen, G.A. (2008). Revenge and student evaluations of teaching. *Teaching of Psychology* 35: 218–222.

Brenman, E. (1985). Cruelty and narrow-mindedness. *International Journal of Psychoanalysis* 66: 273–281.

Britton, R. (2004). Subjectivity, objectivity, and triangular space. *Psychoanalytic Quarterly* 73: 47–61.

Brontë, E. (1847). *Wuthering Heights*. New York, NY: Random House, 2009.

Buckholtz, J. W., Asplund, C.L., Dux, P.E., Zald, D.H., Gore, J.C., Jones, O.D., and Marois, R. (2008). The neural correlates of third-party punishment. *Neuron* 60: 930–940.

Buckholtz, J.W., and Marois, R. (2012). The roots of modern justice: cognitive and neural foundations of social norms and their enforcement. *Nature Neuroscience* 15: 655-661.

Bushman, B.J. (2002). Does venting anger feed or extinguish the flame? Catharsis, rumination, distraction, anger, and aggressive responding. *Personality and Social Psychology Bulletin* 28: 724–731.

Bushman, B.J., Baumeister, R.F., and Phillips, C.M. (2001). Do people aggress to improve their mood? Catharsis beliefs, affect regulation opportunity, and aggressive responding. *Journal of Personality and Social Psychology* 81: 17–32.

Cannon, W.B. (1928). *Bodily Changes in Pain, Hunger, Fear, and Rage*. New York, NY: Appleton-Century.

Carey, B. (2004, July 4). Payback Time: Why Revenge Tastes So Sweet. *New York Times*.

Carlsmith, K.M., Wilson, T.D., and Gilbert, D.T. (2008). The paradoxical consequences of revenge. *Journal of Personality and Social Psychology* 95: 1316–1324.

Carlsmith.Wilson.Gilbert2008.pdf. (n.d.). Retrieved from www.colgate.edu/portaldata/-imagegallerywww/184416d4-5863-4a3e-a73b-b2b6b86e7b60/-ImageGallery/Carlsmith.Wilson.Gilbert2008.pdf

Carrabine, E., Lee, M., South, N., Cox, P., and Plummer, K. (2013). *Criminology: A Sociological Introduction*. Retrieved May 27, 2013, from books.google.com

Casselman, A. (2007, October 11). Animal Insight | Science and Nature | Smithsonian Magazine. Retrieved May 30, 2013, from www.smithsonianmag.com/science-nature/animal-insight.html?c=yandpage=2

Castelnuovo-Tedesco, P. (1974). Stealing, revenge and the Monte Cristo complex. *International Journal of Psychoanalysis* 55: 169–181.

Chagnon, N. A. (1988). Life histories, blood revenge, and warfare in a tribal population. *Science* 239: 985–992.

Chesler, P. (2010). Worldwide trends in honor killings. *Middle East Quarterly* 17: 3–11.

Clarkin, J.F., Yeomans, F.E., and Kernberg, O.F. (2006). *Psychotherapy for Borderline Personality: Focusing on Object Relations*. Washington, DC: American Psychiatric Publishing.

Coates, S., Friedman, R.C., and Wolfe, S. (1991). The etiology of boyhood gender identity disorder: a model for integrating temperament, development, and psychodynamics. *Psychoanalytic Dialogues* 1: 481–523.

Cohen, N. (2012, July 12). Blood feuds still boiling in Albania. *USA Today.com*. Retrieved from usatoday30.usatoday.com/news/world/story/2012-07-29/albania-blood-feuds/56580022/1.

Conrad, J. (1910). *Heart of Darkness and The Secret Sharer*. Pocket Books, New York, 2004.

Cooper, A. (1986). Narcissism. In: *Essential Papers on Narcissism*, ed. A.P. Morrison, pp. 118–134. New York, NY: New York University Press.

Corbett, K. (2009). *Boyhoods: Rethinking Masculinities*. New Haven, CT: Yale University Press.

Dahl, R. (2004). *Matilda*. New York, NY: Penguin Books.

Daly, M. and WIlson, M. (1988). Evolutionary Social Psychology and Family Homicide. *Science*, 242: 519–524.

Dangor, A. (2004). *Bitter Fruit*. New York, NY: Grove Press.

Daniels, M. (1969). Pathological vindictiveness and the vindictive character. *Psychoanalytic Review* 56: 169–196.

de Quervain, D. J.-F., Fischbacher, U., Treyer, V., Schellhammer, M., Schnyder, U., Buck, A., and Fehr, E. (2004). The neural basis of altruistic punishment. *Science* 305: 1254–1258.

de Waal, F. (2013). *The Bonobo and the Atheist: In Search of Humanism Among the Primates*. New York, NY: W.W. Norton.

Diamond, J. (2008). Annals of Anthropology: Vengeance is Ours. *The New Yorker*, 1–10. Accessed 10/17/13 www.unl.edu/rhames/courses/war/diamond-vengeance.pdf.

Diamond, M.J. (1997). Boys to men: the maturing of male identity through paternal watchful protectiveness. *Gender and Psychoanalysis* 3: 243–299.

Dickens, C. (1861). *Great Expectations*. New York, NY: W.W. Norton, 1999.

Dirty Harry. (1971). Directed by Don Siegel, produced by Warner Brothers.

Django Unchained. (2012). Produced by the Weinstein Company, Columbia Pictures, directed by Quentin Tarantino.

Djilas, M. (1958). *Land Without Justice*. Retrieved May 23, 2013, from www.archive.org/stream/milovandjilaslan012052mbp/milovandjilaslan012052mbp_djvu.txt

Dreher, J.-C., Meyer-Lindenberg, A., Kohn, P., and Berman, K.F. (2008). From the cover: age-related changes in midbrain dopaminergic regulation of the human reward system. *Proceedings of the National Academy of Sciences* 105: 15106–15111.

Dumas, A. (1844). *The Count of Monte Cristo*. New York, NY: Bantam Classics, 1984.

Elster, J. (1990). Norms of revenge. *Ethics* 100: 862–885.

Erikson, E. (1950). *Childhood and Society*. New York, NY: W.W. Norton, 1963.

———. (1959). *Identity and the Life Cycle*. Psychological Issues Monograph No. 1. New York, NY: International Universities Press.

Euripides. (431 BCE). *Medea*. Las Vegas, NV: On Demand Publishing, 2013.

Fairbairn, W.D.R. (1952). *Psychoanalytic Studies of the Personality*, pp. 110–112. London, UK: Tavistock.

———. (1963). Synopsis of an object-relations theory of the personality. *International Journal of Psychoanalysis* 44: 224–225.

Feather, Norman T., and McKee, I.R. (2012). Values, right-wing authoritarianism, social dominance orientation, and ambivalent attitudes toward women. *Journal of Applied Social Psychology* 42: 2479–2504.

Fehr, E., and Gächter, S. (2002). Altruistic punishment in humans. *Nature* 415: 137–140.

Fenichel, O. (1945). *The Psychoanalytic Theory of Neurosis*. New York, NY: W.W. Norton.

Ferenczi, S. (1921). The further development of the active therapy in psychoanalysis. In: *Further Contributions to the Theory and Technique of Psychoanalysis*, pp. 217–230. London, UK: Karnac Books, 1980.

———. (1929). The unwelcome child and his death instinct. *International Journal of Psychoanalysis* 10: 125–129.

Fischer, L. (1947). *Gandhi and Stalin: Two Signs at the World's Crossroads*. New York: Harper and Brothers Publishers.

Fiske, R. (2010, September 7). The crimewave that shames the world. *The Independent*. Retrieved from www.independent.co.uk/voices/commentators/fisk/robert-fisk-the-crimewave-that-shames-the-world-2072201.html

Fitzgerald, F.S. (1920). Bernice Bobs Her Hair: Short Story. In: *Flappers and Philosophers*. New York, NY: Charles Scribner's Sons.

Fonagy, P., and Target, M. (1997). Attachment and reflective function: their role in self-organization. *Development and Psychopathology* 9: 679–700.

Foulks, E.F., Freeman, D.M.A., and Freeman, P.A. (1978). Pre-oedipal dynamics in a case of Eskimo arctic hysteria. *Psychoanalytic Study of Society* 8: 41–69.

Fraiberg, S. (1982). Pathological defenses in infancy. *Psychoanalytic Quarterly* 51: 612–635.

Freeman, D.M.A. (1968). Adolescent crises of the Kiowa-Apache Indian male. In: *Minority Group Adolescents in the United States*, ed. E. Brody, pp. 157–204. Baltimore, MD: Williams and Wilkins.

———. (1989). Contributions of cross-cultural studies to clinical theory and practice: the work of Paul Parin. *Psychoanalytic Study of Society* 14: 281–299.

Freeman, D.M.A., Foulks, E.F., and Freeman, P.A. (1976). Ghost sickness and superego development in the Kiowa Apache male. *Psychoanalytic Study of Society* 7: 123–171.

———. (1978). Child development and arctic hysteria in the North Alaskan Eskimo male. *Journal of Psychological Anthropology* 1: 203–210.

Freeman, P.A. (1971). Kiowa Apache concepts and attitudes toward the child. *Papers in Anthropology* 12: 90–160.

Freud, A. (1958). Child observation and prediction of development: a memorial lecture in honor of Ernst Kris. *Psychoanalytic Study of the Child* 13: 92–124.

Freud, S. (1895). Studies on hysteria (with J. Breuer). *Standard Edition* 2: 1–323.

———. (1909a). Analysis of a phobia in a five-year-old boy. *Standard Edition* 10: 5–149.

———. (1909b). Family romances. *Standard Edition* 9: 237–241.

———. (1910). A special type of object choice made by men. *Standard Edition* 11: 153–165.

———. (1911–1913). Psychoanalytic notes on an autobiographical account of a case of paranoia. *Standard Edition* 12: 3–80.

———. (1915). The unconscious. *Standard Edition* 14: 159–216.

———. (1916). The exceptions. *Standard Edition* 14: 311–315.

———. (1917). Mourning and melancholia. *Standard Edition* 14: 237–260.

———. (1918). From the history of an infantile neurosis. *Standard Edition* 17: 7–122.

———. (1919). The uncanny. *Standard Edition* 17: 217–252.

———. (1920a). Beyond the pleasure principle. *Standard Edition* 18: 1–64.

———. (1920b). The psychogenesis of a case of homosexuality in a woman. *Standard Edition* 18: 145–172.

———. (1921). Group psychology and the analysis of the ego. *Standard Edition* 18: 65–143.

———. (1923). The ego and the id. *Standard Edition* 17: 3–68.

———. (1926). Inhibitions, symptoms, and anxiety. *Standard Edition* 20: 77–174.

———. (1930). Civilization and its discontents. *Standard Edition* 21: 59–145.

———. (1931). Female sexuality. *Standard Edition* 21: 223–243.

———. (1932). Why war? *Standard Edition* 22: 197–215.

———. (1933). Femininity. *Standard Edition* 22: 112–135.

———. (1939). An outline of psycho-analysis. *Standard Edition* 23: 211–253.

Freud, S., and Breuer, J. (1893, 1895). Studies on hysteria. *Standard Edition* 2.

Gabbard, G. (1996). *Love and Hate in the Analytic Setting*. Northvale, NJ: Jason Aronson.

———. (1997). Challenges in the analysis of adult patients with histories of childhood sexual abuse. *Canadian Journal of Psychoanalysis* 5: 1–25.

Gaughan, E., Cerio, J., and Myers, R. (2001). *Lethal Violence in Schools: A National Study Final Report*. New York, NY: Alfred University.

Genghis Khan. (2013, June 30). Retrieved July 6, 2013, from medbib.com/Genghis_Khan

Gerber, M., and Jackson, J. (2013). Retribution as revenge and retribution as just deserts. *Social Justice Research* 26: 61–80.

Glover, E. (1947). Basic mental concepts: their clinical and theoretical value. *Psychoanalytic Quarterly* 16: 482–506.

Gollwitzer, M., Meder, M., and Schmitt, M. (2011). What gives victims satisfaction when they seek revenge? *European Journal of Social Psychology* 41: 364–374.

Gordon, L. (1955). Incest as revenge against the pre-oedipal mother. *Psychoanalytic Review* 42: 284–292.

Green, A. (1975). The analyst, symbolization, and absence in the analytic setting (on "Changes in Analytic Practice and Analytic Experience") in memory of D.W. Winnicott. *International Journal of Psychoanalysis* 56: 1–22.

———. (1980). The dead mother. In: *Life Narcissism, Death Narcissism*, transl. A Weller, pp. 185–221. London, UK: Free Association.

———. (1993a). *On Private Madness*. Madison, CT: International Universities Press.

———. (1993b). *Le travail du négative*. Paris, France: Les Editions de Minuit.

———. (1997). The intuition of the negative in playing and reality. *International Journal of Psychoanalysis* 78: 1071–1084.

———. (1998). The primordial mind and the work of the negative. *International Journal of Psychoanalysis* 79: 649–665.

———. (2002). A dual conception of narcissism: positive and negative organizations. *Psychoanalytic Quarterly* 71: 631–649.

Grinberg, L. (1979). Countertransference and projective counteridentification. *Contemporary Psychoanalysis* 15: 226–247.

Hamlin, J.K. (2013). Moral judgment and action in preverbal infants and toddlers: evidence for an innate moral core. *Current Directions in Psychological Science* 22: 186–193.

Hamlin, J.K., Wynn, K., Bloom, P., and Mahajan, N. (2011). How infants and toddlers react to antisocial others. *Proceedings of the National Academy of Sciences* 108: 19931–19936.

Harmon, K. (2011, May 4). Does revenge serve an evolutionary purpose? *Scientific American*. Retrieved May 31, 2013, from www.scientificamerican.com

Hartmann, H. (1939). *Ego Psychology and the Problem of Adaptation.* New York, NY: International Universities Press, 1958.

———. (1950a). Comments on the psychoanalytic theory of the ego. In: *Essays on Ego Psychology,* pp 113–141. New York, NY: International Universities Press, 1964.

———. (1950b). Psychoanalysis and developmental psychology. *Psychoanalytic Study of the Child* 5: 7–17.

Herzog, J.M. (2001). *Father Hunger*. Hillsdale, NJ: Analytic Press.

Hinshelwood, R. (1989). *A Dictionary of Kleinian Thought*. Northvale, NJ: Jason Aronson.

Hoffer, A. (1985). Towards a definition of psychoanalytic neutrality. *Journal of the American Psychoanalytic Association* 33: 771–795.

Homer. *The Iliad*. Retrieved June 10, 2013, from www.gutenberg.org/ebooks/3059.

Honor killing. Wikipedia, the free encyclopedia. Retrieved June 9, 2013, from en.wikipedia.org/wiki/Honor_killing

Horney, K. (1948). The value of vindictiveness. *American Journal of Psychoanalysis* 8: 3–12.

Horowitz, M.J. (2007). Understanding and ameliorating revenge fantasies in psychotherapy. *American Journal of Psychiatry* 164: 24–27.

How To Get Revenge on Your Teacher?—Yahoo! Answers (2013). Retrieved May 24, 2013, from answers.yahoo.com/question/index?qid=20090106131103AAEedK0

Hull, J.W., Lane, R.C., and Okie, J. (1989). Sexual acting out and the desire for revenge. *Psychoanalytic Review* 76: 313–328.

Inglourious Basterds. (2009). Produced by Universal Pictures, directed by Quentin Tarantino.

Jaffe, E. (2011). The complicated psychology of revenge. *Observer* 24: 15–18.

Jensen, K., Call, J., and Tomasello, M. (2007). Chimpanzees are vengeful but not spiteful. *Proceedings of the National Academy of Sciences* 104: 13046–13050.

Juster, N. (2010). *The Odious Ogre*, illus. J. Feiffer. New York, NY: Michael di Capua Books/ Scholastic.

Kagan, J., and Herschkowitz, N. (2005). *A Young Mind in a Growing Child.* Mahwah, NJ: Lawrence Erlbaum Associates.

Kaiser, C.R., Vick, S., and Major, B. (2004). A prospective investigation of the relationship between just world beliefs and the desire for revenge post-September 11, 2001. *Psychological Science* 15: 503–507.

Kandel, E.R. (1979). Psychotherapy and the single synapse. *New England Journal of Medicine* 301: 1028-1037.

Kandel, E.R., Schwartz, J.H., and Jessell, T.M. (1991). *Principles of Neural Science*, 3rd edition. New York, NY: Elsevier.

Kernberg, O.F. (1966). Structural derivatives of object relationships. *International Journal of Psychoanalysis* 47: 236–253.

———. (1967). Borderline personality organization. *Journal of the American Psychoanalytic Association* 4: 641–685.

———. (1970). A psychoanalytic classification of character pathology. *Journal of the American Psychoanalytic Association* 18: 800–822.

———. (1974a). Barriers to falling and remaining in love. *Journal of the American Psychoanalytic Association* 22: 486–511.

———. (1974b). Mature love: prerequisites and characteristics. In: *Object Relations Theory and Clinical Psychoanalysis*, pp. 215–239. New York, NY: Jason Aronson.

———. (1975). *Borderline Conditions and Pathological Narcissism*. New York, NY: Jason Aronson.

———. (1976). *Object Relations Theory and Clinical Psychoanalysis*. New York, NY: Jason Aronson.

———. (1984). *Severe Personality Disorders: Psychotherapeutic Strategies*. New Haven, CT: Yale University Press.

———. (1991). The psychopathology of hatred. *Journal of the American Psychoanalytic Association* 39S: 209-238.

———. (1992). *Aggression in Personality Disorders and Perversions*. New Haven, CT: Yale University Press.

———. (2000). Concerned critique of psychoanalytic education. *International Journal of Psychoanalysis* 81: 97–120.

———. (2004). *Aggressivity, Narcissism, and Self-destructiveness in the Psychotherapeutic Relationship*. New Haven, CT: Yale University Press.

———. (2007). The almost untreatable narcissistic patient. *Journal of the American Psychoanalytic Association* 55: 503–539.

———. (2012). Mentalization, mindfulness, insight, empathy and interpretation. In: *The Inseperable Nature of Love and Aggression*, pp. 57–79. Washington, DC: American Psychiatric Publishing.

Kiernan, B. (2007). *Blood and Soil—A World History of Genocide and Extermination from Sparta to Darfur*. New Haven, CT: Yale University Press.

Kilian, H. (1995). Psychohistory, cultural evolution, and the historical significance of self psychology. In: *The Impact of New Ideas: Progress in Self Psychology, Volume 11,* ed. A Goldberg, pp. 291–301. Hillsdale, NJ: The Analytic Press.

Killingmo, B. (1989). Conflict and deficit: implications for technique. *International Journal of Psychoanalysis* 70: 65–79.

Klein, M. (1933). The early development of conscience in the child. In: *Love, Guilt and Reparation and Other Works—1921–1945*, pp. 262–289. New York, NY: Free Press, 1984.

———. (1940). Mourning and its relation to manic depressive states. In: *Love, Guilt and Reparation and Other Works—1921–1945*, pp. 344–369. New York, NY: Free Press, 1975.

Kleist, H.V. (1808). *Michael Kohlhaas*, transl. J. Geary. Oxford, UK: Oxford University Press, 1967.

Knutson, B. (2004). Behavior: sweet revenge. *Science* 305: 1246–1247.

Kohut, H. (1971). *The Analysis of the Self.* New York, NY: International Universities Press.

———. (1972). Thoughts on narcissism and narcissistic rage. *Psychoanalytic Study of the Child* 27: 360–400.

Kohut, H., and Wolf, E.I. (1978). The disorders of the self and their treatment. *International Journal of Psychoanalysis* 59: 413–425.

Kolansky, H., and Eisner, H. (1974). The psychoanalytic concept of preoedipal developmental arrest. Paper presented at the Fall Meetings of the American Psychoanalytic Association, New York, December, 1974. Cited in: *Inner Torment: Living Between Conflict and Fragmentation* by S. Akhtar, p. 231. Northvale, NJ: Jason Aronson, 1999.

Kosawa, H. (1931). Two kinds of guilt feelings—the Ajase complex. *Japanese Journal of Psychoanalysis* 1: 5–9, 1954.

Kraepelin, E. (1905). *Einfuehrung in die Psychiatrische Klinik*. Leipzig, Germany: Barth.

———. (1921). *Manic Depressive Illness and Paranoia*. Edinburgh, Scotland: E.S. Livingstone.

Kramer, E. (1987). The analyst's resolution of revenge resulting from the treatment of his parents. *Modern Psychoanalysis* 12: 207–219.

Kris, E. (1950). Notes on the development and on some current problems of psychoanalytic child psychology. *Psychoanalytic Study of the Child* 5: 24–46.

Kulish, N., and Holtzman, D. (1998). Persephone, the loss of virginity, and the female oedipal complex. *International Journal of Psychoanalysis* 79: 57–71.

LaFarge, L. (2006). The wish for revenge. *Psychoanalytic Quarterly* 75: 447–475.

Lansford, J.E., Skinner, A.T., Sorbring, E., Giunta, L.D., Deater-Deckard, K., Dodge, K.A., and Chang, L. (2012). Boys' and girls' relational and physical aggression in nine countries. *Aggressive Behavior* 38: 298–308.

Larsson, S. (2004). *The Girl with the Dragon Tattoo*. New York, NY: Vintage, 2011.

Lerner, M. (1980). *The Belief in a Just World: A fundamental delusion*. New York: Plenum.

Lipton, E.L. (1983). On ventriloquism. *Psychoanalytic Study of the Child* 38: 601–616.

Loewenstein, R. (1951). The problem of interpretation. *Psychoanalytic Quarterly* 20: 1–23.

Lyons-Ruth, K. (1991). Rapprochement or approchement: Mahler's theory reconsidered from the vantage point of recent research in early attachment relationships. *Psychoanalytic Psychology* 8: 1–23.

Mahler, M., Pine, F., and Bergman, A. (1975). *The Psychological Birth of the Human Infant*. New York, NY: Basic Books.

Mahler, M.S. (1952). On childhood psychosis and schizophrenia: autistic and symbiotic infantile psychosis. *Psychoanalytic Study of the Child* 7: 286–305.

Mahler, M.S., and Gosliner, B.J. (1955). On symbiotic child psychosis: genetic, dynamic and restitutive aspects. *Psychoanalytic Study of the Child* 10: 195–212.

Maltsberger, J.T., and Buie, D.H. (1980). The devices of suicide-revenge, riddance, and rebirth. *International Review of Psychoanalysis* 7: 61–72.

Manninen, V. (1996). The supremacy of evil: The ultimate masculine fear in the light of Herman Melville's "Moby Dick." *The Scandinavian Psychoanalytic Review* 19: 73–96.

McCullough, M.E. (2008). *Beyond Revenge: The Evolution of the Forgiveness Instinct*. San Francisco, CA: Jossey-Bass.

McCullough, M.E., Kurzban, R., and Tabak, B. (2010). Evolved mechanisms for revenge and forgiveness. In: *Understanding and Reducing Aggression, Violence, and Their Consequences*, eds. P.R. Shaver and M. Mikulincer, pp. 221–239. Washington, DC: American Psychological Association.

———. (2013). Cognitive systems for revenge and forgiveness. *Behavioral and Brain Sciences* 36: 1–15.

McKee, I.R., and Feather, N.T. (2008). Revenge, retribution, and values: social attitudes and punitive sentencing. *Social Justice Research* 21: 138–163.

Melville, H. (1851). *Moby Dick; or, The Whale*. New York, NY: Putnam, 2002.

Milton, J. (1667). *Paradise Lost*. Accessed 10/17/13. www.paradiselost.org/.

Mish, F.C. (ed.). (1998). *Merriam Webster's Collegiate Dictionary* (tenth ed.). Springfield, MA: Merriam Webster Press.

Moss, D.B. (1986). Revenge and forgiveness. *American Imago* 43: 191–210.

National Research Council and Institute of Medicine. (2000). *From Neurons to Neighborhoods: The Science of Early Development*, eds. J.P. Shonkoff and D.A. Phillips. Washington, DC: National Academy Press.

Nelson, B. (2009). *Being falsely accused by students seeking revenge* | MenTeach—Recruiting male teachers for education. Retrieved June 10, 2013, from www.menteach.org/node/973

Nichols, P. (1967). *Joe Egg*. New York, NY: Grove Weidenfeld.

Nietzsche, F. (1905). *Thus Spake Zarthustra*. New York, NY: Modern Library Series, 1955.

Novick, J., and Novick, K.K. (2000). Love in the therapeutic alliance. *Journal of the American Psychoanalytic Association* 48: 189–218.

———. (2002). Two systems of self-regulation: psychoanalytic approaches to the treatment of children and adolescents. *Journal of Psychoanalytic Social Work* 8: 95–122.

———. (2003). Two systems of self-regulation and the differential application of psychoanalytic technique. *American Journal of Psychoanalysis* 63: 1–19.

———. (2005). Soul blindness: a child must be seen to be heard. In: *Divorce and Custody: Contemporary Developmental Psychoanalytic Perspectives*, eds. L. Gunsberg and P. Hymowitz, pp. 81–91. Washington, DC: American Psychological Association.

Novick, K. (2013). Green wounds: revenge as a preserver of the self. Paper presented at the 44th Annual Mahler Symposium, April 20, 2013, Philadelphia, PA.

Novick, K.K., and Novick, J. (2003). Two systems of self-regulation and the differential application of psychoanalytic technique. *American Journal of Psychoanalysis* 63: 1–20.

———. (2005). *Working with Parents Makes Therapy Work*. Lanham, MD: Jason Aronson.

———. (2010). *Emotional Muscle: Strong Parents, Strong Children*. Bloomington, IN: XLibris.

———. (2011). Building emotional muscle in children and parents. *Psychoanalytic Study of the Child* 65: 131–151.

———. (2013). A new model of techniques for concurrent psychodynamic work with parents of child and adolescent patients. *Psychodynamic Psychotherapy: Child and Adolescent Psychiatric Clinics of North America* 22: 331–349.

Ornstein, A., Gropper, C., and Bogner, J.Z. (1983). Shoplifting: an expression of revenge and restitution. *Annual of Psychoanalysis* 11: 311–331.

Orth, U. (2004). Does perpetrator punishment satisfy victims' feelings of revenge? *Aggressive Behavior* 30: 62–70.

O'Toole, G. (2010). *An Eye for an Eye Will Make the Whole World Blind*. Retrieved June 8, 2013, from quoteinvestigator.com/2010/12/27/eye-for-eye-blind/

Parens, H. (1971). A contribution of separation-individuation to the development of psychic structure. In: *Separation-Individuation: Essays in Honor of Margaret S. Mahler*, ed. J.B. McDevitt and C.F. Settlage, pp. 100–112. New York, NY: International Universities Press.

———. (1973). Aggression: a reconsideration. *Journal of the American Psychoanalytic Association* 21: 34–60.

———. (1979). *The Development of Aggression in Early Childhood*. New York, NY: Jason Aronson, 2008.

———. (1991). A view of the development of hostility in early life. *Journal of the American Psychoanalytic Association* 39: 75–108.

———. (1993). Toward preventing experience-derived emotional disorders: education for parenting. In: *Prevention in Mental Health*, eds. H. Parens and S. Kramer, pp. 121–148. Northvale, NJ: Jason Aronson.

———. (2000). *The Multi-Trends Theory of Aggression*. PowerPoint presentation (unpublished; shown a number of times in lectures).

———. (2007a). Malignant prejudice—guidelines toward its prevention. In: *The Future of Prejudice: Psychoanalysis and the Prevention of Prejudice*, eds. H. Parens, A. Mahfouz, S. Twemlow, and D. Scharff, pp. 269–289. Lanham, MD: Jason Aronson.

———. (2007b). Roots of prejudice: findings from observational research. In: *The Future of Prejudice: Psychoanalysis and the Prevention of Prejudice*, eds. H. Parens, A. Mahfouz, S. Twemlow, and D. Scharff, pp. 81–95. Lanham, MD: Jason Aronson.

———. (2008). *The Urgent Need for Universal Parenting Education—A Documentary*. DVD produced by H. Parens, and P. Gilligan, Thomas Jefferson University, Medical School Media Division, Philadelphia, PA.

———. (2011a). Does the death-instinct-based theory of aggression hold up? In: *On Freud's "Beyond the Pleasure Principle,"* eds. S. Akhtar and M.K. O'Neil, pp. 154–172. London, UK: Karnac Books.

———. (2011b). *Handling Children's Aggression Constructively—Toward Taming Human Destructiveness*. Lanham, MD: Jason Aronson.

———. (2013a). *War Is Not Inevitable* (in press).

———. (2013b). War is not inevitable. *Peace Review* 25: 187–194.

Parens, H., Pollock, L., and Prall, R.C. (1974). Film #2: *Toward an Epigenesis of Aggression in Early Childhood*. Audiovisual medical section, Eastern Pennsylvania Psychiatric Institute, Philadelphia, PA.

Parens, H., Scattergood, E., Duff, A., and Singletary, W. (1995). *Parenting for Emotional Growth: The Textbook*. In Parens, H. (2010). CD: *Parenting for Emotional Growth: A Textbook, Two Series of Workshops, and A Curriculum for Students in Grades K Thru 12*. ISBN 0-9726910-0-6. Production Manager, Liz Mikita; Thomas Jefferson University, Media Division, Philadelphia, PA.

Parin, P., Morgenthaler, F., and Parin-Matthey, G. (1980). *Fear Thy Neighbor as Thyself: Psychoanalysis and Society Among the Anyi of West Africa*. Chicago, IL: University of Chicago Press.

Piaget, J. (1954). *Les Relations Entre l'Affectivité et l'Intelligence dans le Développement Mental de l'Enfant*. Paris: Centre de Documentation Universitaire. Published in English as "The relations of affectivity to intelligence in the mental development of the child." *Bulletin Menninger Clinic* 26: 129–137.

Pilkey, D. (2013). *Captain Underpants and the Revolting Revenge of the Radioactive Robo-Boxers*. New York, NY: The Blue Sky Press/Scholastic.

Pine, F. (1988). The four psychologies of psychoanalysis and their place in clinical work. *Journal of the American Psychoanalytic Association* 36: 571–596.

———. (1995). On the origin and evolution of a species of hate: a clinical-literary excursion. In: *The Birth of Hatred: Developmental, Clinical, and Technical Aspects of Intense Aggression*, eds. S. Akhtar, S. Kramer, and H. Parens, pp. 103–132. Northvale, NJ: Jason Aronson.

Pinheiro, P. (2005). UNICEF Study on violence against children. www.un.org/news, 10/17/05.

Pinker, S. (2011). *Better Angels of Our Nature: Why Violence Has Declined*. New York, NY: Penguin Books.

Pirandello, L. (1921). *Six Characters in Search of an Author*. New York, NY: Signet, 1998.

Poe, E.A. (1846). "The Cask of Amontillado." In: *The Fall of the House of Usher and Other Writings: Poems, Tales, Essays, and Reviews*. London, UK: Penguin Classics, 2003.

———. (1951). *Great Tales and Poems of Edgar Allan Poe*. New York, NY: Pocket Books, 2003.

Poland, W.S. (1975). Tact as a psychoanalytic function. *International Journal of Psychoanalysis* 56: 155–161.

Pope, A. (1734). *Epistle to Cobham*. Published anonymously.

Price, M. (2009). Revenge and the people who seek it. *Monitor* 40: 34.

Procci, W. (1987). Mockery through caricature: a variant of introjection utilized by a masochistic woman. *Journal of American Academy of Psychoanalysis* 15: 51–66.

Psycho (1960). Directed by A. Hitchcock, produced by Shamley Productions.

Puzo, M. (1969). *The Godfather*. New York: G. P. Putnam's Sons.

della Quercia, J. (2010). 6 Historic Acts of Revenge That Put "Kill Bill" to Shame. Cracked.com. *crakcked.com Newsletter*. Retrieved June 11, 2013, from www.cracked.com/article_18430_6-historic-acts-revenge-that-put-kill-bill-to-shame.html#ixzz2VsEh63Kq.

Raab, S. (2005). *Five Families: The Rise, Decline, and Resurgence of America's Most Powerful Mafia Empires*. New York, NY: Thomas Dunne Books.

Ramzy, I., and Wallerstein, R. (1958). Pain, fear, and anxiety: a study of interrelationships. *Psychoanalytic Study of the Child* 13: 147–189.

Rank, O. (1913). 'Der Familienroman' in der psychologie des attentäters'. *International Zeitschrift Psychoanalyze* 1: 565–567.

Rapaport, D. (1960). The structure of psychoanalytic theory. *Psychological Issues* 6: 39–72.

Reis, D.J. (1973). "The chemical coding of aggression in the brain." Paper circulated for *Colloquium on Aggression of the American Psychoanalytic Association*.

Repetto, T. (2004). *American Mafia: A History of Its Rise to Power*. New York, NY: Henry Holt and Company.

Rilling, J., Gutman, D., Zeh, T., Pagnoni, G., Bornes, G., and Kilts, D. (2002). A neural basis for social cooperation. *Neuron* 35: 395–405.

Rilling, J., and Sanfey, A. (2011). The neuroscience of social decision-making. *Annual Review of Psychology* 62: 23–48.

Rochlin, G. (1953). Loss and restitution. *Psychoanalytic Study of the Child* 8: 288–309.

———. (1961). The dread of abandonment. *Psychoanalytic Study of the Child* 16: 451–470.

———. (1973). *Man's Aggression: The Defense of the Self.* Boston, MA: Gambit.

Rosen, I.C. (2007). Revenge—the hate that dare not speak its name: a psychoanalytic perspective. *Journal of the American Psychoanalytic Association* 55: 595–619.

Rosenfeld, H. (1971). A clinical approach to the psychoanalytic theory of the life and death instincts: an investigation into aggressive aspects of narcissism. *International Journal of Psychoanalysis* 52: 169–178.

———. (1987). *Impasse and Interpretation: Therapeutic and Anti-therapeutic Factors in the Psychoanalytic Treatment of Psychotic, Borderline, and Neurotic Patients*. London, UK: Tavistock.

Samson. Wikipedia, the free encyclopedia. Retrieved June 9, 2013, from en.wikipedia.org/wiki/Samson

Sandler, J., and Freud, A. (1983). Discussions with Anna Freud on 'the ego and the mechanisms of defense': the ego and the id at puberty. *International Journal of Psychoanalysis* 64: 401–406.

Sandler, J., Kennedy, H., and Tyson, R.L. (1980). *The Technique of Child Psychoanalysis: Discussions with Anna Freud.* Cambridge, MA: Harvard University Press.

Sanfrey, A.G., Riling, J., Aronson, J., Nystrom, L., and Cohen, J. (2003). The neural basis of economic decision-making in the ultimate game. *Science* 300: 1755–1758.

Sarnoff, C.A. (1970). Symbols and symptoms phytophobia in a two-year-old girl. *Psychoanalytic Quarterly* 39: 550–562.

Schecter, M. (1972). The analysis of a boy with neurodermatitis. *Psychoanalytic Study of the Child* 27: 529–564.

Schiller, B.M. (2012). Representing female desire within a labial framework of sexuality. *Journal of the American Psychoanalytic Association* 60: 1161–1197.

Schwartz, B. (1978). Vengeance and forgiveness: the uses of beneficence in social control. *School Review* 86: 655–668.

Searles, H.F. (1956). The psychodynamics of vindictiveness. In: *Collected Papers on Schizophrenia and Related Subjects*, ed. H. F. Searles. New York, NY: International Universities Press.

Seton, P. (2001). On the importance of getting even: a study of the origins and intention of revenge. *Smith College Studies in Social Work* 72: 79–97.

Shakespeare, W. (1592). *William Shakespeare, The Complete Works.* New York, NY: Random House, 1952.

———. (1596). *The Merchant of Venice*. New York, NY: Simon and Schuster, 2010.

———. (1602). *Hamlet*. New York, NY: Simon and Schuster; New Folger Edition, 2003.

Shamlan, A. (2013, May 5). Revenge killings hit Yemen hard | ArabNews. *Arab News*. Retrieved from www.arabnews.com/news/450440

Shengold, L. (1989). *Soul Murder: The Effects of Childhood Abuse and Deprivation.* New Haven, CT: Yale University Press.

Sheppard, K., and Boon, S.D. (2012). Predicting appraisals of romantic revenge: the roles of honesty–humility, agreeableness, and vengefulness. *Personality and Individual Differences* 52: 128–132.

Shteynberg, G., Gelfand, M.J., and Kim, K. (2009). Peering into the "Magnum Mysterium" of culture: the explanatory power of descriptive norms. *Journal of Cross-Cultural Psychology* 40: 46–69.

Siassi, S. (2006). Identity, destiny, and terrorism: the effect of social terror on identity formation. Panel report, S. Akhtar, moderator. *International Journal of Psychoanalysis* 87: 1709-1711.

———. (2013). *Forgiveness in Intimate Relationships: A Psychoanalytic Perspective*. London, UK: Karnac Books.

Singer, M. (1977a). The experience of emptiness in narcissistic and borderline states: deficiency and ego-defect versus dynamic-defensive models. *International Review of Psychoanalysis* 4: 459–470.

———. (1977b). The experience of emptiness in narcissistic and borderline states: the struggle for a sense of self and the potential for suicide. *International Review of Psychoanalysis* 4: 471–479.

———. (1979). Some metapsychological and clinical distinctions between borderline and neurotic conditions with special reference to the self experience. *International Journal of Psychoanalysis* 60: 489–499.

———. (1982). Anal sadism, rapproachment and self-representation: analysis of a preverbal complaint of emptiness. *Journal of the Philadelphia Psychoanalytic Association* 8: 173–192.

———. (1988). Fantasy or structural defect? The borderline dilemma as viewed from analysis of an experience of nonhumanness. *Journal of the American Psychoanalytic Association* 36: 31–59.

———. (1996). *A Revised Theory of Borderline Structure: Its Underlying Unity with Neurosis and Perversions*. Presented at the December Meetings of the American Psychoanalytic Association, New York, NY.

Singer, T., Seymour, B., O'Doherty, J.P., Stephan, K.E., Dolan, R.J., and Frith, C.D. (2006). Empathic neural responses are modulated by the perceived fairness of others. *Nature* 439: 466–469.

Slap, J., and Slap-Shelton, L. (1991). *The Schema in Clinical Psychoanalysis*. Hillsdale, NJ: Analytic Press.

Socarides, C.W. (1966). On vengeance: the desire to "get even." *Journal of the American Psychoanalytic Association* 35: 98–107.

Spitz, R. (1946). Anaclitic depression: an inquiry into the genesis of psychiatric condition in early childhood. *Psychoanalytic Study of the Child* 2: 313–342.

———. (1951). The psychogenic diseases in infancy. *Psychoanalytic Study of the Child* 6: 255–275.

Spitz, R., and Cobliner, W.G. (1965). *The First Year of Life: A Psychoanalytic Study of Normal and Deviant Development of Object Relations*. New York, NY: International Universities Press.

Steig, W. (1988). *Spinky Sulks*. New York, NY: Farrar, Straus and Girroux.

Steiner, J. (1993). *Psychic Retreats: Pathological Organizations in Psychotic, Neurotic, and Borderline Patients*. London, UK: Routledge.

———. (1996). Revenge and resentment in the 'Oedipus Situation.' *International Journal of Psychoanalysis* 77: 433–443.

Stern, D.N. (1985). *The Interpersonal World of the Infant*. New York, NY: Basic Books.

Stillwell, A.M., Baumeister, R.F., and Del Priore, R.E. (2008). We're all victims here: toward a psychology of revenge. *Basic and Applied Social Psychology* 30: 253–263.

Stone, M. (1976). *When God Was a Woman*. New York, NY: Dorset Press.

———. (1989). Murder. *Psychiatric Clinics of North America* 12: 643–651.

Strelan, P., Feather, N.T., and McKee, I. (2011). Retributive and inclusive justice goals and forgiveness: the influence of motivational values. *Social Justice Research* 24: 126–142.

Strelan, P., and Sutton, R.M. (2011). When just-world beliefs promote and when they inhibit forgiveness. *Personality and Individual Differences* 50: 163–168.

Strobel, A., Zimmermann, J., Schmitz, A., Reuter, M., Lis, S., Windmann, S., and Kirsch, P. (2011). Beyond revenge: neural and genetic bases of altruistic punishment. *NeuroImage*, 54 (1), 671–680.

Tausk, V. (1933). On the origin of the "Influencing Machine in Schizophrenia." *Psychoanalytic Quarterly* 2: 519–556.

Tronick, E.Z. (1989). Emotions and emotional communication in infants. *American Psychologist* 44: 112–119.

———. (2007). *The Neurobehavioral and Social-Emotional-Development of Infants and Children*. New York, NY: W.W. Norton.

Tronick, E., Als, H., Adamson, L., Wise, S., and Brazelton, T.B. (1978). The infant's response to entrapment between contradictory messages in face-to-face interaction. *Journal of the American Academy* of *Child Psychiatry* 17: 1–13.

Tronick, E. and Weinberg, M. (1997). Depressed mothers and infants: the failure to form dyadic states of consciousness. In: *Postpartum Depression and Child Development*, eds. L. Murray and P. Cooper, pp. 54–81. New York, NY: Guilford Press.

Tutu, D. (1999). *No Future Without Forgiveness*. New York, NY: Doubleday.

Vivona, J. (2012). Is there a nonverbal period of development? *Journal of the American Psychoanalytic Association* 60: 231–265.

Wallace, A. (1961). *Culture and Personality*. New York, NY: Random House.

Walster, E., Walster, G., and Berscheid, E. (1978). *Equity: Theory and Research*. Boston, MA: Allyn and Bacon.

Wandimoyi, A. (2012, October 3). When chimpanzees attack: 10 killed in possible "revenge" for past human brutality—all news is global. *World Crunch*. Retrieved May 30, 2013, from worldcrunch.com/culture-society.

Wangh, M. (1962). The 'evocation of a proxy': a psychological maneuver, its use as a defense, its purposes and genesis. *Psychoanalytic Study of the Child* 17: 451–469.

Weiss, E. (1934). Bodily pain and mental pain. *International Journal of Psychoanalysis* 15: 1–13.

Wilkowski, B. M., Hartung, C. M., Crowe, S. E., and Chai, C. A. (2012). Men don't just get mad; they get even: revenge but not anger mediates gender differences in physical aggression. *Journal of Research in Personality* 46: 546–555.

Winnicott, D. W. (1953). Transitional objects and transitional phenomena. *International Journal of Psychoanalysis* 34: 89–97.

———. (1956). The antisocial tendency. In: *Collected Papers: Through Paediatrics to Psychoanalysis,* pp. 306–316. New York, NY: Basic Books, 1958.

Wolf, E. (1988). *Treating the Self: Elements of Clinical Self Psychology*. New York, NY: Guilford Press.

Wurmser, L. (1994). A time of questioning: the severely disturbed patient within classical analysis. *The Annual of Psychoanalysis* 22: 173–207.

Zdaniuk, A., and Bobocel, D.R. (2012). Vertical individualism and injustice: the self-restorative function of revenge. *European Journal of Social Psychology* 42: 640–651.

Zilboorg, G. (1936). Differential diagnostic types of suicide. *Archives of Neurological Psychiatry* 35: 270–291.

Index

About the Contributors

Salman Akhtar, M.D., professor of psychiatry, Jefferson Medical College; training and supervising analyst, Psychoanalytic Center of Philadelphia, Philadelphia, PA.

April E. Fallon, Ph.D., faculty member, Fielding Graduate University and Drexel University School of Medicine, Philadelphia, PA.

Frederick Fisher, M.D., faculty member, Psychoanalytic Center of Philadelphia, Philadelphia, PA.

Daniel M. A. Freeman, M.D., faculty member, Psychoanalytic Center of Philadelphia; clinical associate professor of psychiatry, Drexel University School of Medicine, Philadelphia, PA.

Rama Rao Gogineni, M.D., associate professor, Cooper Medical School of Rowan University, Camden, NJ; faculty member, Psychoanalytic Center of Philadelphia, Philadelphia, PA.

Eve Holwell, B.A., medical student, Jefferson Medical College, Philadelphia, PA.

Otto Kernberg, M.D., professor of psychiatry, Weil Medical College of Cornell University; training and supervising, Columbia University Center for Psychoanalytic Training and Research, New York, NY.

Kerry Kelly Novick, A.B., B.A., training and supervising analyst, International Psychoanalytic Association; faculty member, Michigan Psychoanalytic Institute, Ann Arbor, MI.

Henri Parens, M.D., professor of psychiatry, Jefferson Medical College; training and supervising analyst, Psychoanalytic Center of Philadelphia, Philadelphia, PA.

Barbara Shapiro, M.D., faculty member, Psychoanalytic Center of Philadelphia; associate professor of pediatrics and psychiatry, Perelman School of Medicine, University of Pennsylvania, Philadelphia, PA.

Melvin Singer, M.D., training and supervising analyst, Psychoanalytic Center of Philadelphia; clinical associate professor of psychiatry, Perelman School of Medicine, University of Pennsylvania, Philadelphia, PA.